# Workbook

**MIDDLE GRADES**

**MATH** *Thematics*

**Book 3**

The **STEM** Project

**McDougal Littell**

A HOUGHTON MIFFLIN COMPANY

Evanston, Illinois • Boston • Dallas

McDougal Littell: www.mcdougallittell.com
Middle School Mathematics: www.mlmath.com

ISBN 0-618-21250-7

Printed in the United States of America.

ISBN-13: 978-0-618-21250-7   ISBN-10: 0-618-21250-7

Printed in the United States of America

10 11 12 13 14 -VEI- 10 09 08 07

# Contents

**MODULE 1**                                                      LABSHEET **2A**

# Grammy Award Winners   (Use with Exercises 1 and 2 on page 22.)

**Directions**  Use the data below of female Grammy Award winners to
create and compare stem-and-leaf plots.

| Grammy Awards, 1975–1996 | | | | |
|---|---|---|---|---|
| | **Best Female Country Performance** | | **Best Female Pop Performance** | |
| Year | Winner | Age | Winner | Age |
| 1975 | Linda Ronstadt | 29 | Janis Ian | 24 |
| 1976 | Emmylou Harris | 29 | Linda Ronstadt | 30 |
| 1977 | Crystal Gayle | 27 | Barbra Streisand | 35 |
| 1978 | Dolly Parton | 33 | Anne Murray | 33 |
| 1979 | Emmylou Harris | 32 | Dionne Warwick | 38 |
| 1980 | Anne Murray | 35 | Bette Midler | 35 |
| 1981 | Dolly Parton | 36 | Lena Horne | 64 |
| 1982 | Juice Newton | 31 | Melissa Manchester | 32 |
| 1983 | Anne Murray | 38 | Irene Cara | 24 |
| 1984 | Emmylou Harris | 37 | Tina Turner | 45 |
| 1985 | Rosanne Cash | 30 | Whitney Houston | 21 |
| 1986 | Reba McEntire | 32 | Barbra Streisand | 44 |
| 1987 | K.T. Oslin | 46 | Whitney Houston | 23 |
| 1988 | K.T. Oslin | 47 | Tracy Chapman | 24 |
| 1989 | k.d. lang | 28 | Bonnie Raitt | 40 |
| 1990 | Kathy Mattea | 31 | Mariah Carey | 19 |
| 1991 | Mary Chapin-Carpenter | 34 | Bonnie Raitt | 42 |
| 1992 | Mary Chapin-Carpenter | 35 | k.d. lang | 31 |
| 1993 | Mary Chapin-Carpenter | 36 | Whitney Houston | 29 |
| 1994 | Mary Chapin-Carpenter | 37 | Sheryl Crow | 31 |
| 1995 | Alison Kraus | 24 | Annie Lennox | 41 |
| 1996 | LeAnn Rimes | 14 | Toni Braxton | 28 |

## Baseball Players' Life Spans
(Use with Project Questions 2 and 3 on page 25.)

**Directions** Use the data below to compare life spans of baseball players and prove or disprove a statement.

### Life Spans of Major League Third Basemen and Shortstops
### (1920–1923 Season)

| Short Stops' Life Spans (in years) | | | | | | | | Third Basemen's Life Spans (in years) | | | | | | | | | | |
|---|---|---|---|---|---|---|---|---|---|---|---|---|---|---|---|---|---|---|
| 2 | 9 | | | | | | | 2 | 9 | | | | | | | | | |
| 3 | 0 | | | | | | | 3 | 1 | | | | | | | | | |
| 4 | 4 | | | | | | | 4 | 0 | 3 | 9 | | | | | | | |
| 5 | 1 | 4 | 9 | | | | | 5 | | | | | | | | | | |
| 6 | 1 | 1 | 2 | 4 | 5 | 5 | 7 | 6 | | | | | | | | | | |
| 7 | 1 | 2 | 3 | 5 | 9 | | | 7 | 2 | 4 | 4 | 5 | 7 | 7 | 7 | 8 | 9 | |
| 8 | 1 | 1 | 3 | 4 | 9 | | | 8 | 1 | 3 | 4 | 4 | 5 | 5 | 7 | 7 | 8 | 8 | 9 | 9 |
| 9 | 0 | 5 | | | | | | 9 | 1 | 2 | 3 | | | | | | | |

2|9 represents a life span of 29 years

### Life Spans of Major League Third Basemen and Shortstops (1920–1923 Season)

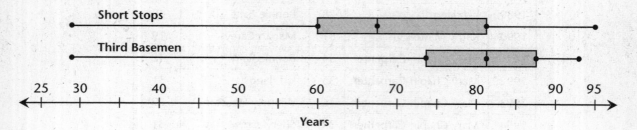

Short Stops

Third Basemen

25  30    40    50    60    70    80    90  95

Years

## MODULE 1

# Heptathlon Events

(Use with Question 12 on page 32.)

**Directions**  Each scatter plot below compares performances of athletes in two different 1996 Olympic heptathlon events. Complete parts (a) and (b) for each scatter plot.

**a.** Describe what pattern, if any, the data points appear to show.

**b.** If the data points appear to fall along a line, draw a fitted line. What does your fitted line tell you about performances in the heptathlon events?

**1996 Olympic Heptathlon Performances**

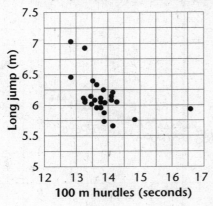

**1996 Olympic Heptathlon Performances**

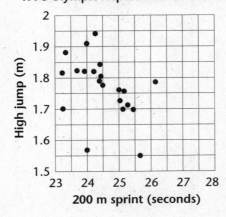

**MODULE 1**                                    **LABSHEET** **3B**

# World Record Marathon Times

(Use with Exercises 1–3 on page 35.)

**Directions**  Use the scatter plot below to compare record marathon times for men and women of different ages.

**Record Marathon Times, 1996**

▲ Women
○ Men

Time (hours) *(y-axis: 0 to 10)*

Age (years) *(x-axis: 0 to 95)*

**MODULE 1**                                                    LABSHEET  6A

# Map of Missouri and the Lake of the Ozarks

(Use with Question 2 on page 69.)

**Directions** Use the map to complete parts (a)–(c).

**a.** Use the map scale to estimate the perimeter of the rectangle drawn around the Lake of the Ozarks.

**b.** Estimate the length in miles of the state's border. (You may want to use string and a ruler to make your measurements.)

**c.** The travel brochure claims that the shoreline is almost as long as the border of the state. Do you think the claim could be true? Explain.

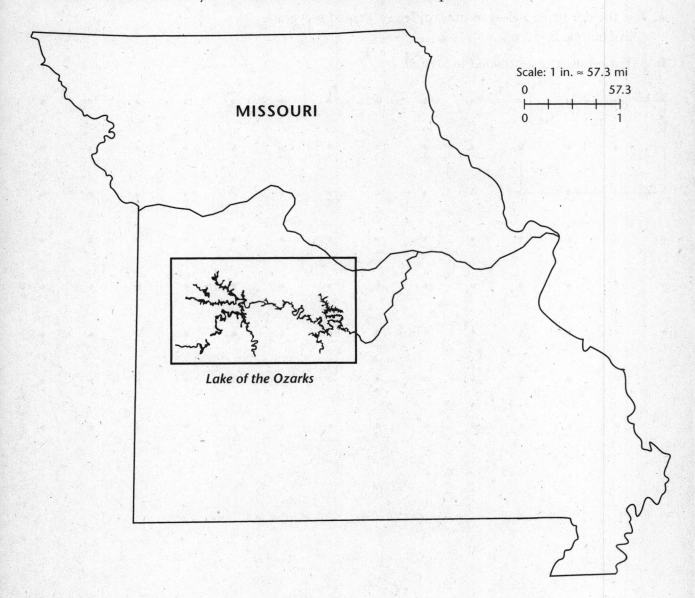

Lake of the Ozarks

**MODULE 1**                                    **LABSHEET 6B**

## Polygon Dot Paper  (Use with Standardized Testing on page 76.)

**Directions**  Use the steps for Pick's Formula below to complete parts (a) and (b).

**Step 1**  Count the number of dots on the perimeter of the polygon below and divide by 2.

**Step 2**  Add the number of dots inside the polygon to your answer from Step 1.

**Step 3**  To find the area of any polygon, you always subtract the same number from your answer from Step 2.

**a.** Use the dot paper below to draw different shaped polygons. (An example is given.)

**b.** What number is subtracted in Step 3?

Name _____ Problem _____

 **TEACHER** **ASSESSMENT SCALES**

 *The star indicates that you excelled in some way.*

 ## Problem Solving

────①────②────③────④────⑤────★→

**①** You did not understand the problem well enough to get started or you did not show any work.

**③** You understood the problem well enough to make a plan and to work toward a solution.

**⑤** You made a plan, you used it to solve the problem, and you verified your solution.

 ## Mathematical Language

────①────②────③────④────⑤────★→

**①** You did not use any mathematical vocabulary or symbols, or you did not use them correctly, or your use was not appropriate.

**③** You used appropriate mathematical language, but the way it was used was not always correct or other terms and symbols were needed.

**⑤** You used mathematical language that was correct and appropriate to make your meaning clear.

 ## Representations

────①────②────③────④────⑤────★→

**①** You did not use any representations such as equations, tables, graphs, or diagrams to help solve the problem or explain your solution.

**③** You made appropriate representations to help solve the problem or help you explain your solution, but they were not always correct or other representations were needed.

**⑤** You used appropriate and correct representations to solve the problem or explain your solution.

 ## Connections

────①────②────③────④────⑤────★→

**①** You attempted or solved the problem and then stopped.

**③** You found patterns and used them to extend the solution to other cases, or you recognized that this problem relates to other problems, mathematical ideas, or applications.

**⑤** You extended the ideas in the solution to the general case, or you showed how this problem relates to other problems, mathematical ideas, or applications.

## Presentation

────①────②────③────④────⑤────★→

**①** The presentation of your solution and reasoning is unclear to others.

**③** The presentation of your solution and reasoning is clear in most places, but others may have trouble understanding parts of it.

**⑤** The presentation of your solution and reasoning is clear and can be understood by others.

**Content Used:** _____    **Computational Errors:**    Yes ☐   No ☐

**Notes on Errors:** _____

_____

# STUDENT    SELF-ASSESSMENT SCALES

If your score is in the shaded area, explain why on the back of this sheet and stop.

☆ The star indicates that you excelled in some way.

 ## Problem Solving

**①**      **②**      **③**      **④**      **⑤**

**1** I did not understand the problem well enough to get started or I did not show any work.

**2** I understood the problem well enough to make a plan and to work toward a solution.

**3** I made a plan, I used it to solve the problem, and I verified my solution.

 ## Mathematical Language

**①**      **②**      **③**      **④**      **⑤**

**1** I did not use any mathematical vocabulary or symbols, or I did not use them correctly, or my use was not appropriate.

**2** I used appropriate mathematical language, but the way it was used was not always correct or other terms and symbols were needed.

**3** I used mathematical language that was correct and appropriate to make my meaning clear.

 ## Representations

**①**      **②**      **③**      **④**      **⑤**

**1** I did not use any representations such as equations, tables, graphs, or diagrams to help solve the problem or explain my solution.

**2** I made appropriate representations to help solve the problem or help me explain my solution, but they were not always correct or other representations were needed.

**3** I used appropriate and correct representations to solve the problem or explain my solution.

 ## Connections

**①**      **②**      **③**      **④**      **⑤**

**1** I attempted or solved the problem and then stopped.

**2** I found patterns and used them to extend the solution to other cases, or I recognized that this problem relates to other problems, mathematical ideas, or applications.

**3** I extended the ideas in the solution to the general case, or I showed how this problem relates to other problems, mathematical ideas, or applications.

 ## Presentation

**①**      **②**      **③**      **④**      **⑤**

**1** The presentation of my solution and reasoning is unclear to others.

**2** The presentation of my solution and reasoning is clear in most places, but others may have trouble understanding parts of it.

**3** The presentation of my solution and reasoning is clear and can be understood by others.

        

## MODULE 1 SECTION 1        PRACTICE AND APPLICATIONS

### For use with Exploration 1

1. Suppose a gardener wants to estimate how many seedlings he can plant in a rectangular garden plot.

   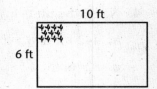

   a. Describe a strategy for solving the problem.

   b. Use your strategy to estimate how many seedlings should be planted in the garden at the right.

2. Suppose you have a 2 gallon, a 3 gallon, and a 5 gallon container.

   a. Describe how you can use the containers to measure 1 gallon of water into the 2 gallon container.

   b. What is the least number of "pourings" you could use to measure one gallon of water?

   c. Write a list of instructions for solving the problem.

3. In 1772, Johann Elert Bode reasoned that the distances of the planets from the sun followed the pattern shown below. The actual distance from Earth to the sun is given as 10 units.

   | Planet | Bode's pattern | Actual distance |
   |--------|----------------|-----------------|
   | Mercury | 0 + 4 = 4 | 4 |
   | Venus | 3 + 4 = 7 | 7 |
   | Earth | 6 + 4 = 10 | 10 |
   | Mars | 12 + 4 = 16 | 16 |
   | — | __ + __ = __ | — |
   | Jupiter | __ + __ = __ | — |

   a. What is Bode's pattern?

   b. What numbers belong between Mars and Jupiter?

   c. Jupiter's actual distance from the sun matches the prediction from Bode's pattern. What is the actual distance?

   d. Predict Bode's pattern for the next planet, Saturn.

   *(continued)*

## MODULE 1  SECTION 1                    PRACTICE AND APPLICATIONS

**For use with Exploration 2**

4. Name the units in each rate. Then write a unit rate.

  **a.** 442 mi in 8.5 h                    **b.** 3 lb for $8.43

  **c.** 82 mi for 4.5 gal                  **d.** 87 chirps in 3 min

5. Complete each equation.

  **a.** 1.5 mi/min = ___?___ mi/h          **b.** $1.92 per lb = ___?___ per oz

  **c.** $18,500 salary per year = ___?___ per week    **d.** 42 h/week = ___?___ h/day

6. It takes the space shuttle about 8 minutes to climb 70 miles. What is the shuttle's rate of ascent?

7. The Humphrey family traveled 320 miles in 7.5 hours.

  **a.** What was their average rate of speed?

  **b.** At the same average rate of speed, how far can they travel in 9 hours?

  **c.** Change the rate to miles per minute.

  **d.** How long does it take to travel exactly one mile?

8. Write a word problem for which you need to perform each calculation. Solve the problem.

  **a.** 70 mi/h • 3.5 h                    **b.** 21 mi/gal • 6.2 gal

  **c.** $2.50 per lb • 4 lb                **d.** $5.25 per hour • 4 h

9. The longest nonstop flight currently operating is between Johannesburg, South Africa, and New York.

  **a.** If the 7983 mile flight takes 15 hours 5 minutes, what is the average rate of speed per hour?

  **b.** What is average rate of speed per minute?

  **c.** At the same rate of speed, how far could the airplane travel in 20 hours?

Name _____                                 Date _____

## For use with Exploration 1

The heights of an 8th grade class are given below. Use the data for Exercises 1–2.

**Heights of Eighth Grade Class, in Inches**

| 60 | 62 | 64 | 63 | 70 | 66 | 68 | 67 | 67 | 59 | 71 | 58 | 67 | 72 | 71 | 59 | 73 |
|----|----|----|----|----|----|----|----|----|----|----|----|----|----|----|----|----|
| 56 | 58 | 55 | 59 | 61 | 62 | 60 | 61 | 59 | 64 | 65 | 58 | 62 | 61 | 68 | 60 | 60 |

1. Make a stem-and-leaf plot of the data set.

2. **a.** Find the range of the data in the stem-and-leaf plot.

   **b.** Find the mean, median, and mode of the data.

   **c.** Which average to you think best represents the data? Explain.

The tables below show points scored for the first 13 games of the Chicago Bulls and the Utah Jazz during the 1996–1997 National Basketball Association playoff series. Use the same data set for Exercises 3–5. (Note: these games were not played against each other.)

**NBA Playoff Scores**

| Chicago | 98 | 109 | 96 | 100 | 95 | 100 | 89 | 107 | 84 | 75 | 98 | 80 | 100 |
|---------|-----|-----|-----|-----|-----|-----|-----|-----|-----|-----|-----|-----|-----|
| Utah | 106 | 105 | 104 | 93 | 103 | 84 | 110 | 98 | 101 | 104 | 100 | 92 | 96 |

3. **a.** Use the data to make a stem-and-leaf plot for each team.

   **b.** Compare the shapes of the two stem-and-leaf plots. What do the shapes tell you about the scores of each team?

   **c.** Compare the ranges of the two data sets. What do the ranges tell you about the number of points each team scores per game?

4. **a.** Find the mean, median, and mode of the data for each team.

   **b.** Which average from part (a) do you think best represents the data? Explain.

5. Chicago went on to defeat Utah in the championship series. Explain why you could not use the previous playoff scores to predict this.

*(continued)*

**MODULE 1   SECTION 2**                           **PRACTICE AND APPLICATIONS**

## For use with Exploration 2

The box-and-whisker plot below represents the heights of 8th graders from Exploration 1.

**Heights of Eighth Grade Class (in inches)**

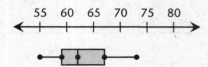

**6. a.** About what percent of the heights are included in the box portion of the box-and-whisker plot?

   **b.** What do the sizes of the box portions tell you about the heights of the eighth grade students?

   **c.** About what percent of students were between 62 inches and 73 inches tall?

   **d.** How are the least and greatest values from the stem-and-leaf plot from Exploration 1 shown in the box-and-whisker plot?

**Use the data for the NBA playoff scores from Exploration 1 and the box-and-whisker plots below for Exercises 7–9.**

**NBA Playoff Game Scores**

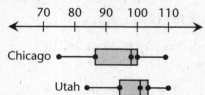

**7.** For each box-and-whisker plot, find the values below.

   **a.** the lower extreme            **b.** the upper extreme

   **c.** the lower quartile           **d.** the upper quartile

**8. a.** About what percent of Chicago's scores were below 100?

   **b.** About what percent of Utah's scores were above 101?

**9. a.** **Writing** Explain how to use the box-and-whisker plot to compare the median score for each team.

   **b.** Which team had at least 50% of its scores greater than its mean?

## MODULE 1  SECTION 3                    PRACTICE AND APPLICATIONS

### For use with Exploration 1

**The scatter plot for Exercises 1–2 shows the winning times for the men's and women's 200-Meter Butterfly swimming events in the 1968–1996 Olympic Games.**

**1. a.** What is the approximate fastest winning time of the men's event?

   **b.** What is the approximate fastest winning time of the women's event?

**2. a.** In what years do the times seem to change very little for each group?

   **b.** Which group had the most change in the winning times?

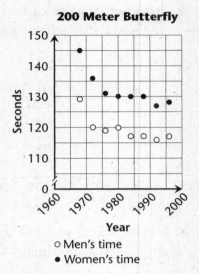

**200 Meter Butterfly**

○ Men's time
● Women's time

**The table below shows the number of wins and the number of runs scored for the American League in 1996. Use the data set for Exercises 3–4.**

|                  | Wins | Runs |                   | Wins | Runs |                   | Wins | Runs |
|------------------|------|------|-------------------|------|------|-------------------|------|------|
| New York Yankees | 92   | 871  | Cleveland Indians | 99   | 952  | Texas Rangers     | 90   | 928  |
| Baltimore Orioles| 88   | 949  | Chicago White Sox | 85   | 898  | Seattle Mariners  | 85   | 993  |
| Boston Red Sox   | 85   | 928  | Milwaukee Brewers | 80   | 894  | Oakland Athletics | 78   | 861  |
| Toronto Blue Jays| 74   | 766  | Minnesota Twins   | 78   | 877  | California Angels | 70   | 762  |
| Detroit Tigers   | 53   | 783  | Kansas City Royals| 75   | 746  |                   |      |      |

**3.** Construct a scatter plot that compares wins with the number of runs scored. Put the number of runs scored on the horizontal axis.

**4. a.** Find the range for the number of runs scored. What is the greatest number of runs scored? the least?

   **b.** Do the number of runs scored seem to be related to the number of wins? Can this be expected? Explain your thinking.

*(continued)*

**MODULE 1  SECTION 3**                    **PRACTICE AND APPLICATIONS**

## For use with Exploration 2

**5.** Tell whether each scatter plot appears to have a straight-line pattern, a curved pattern, or no pattern.

**a.**

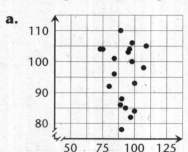

**b.**

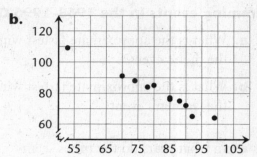

**6.** Use the scatter plot in Exercise 5 part (b) to fill in the blanks for the approximate coordinates that would fit the straight-line pattern.

    **a.** (65, __?__ )          **b.** (100, __?__ )          **c.** ( __?__ , 80)

**7. a.** Draw a fitted line on your scatter plot for wins versus runs from Exercises 3 and 4.

    **b.** Does the line in the scatter plot in part (a) represent the data well? Explain what it shows about the runs scored compared to the wins.

    **c.** Use part (a) to determine what number of wins you would expect from a team that has scored 1050 runs.

**The table represents record times in freestyle swimming for men and women.**

**8. a.** Construct a scatter plot with men's time and the women's time on the same graph. Use a different mark or color for the women's plot.

| Meters | Men's time (seconds) | Women's time (seconds) |
|--------|----------------------|------------------------|
| 50 | 22 | 25 |
| 100 | 48 | 54 |
| 200 | 107 | 112 |
| 400 | 224 | 245 |
| 800 | 466 | 496 |

    **b.** Describe the pattern you see in each scatter plot. Draw a fitted line for each if it makes sense.

    **c.** What can you conclude about the men's and women's time as the number of meters increase?

**MODULE 1  SECTION 4**                    **PRACTICE AND APPLICATIONS**

## For use with Exploration 1

**1.** Find the circumference of each circle. Use π = 3.14.

   **a.** diameter = 15 cm            **b.** radius = 4 in.

**2. a.** How far would a bicycle with 30 inch tires travel in one complete turn of its wheels?

   **b.** How many turns would the smallest bicycle with tire diameter 0.76 inches have to make to go the same distance?

**3.** A certain single mirror telescope has a diameter of 19 feet 8 inches. What is the circumference of a circle with that diameter?

## Evaluate each expression. Use π = 3.14.

**4.** $2\pi r$ when $r = 8$                    **5.** $9 + x$ when $x = 104$

**6.** $\dfrac{22}{z}$ when $z = 4$               **7.** $6r^2$ when $r = 0.4$

**8.** $10 - w$ when $w = 3$            **9.** $xyz$ when $x = 4, y = 3, z = 0.5$

## Use symbols to write an expression for each word phrase. (*n* = variable)

**10.** six more than eighteen         **11.** three less than a number

**12.** nine divided by a number      **13.** seven times a number

**14.** four more than the product of a number and three

**15.** Suppose two circles are enclosed in a rectangle as shown. Find the perimeter of the rectangle.

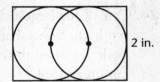

2 in.

*(continued)*

       

## MODULE 1 SECTION 4                                    PRACTICE AND APPLICATIONS

### For use with Exploration 2

**16.** Find the volume of each figure. Use $\pi = 3.14$.

**a.**

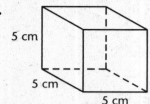

5 cm
5 cm
5 cm

**b.**

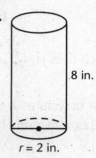

8 in.

$r = 2$ in.

**c.**

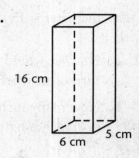

16 cm
6 cm
5 cm

### Find the volume of each cylinder. Use $\pi = 3.14$.

**17.** $r = 4$ cm
$h = 12$ cm

**18.** $r = 5.2$ cm
$h = 5.2$ cm

**19.** $r = 18$ cm
$h = 10$ cm

### Find the volume of each rectangular prism. Use $\pi = 3.14$.

**20.** $l = 18$ cm
$w = 18$ cm
$h = 8$ cm

**21.** $l = 7$ cm
$w = 9$ cm
$h = 6$ cm

**22.** $l = 6$
$w = 12.5$ cm
$h = 10$ cm

**23. a.** A cereal box measures $2\frac{3}{4}$ inches by $8\frac{1}{4}$ inches by 12 inches.
Find its volume.

**b.** The box contains 15 ounces of cereal, the "net weight." Why
doesn't the manufacturer list the volume on the box?

**24.** One of the largest cheeses ever made was 14.5 ft tall, 6.5 ft wide, and
6 ft high. It was made in January of 1964 for the World's Fair in New
York. It toured the country and was displayed until 1968, when it was
cut up and sold.

**a.** Estimate the volume of the cheese.

**b.** The whole cheese weighed 34,591 pounds. Find the weight of one
cubic foot of cheese. Round to the nearest tenth of a cubic foot.

**c.** Use your answer to part (b) to help you estimate how many
8 ounce blocks of cheese fit into a volume of 1 cubic foot.

## MODULE 1  SECTION 5                          PRACTICE AND APPLICATIONS

### For use with Exploration 1

1. The depth of the roots of a tree is about one third the height of the tree. Which equation represents this rule of thumb? Let $r$ = the depth of the roots and $t$ = the height of the tree.

   **A.** $t = \frac{1}{3}r$                    **B.** $r = \frac{1}{3}t$                    **C.** $r = 3t$

**For Exercises 2–6, change each word sentence into a mathematical equation. Tell what each variable represents.**

2. The total cost of tickets for the 8th grade to attend a concert is $6 per student times the number of students.

3. To estimate the amount of interest on a savings account for one year, multiply the interest rate of 0.05 by the amount of savings.

4. The total distance of a car trip divided by 50 gives the approximate number of hours the trip will take.

5. To estimate the circumference of a circle, multiply the diameter by 3.

### For use with Exploration 2

6. Use variables and symbols to write each equation modeled with the algebra tiles below. Solve each equation.

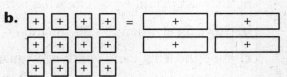

**Use inverse operations to solve each equation.**
**Check your solutions.**

**7.** $5 + x = 27$               **8.** $7t = 28$                  **9.** $2y - 4 = 20$

**10.** $x - 8 = 4$               **11.** $17 = 3t$                  **12.** $18 = m - 4$

**13.** $5 + 2d = 22$             **14.** $\frac{r}{3} = 18$         **15.** $\frac{p}{4} - 1 = 19$

16. To estimate your safe heart rate during exercise, subtract your age from 220 and then multiply by 0.55. Write an equation and find your safe heart rate if you are 35 years old.

*(continued)*

## MODULE 1  SECTION 5                         PRACTICE AND APPLICATIONS

### For use with Exploration 3

**17.** Which of the terms below are like terms?

$$x^2 \quad \frac{3}{4}x \quad xy \quad xy^2 \quad x^2y \quad 5x^2$$

**If possible, combine like terms to simplify each expression.**

**18.** $5x + 12 - 4$

**19.** $6t - 7st$

**20.** $2y + 4x - 2y$

**21.** $12x^2 - 8x + 6y^2$

**22.** $8t + 16 - 3t$

**23.** $2x^2 + 8x + 5x^2$

**24.** $5xy^2 + 6xy^2$

**25.** $12x + 8x + 6$

**26.** $3x^2 + 12 - 3x^2$

**27.** The perimeter of a square is given by the formula $P = 4l$, where $l =$ the length. Find the perimeter of a square with $l = 12$ cm.

**28.** Find the perimeter of each rectangle below.

**a.**

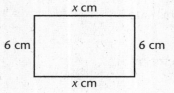

**b.**

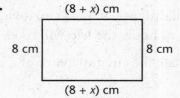

**29.** The perimeter of a rectangle is represented by the formula $P = 2l + 2w$.

**a.** If $l = 8$ cm and $w = 7$ cm, what is the perimeter?

**b.** Solve for $w$ when $P = 80$ cm and $l = 16$ cm.

**c.** Find the length and width of a square with perimeter 81 cm.

**MODULE 1 SECTION 6**          **PRACTICE AND APPLICATIONS**

## For use with Exploration 1

1. Which of the figures are polygons? Which appear to be regular polygons? Explain your thinking.

    **a.**          **b.** 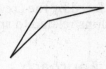         **c.**

**Find the perimeter and area of each rectangle.**

2. $l = 8$ cm             3. $l = 8.4$ cm             4. $l = 11$ cm
   $w = 12$ cm            $w = 4.2$ cm           $w = 11$ cm

5. **a.** Draw a 6 unit by 4 unit rectangle on the coordinate grid. Find the perimeter and area of the rectangle.

    **b.** Draw a polygon inside your rectangle that has a perimeter greater than the perimeter of the rectangle.

    **c.** Find the perimeter and area of your polygon.

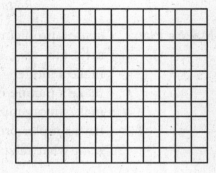

6. Find the exact length of a rectangle with an area of 24 square units and a width of $\frac{1}{2}$ unit.

7. Find the perimeter of a rectangle with an area of 24 square units and a width of 3 units.

8. Find the perimeter of a square with area 49 cm$^2$.

9. Determine the width and length of a rectangle with a perimeter of 48 and the greatest possible area.

        

## MODULE 1 SECTION 1                                    STUDY GUIDE

# We've Got a Problem Here     Problem Solving and Rates

**GOAL**   **LEARN HOW TO:** • use a 4-step problem solving approach
                           • use rates to solve problems

   **AS YOU:** • study a problem faced by the crew of *Apollo 13*
               • perform calculations related to space flight

## Exploration 1: Problem Solving Approach

### Problem Solving

You can use this 4-step approach when solving problems:

**Understand the Problem**   *Identify* questions that need to be answered.
                            *Find* the information you need to answer them.
                            *Restate* the problem in your own words.

**Make a Plan**   *Choose* a problem solving strategy.
   • act it out                          • examine a related problem
   • make a model                        • use an equation
   • make a picture or diagram           • guess and check
   • make an organized list              • work backward
   • try a simpler problem               • use logical reasoning
   *Decide* what calculations, if any, are needed.

**Carry Out the Plan**   You may need to change your strategy or use a
                        different approach, depending on how well your
                        original plan works.

**Look Back**   Is your solution reasonable?
               Is there another way you could have solved the problem?
               Are there other problems you can solve the same way?

## Exploration 2: Using Rates

### Rates

A **rate** is a ratio that compares two quantities measured in different units.
Rates describe how one quantity depends on another. A *unit rate* gives an
amount per one unit. For example, if you pay $6.50 for 5 pairs of socks
the rate is $\frac{\$6.50}{5 \text{ pairs}}$ and the unit rate is $\frac{\$1.30}{1 \text{ pair}}$, or $1.30/pair.

| MODULE 1  SECTION 1 | PRACTICE & APPLICATION EXERCISES | STUDY GUIDE |

## Exploration 1

**1.** Mark can do 50 sit-ups in 5 min. Describe a strategy for determining how many sit-ups he can do in 2 min. Use your strategy to solve the problem.

**2.** Marv and Gloria are in a band. They are performing a song in which Marv plays one note every 6 counts. Gloria plays one note every 10 counts. If there are 4 counts to a measure, in which measure will they both play together for the first time?

## Exploration 2

**Name the units in each rate. Then write a unit rate.**

**3.** 186 pages from 31 students          **4.** 18.75 miles in 25 min

**5.** $15.81 for 3 boxes                 **6.** 192 mi per 6 gal of gas

**Copy and complete each equation.**

**7.** $.50/day = ___?___ per week        **8.** 3600 lb/h = ___?___ lb/min

**9.** $5.52/ft = ___?___ per in.          **10.** 3 vials/oz = ___?___ vials/c

## Spiral Review

**11.** Plot the points on graph paper and connect them alphabetically. Then connect point $O$ to point $A$ to see a rough outline of the Space Shuttle. **(Toolbox, p. 602)**

$A(1, 0)$     $B(3, 2)$     $C(4, 2)$     $D(5, 3)$     $E(7, 3)$

$F(9, 3)$     $G(11, 3)$     $H(13, 5)$     $I(15, 5)$     $J(13, 3)$

$K(13, 2)$     $L(14, 2)$     $M(14, 1)$     $N(13, 1)$     $O(13, 0)$

**12.** Find the mean, the median, the mode, and the range of the values shown below. **(Toolbox, p. 606)**

325, 320, 300, 370, 270, 290, 320, 260, 270, 270, 250, 260, 240, 225, 250

**Write each percent as a fraction in lowest terms.** **(Toolbox, p. 599)**

**13.** 75%          **14.** 50%          **15.** 15%          **16.** 28%

**MODULE 1  SECTION 2**                                    **STUDY GUIDE**

# Amazing Musicians    Displaying Data

**GOAL**   **LEARN HOW TO:** • make and use stem-and-leaf plots
                • use box-and-whisker plots to analyze and compare data

**As you:** • analyze the ages of famous pop and country musicians
           • investigate the achievements of famous musicians

## Exploration 1: Stem-and Leaf Plots

A stem-and-leaf plot displays data in an organized format. The data items
are usually ordered from least to greatest.

Usually the digit in the ones place forms the **leaf** for each data value. The
leaves are ordered horizontally from least to greatest.

Then the remaining digit or digits of each data value form the **stem** for
the corresponding leaf. The stems are ordered vertically, usually from least
to greatest.

### Example

The following list of numbers represents the number of years the top 15 players in the
National Hockey League have played on major teams of the NHL at the start of the
1992–93 season.  Source: *The Essential Researcher*

   13, 26, 18, 18, 22, 17, 23, 17, 17, 24, 21, 20, 20, 15, 12

Use a stem-and-leaf plot to find the mean, the median, and the mode of this data.

### ■ Sample Response ■

In the stem-and-leaf plot below, each **stem** represents a tens digit and each **leaf**
represents the corresponding ones digit.

**Year Played in NHL by Top 15 Players**

```
1 | 2 3 5 7 7 7 8 8          ← The leaves are written in order from
2 | 0 0 1 2 3 4 6                least to greatest.
```

 1 | 2 represents the data value 12.

The median is the number represented by the 8th leaf (of 15) counting from left to
right beginning in the top row. This leaf represents the data value 18.

The mode is identified by the leaf (or leaves) that occurs in one row more often than
all the other leaves in the plot. Here, the leaf 7 occurs three times in the first row.
This leaf represents the data value 17.

The mean of the data is $18\frac{13}{15}$.

## MODULE 1   SECTION 2              STUDY GUIDE

## Exploration 2: Box-and-Whisker Plots

A box-and-whisker plot shows how data are distributed by dividing the
data items into 4 regions. The five values that separate these regions are
the *lower extreme, lower quartile, median, upper quartile,* and *upper
extreme.* Each group contains about the same number of data items, or
about 25% of all the data items. The lower and upper extremes are the
least and greatest data values, respectively. While the median is the middle
item (or mean of the two middle items) of all the data values, the lower
quartile is the median of the data values that occur before the median in
an ordered list. Similarly, the upper quartile is the median of the data
values that occur after the median in an ordered list.

### Example

Use the box-and whisker-plot below to identify the lower and upper extremes, the
lower and upper quartiles, and the median of the data.

**Number of Dollars Donated to the Family Crisis Center**

### ■ Sample Response ■

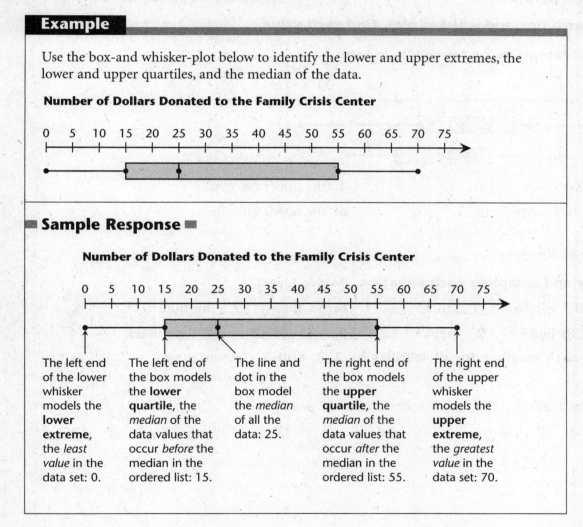

**Number of Dollars Donated to the Family Crisis Center**

| The left end of the lower whisker models the **lower extreme,** the *least value* in the data set: 0. | The left end of the box models the **lower quartile,** the *median* of the data values that occur *before* the median in the ordered list: 15. | The line and dot in the box model the *median* of all the data: 25. | The right end of the box models the **upper quartile,** the *median* of the data values that occur *after* the median in the ordered list: 55. | The right end of the upper whisker models the **upper extreme,** the *greatest value* in the data set: 70. |

        

## MODULE 1  SECTION 2 | PRACTICE & APPLICATION EXERCISES | STUDY GUIDE

### Exploration 1

**Use the data in the table for Exercises 1 and 2.**

1. Make two stem-and-leaf plots, one for the Test A scores and one the Test B scores. What do the shapes of of the stem-and-leaf plots tell you about the distribution of the scores on two tests?

2. Find the mean, the median, and the mode for each set of scores.

| Scores on Tests A and B | | | |
|---|---|---|---|
| Test A | | Test B | |
| 88 | 86 | 55 | 75 |
| 96 | 75 | 88 | 99 |
| 100 | 76 | 66 | 98 |
| 68 | 72 | 78 | 75 |
| 50 | 75 | 85 | 65 |

### Exploration 2

**For each box-and-whisker plot, find each value.**

**Age of Patients Having Appendicitis in April**

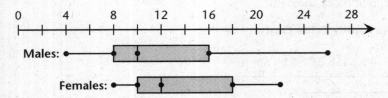

3. the lower extreme

4. the upper extreme

5. the lower quartile

6. the upper quartile

### Spiral Review

**Copy and complete each equation.** (Module 1, p. 8)

7. 3.5 m/min = ___?___ m/h

8. 45 mi/h = ___?___ mi/min

9. 288 lb/ft$^2$ = ___?___ lb/in.$^2$

10. \$.45 per day = ___?___ per week

**Test each number for divisibility by 2, 3, and 5.** (Toolbox, p. 595)

11. 405          12. 31,212          13. 330          14. 567

**Replace each ___?___ with > or <.** (Toolbox, p. 601)

15. −9 ___?___ −3          16. 45 ___?___ −323          17. −1 ___?___ −17

**MODULE 1  SECTION 3**                                            **STUDY GUIDE**

# Athletic Triumphs  Scatter Plots

**GOAL**  **LEARN HOW TO:** • organize data in a scatter plot
   • use a fitted line to make predictions

**AS YOU:** • analyze data about height and jumping distance
   • analyze data about students' heights and their jump heights

## Exploration 1: Making a Scatter Plot

**Scatter Plots**

A **scatter plot** is a graph used to compare two sets of data and look for the relationships between them.

On a scatter plot, one set of data is modeled along the horizontal axis and the other set is modeled along the vertical axis. The numbers written along each axis are called its **scale**. The range of each data set determines the scale of each axis of the scatter plot.

## Exploration 2: Fitting a Line

If the data points on a scatter plot appear to fall along a line, then a **fitted line** can be drawn to show the *pattern* in the data and help make *predictions*.

### Example

Use the data in the table to make a scatter plot. If it makes sense to do so, draw a fitted line for the data. Then describe the relationship and make a prediction based on it.

**Age and Height of First 8 Children seeing Dr. Smith on Tuesday**

| Age (yr) | Height (in.) |
|:--------:|:------------:|
| 2 | 33 |
| 2 | 37 |
| 4 | 37 |
| 4 | 39 |
| 6 | 45 |
| 6 | 47 |
| 8 | 47 |
| 8 | 50 |

**Age and Height of First 8 Children Seeing Dr. Smith on Tuesday**

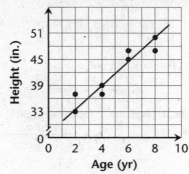

The relationship between age and height in children under the age of 10 appears to be linear. From the scatter plot, you could predict that the height of a 7 year old child would be about 47 in.

## MODULE 1   SECTION 3 | PRACTICE & APPLICATION EXERCISES | STUDY GUIDE

### Explorations 1 and 2

The scatter plot at the right shows the relationship between the high temperature and the number of ice cream cones sold between 2 P.M. and 3 P.M. each day during a two week period.

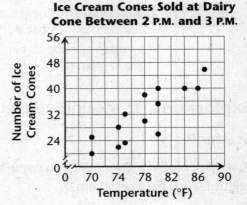

**Ice Cream Cones Sold at Dairy Cone Between 2 P.M. and 3 P.M.**

1. What was the approximate temperature when the greatest number of cones was sold?

2. Does it make sense to draw a fitted line for the scatter plot? Explain.

3. Suppose it is 2 P.M. and the temperature is 81°. How many ice cream cones can the owner expect to sell in the next hour?

### Spiral Review

4. Use the box-and-whisker plot to tell whether each statement below is *true* or *false*. Explain your thinking. **(Module 1, p. 18)**

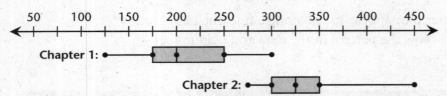

   a. All of the students totaled more than 200 points during Chapter 1.

   b. About half of the students totaled less than 325 points during Chapter 2.

   c. About 25% of all the scores in Chapter 1 were less than 175.

**Find each answer.** (Toolbox, p. 592)

**5.** $5^3$                 **6.** $6^2$                 **7.** $5 \cdot 3^2$                 **8.** $6.28 \cdot 1.4$

**Find the area of each figure.** (Toolbox, p. 605)

**9.**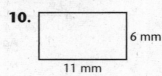
4 cm
4 cm

**10.**
6 mm
11 mm

**11.**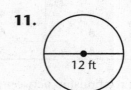
12 ft

Name _____          Date _____

# Amazing Appetites   Circumference and Volume

**GOAL**  **LEARN HOW TO:** • find circumference
• write and evaluate expressions
• find the volume of rectangular prisms and circular cylinders

**AS YOU:** • investigate a claim made in a tall tale
• investigate eating records

## Exploration 1: Finding Circumference

### Variables and Expressions

A **variable** is a symbol used to represent a quantity that is unknown or
that changes. An **expression** is a mathematical phrase that can contain
numbers, variables, and operation symbols.

**Example**

Each entry in the first row of the table is an expression. Below each expression is a list
of the variables in that expression, if there are any.

| 2xyz | 7 | 3(4) | 8 + d |
|------|---|------|-------|
| The variables are $x$, $y$, and $z$. | There are no variables. | There are no variables. | The variable is $d$. |

To **evaluate an expression** means to find its value for given values of the
variables in the expression.

**Example**

Evaluate the expression $5n^2$ when $n = 3$.

■ **Sample Response** ■

$5n^2 = 5(3^2)$     ← Substitute 3 for $n$.

$\quad = 5(3)(3)$     ← The **exponent** 2 means to use 3 as a factor 2 times.

$\quad = 45$

The value of the expression $5n^2$ when $n = 3$ is 45.

**MODULE 1  SECTION 4**                                    **STUDY GUIDE**

## Circumference

The **circumference** of a circle is the distance around it. $\pi$ is the ratio of the circumference of a circle to its diameter. $\pi$ is approximately equal to 3.14. The formula for finding the circumference is $C = \pi d$.

### Example

Find the circumference of this circle.

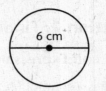
6 cm

### ■ Sample Response ■

$C = \pi d$          ← Use the formula for circumference.

$\approx (3.14)(6)$     ← Substitute 6 for $d$ and 3.14 for $\pi$.

$= 18.84$

The circumference is about 18.84 cm.

## Exploration 2: Finding Volume

### Prisms and Cylinders

A **prism** is a figure made up of flat faces that are shaped like polygons. The two *bases are congruent and parallel*. In a rectangular prism, the bases are rectangles. In this book, all the prisms are right prisms.

To find the volume of a right prism, use the formula volume = area of the base × height or $V = Bh$, where $B$ is the area of a base and $h$ is the height.

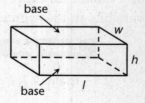

A **cylinder** is a space figure that has a curved surface and two parallel, congruent bases. In this book, all the cylinders are circular cylinders. That means their bases are circles.

To find the volume of a cylinder use the formula volume = area of the base × height. Since the area of a circle is $A = \pi r^2$, the volume of a circular cylinder can be written as $V = \pi r^2 h$.

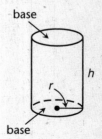

Name _____ Date _____

## Exploration 1

1. Find the circumference of a dinner plate whose diameter is 25.6 cm.

2. A bicycle whose wheels have a diameter of 15 in. was ridden a distance of 235.5 in. How many complete turns did the wheels make?

**For Exercises 3 – 6, evaluate each expression for the given values of the variables.**

3. $2\pi r$ when $r = 8$

4. $12 + t$ when $t = 34$

5. $4 - m$ when $m = 1.7$

6. $bh$ when $b = 4$, $h = 1.4$

7. Use symbols to write an expression for the word phrase *five less than the sum of a number and eight.*

## Exploration 2

**Find the volume of each figure.**

8.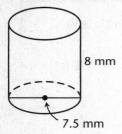
8 mm
7.5 mm

9.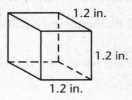
1.2 in.
1.2 in.
1.2 in.

10.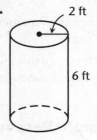
2 ft
6 ft

## Spiral Review

11. The table shows the keyboarding speeds in words per minute (wpm) for 8 students. Make a scatter plot using the data. Put hours of practice on the horizontal axis. If it makes sense to draw a fitted line, do so. (Module 1, p. 34)

| Hours of practice | 8 | 5 | 10 | 1 | 7 | 5 | 2 | 6 |
|---|---|---|---|---|---|---|---|---|
| Speed (wpm) | 45 | 35 | 60 | 18 | 45 | 33 | 25 | 40 |

**Find each quotient.** (Toolbox, p. 594)

12. $2.5 \div 30$

13. $64.8 \div 3.6$

14. $5.1 \div 17$

15. $8.9 \div 1.2$

**Find each answer.** (Toolbox, p. 600)

16. $9(1 + 1^5)$

17. $18 - 7 + \dfrac{32}{8}$

18. $12(3) \div 9$

19. $7 \cdot 3 - 2$

## MODULE 1  SECTION 5

# Extraordinary Rules of Thumb    Equations and Expressions

**GOAL**  **LEARN HOW TO:** • write equations from words
  • solve equations
  • simplify expressions

**As you:** • investigate rules of thumb
  • work with algebra and a rule of thumb about temperature
  • work with a rule of thumb about laundry

## Exploration 1: Writing Equations

### Writing Equations for Word Sentences

To write an equation, first choose a variable to represent each of the quantities that are unknown or that may change. Then use mathematical expressions to represent the word relationships between the quantities.

---

**Example**

Change the statement below into a mathematical equation. Tell what each variable represents.

*The total cost for a family to join a local health club is $100 the first month and $47 for each month thereafter.*

---

**■ Sample Response ■**

**Step 1**   Choose a variable to represent each of the unknowns.

Let $c$ = the total cost and let $m$ = the number of months.

**Step 2**   Represent the word relationships with symbols and variables.

$c = 100 + 47m$

---

## Exploration 2: Solving Equations

To **solve an equation** means to find the **solution** of the equation, or the value of the variable that makes the equation true.

You can find a solution by using **inverse operations**. Inverse operations are operations that undo each other. Addition and subtraction are inverse operations. So are multiplication and division.

**MODULE 1   SECTION 5**                                    **STUDY GUIDE**

### Example

Use inverse operations to solve $3x + 1 = 7$.

### ■ Sample Response ■

$$3x + 1 = 7$$
$$3x + 1 - 1 = 7 - 1 \qquad \leftarrow \text{The inverse of addition is subtraction.}$$
$$3x = 6 \qquad \leftarrow \text{Simplify.}$$
$$\frac{3x}{3} = \frac{6}{3} \qquad \leftarrow \text{The inverse of multiplication is division.}$$
$$x = 2 \qquad \leftarrow \text{Simplify.}$$

## Exploration 3: Simplifying Expressions

The parts of an expression that are added together are called **terms**. Terms with identical variable parts are called **like terms**. Like terms can be combined by adding or subtracting *coefficients*. A **coefficient** is the numeral part of the term.

*Expression*: $3y + 5 + 2y + 6 + y^3$

*Terms*: $3y, 5, 2y, 6, y^3$

*Like terms*: $3y$ and $2y$; $5$ and $6$

*Coefficients*: $3, 5, 2, 6,$ and $1$

To simplify some expressions and to solve some equations, you can combine like terms by adding and subtracting coefficients.

### Example

Combine like terms to simplify the equation $4x + 4 + 5x + 9 = 22$. Then solve it.

### ■ Sample Response ■

On the left side of the equation, the like terms are $4x$ and $5x$, and $4$ and $9$.

$$4x + 4 + 5x + 9 = 22$$
$$(4x + 5x) + (4 + 9) = 22 \qquad \leftarrow \text{Group the like terms.}$$
$$9x + 13 = 22 \qquad \leftarrow \text{Combine the like terms.}$$
$$9x + 13 - 13 = 22 - 13 \qquad \leftarrow \text{The inverse of addition is subtraction.}$$
$$9x = 9 \qquad \leftarrow \text{Simplify.}$$
$$\frac{9x}{9} = \frac{9}{9} \qquad \leftarrow \text{The inverse of multiplication is division.}$$
$$x = 1 \qquad \leftarrow \text{Simplify.}$$

Name _____     Date _____

## Exploration 1

**Change each word sentence into a mathematical equation. Tell what each variable represents.**

1. Theresa just started her new job. She will earn $6.25 an hour.

2. The cost of going to the zoo is $4.50 for each adult and $2.50 for each child.

## Exploration 2

**Use inverse operations to solve each equation. Check your solutions.**

3. $4m + 8 = 24$      4. $7h = 56$      5. $\frac{y}{13} = 9$

## Exploration 3

**In Exercises 6–8, combine like terms to simplify each expression.**

6. $8m + 4m - 7$      7. $8 + 5ty - y + 4ty$      8. $\frac{1}{2} + 3w^2 - 4w$

9. Simplify the equation $3h + 5 + 2h = 20$ by combining like terms. Then solve it.

## Spiral Review

10. Use $C = \pi d$ to find the diameter of a circle with a circumference of 45.9 mm. Use 3.14 for $\pi$. **(Module 1, p. 46)**

11. The volume of a rectangular prism is 385 cm³. The area of the base is 35 cm². What is the height of the prism? **(Module 1, p. 47)**

12. The equation for finding the area of a triangle is $A = \frac{1}{2}bh$, where $A$ is the area of the triangle, $b$ is the length of the base of the triangle, and $h$ is the height of the triangle. Find the area of each triangle below. **(Toolbox, p. 605)**

a.
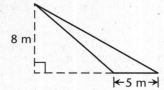

b.
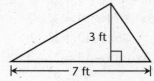

Name _____      Date _____

# Amazing Lake    Area and Perimeter

**GOAL**   **LEARN HOW TO:** • model the relationship between the area and the perimeter of various polygons
• use tables, graphs, and equations to model relationships

     **As you:** • learn about the Lake of the Ozarks

## Exploration 1: Exploring Area and Perimeter

### Area and Perimeter of Polygons

A **polygon** is a closed figure with three or more segments that do not cross. A **regular polygon** is a polygon with *all sides congruent and all angles congruent.*

Polygon
(closed, 3 or
more sides)

Not a Polygon
(open, crosses itself,
not formed by
segments)

Regular Polygon
(all angles are
congruent, all sides
are congruent)

A polygon with a greater area than another polygon does not necessarily have a greater perimeter, as shown in the Example below.

---

**Example**

The area of polygon *ABCD* is greater than the area of polygon *EFGHIJ*.

The perimeter of polygon *ABCD* is less than the perimeter of polygon *EFGHIJ*.

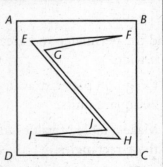

---

    

## MODULE 1   SECTION 6 STUDY GUIDE

**Mathematical Models**

Tables, equations, and graphs can be used as mathematical models to study mathematical relationships.

### Example

Three ways to model a relationship between the perimeter and the area of a square are shown below.

**Equations:**

$P = 2l + 2w$

$A = l \cdot w$

**Table:**

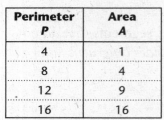

| Perimeter P | Area A |
|:-----------:|:------:|
| 4 | 1 |
| 8 | 4 |
| 12 | 9 |
| 16 | 16 |

**Graph:**

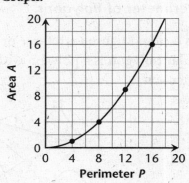

When data points fall in a curved pattern, a smooth curve can be drawn through the points as shown in the graph above.

## MODULE 1   SECTION 6 | PRACTICE & APPLICATION EXERCISES

## Exploration 1

**1.** Find the perimeter and area of a rectangle that is 34 ft long and 23 ft wide.

**2.** Find the perimeter and area of a rectangle that is 34 ft long and 34 ft wide.

**3. a.** On graph paper, draw 6 different rectangles that have an area of 20 square units.

**b.** Make a table of values for lengths, widths, and perimeters for these rectangles.

**c.** On a graph, plot points for the width and the perimeter of the rectangles. Put width on the horizontal axis. Then draw a smooth curve through the points.

**MODULE 1  SECTION 6**  PRACTICE & APPLICATION EXERCISES  **STUDY GUIDE**

**4.** Find the perimeter of a rectangle whose area is 55 square units and whose length is 11 units.

**5.** Tell whether each of the figures below is a polygon. Explain why or why not. If it is a polygon, tell if it is a regular polygon.

**a.**
**b.**
**c.**

## Spiral Review

**Simplify each expression.** (Module 1, p. 62)

**6.** $6n + 8n$

**7.** $9x + x - 3$

**8.** $4y^2 - 3y + 4y^2$

**Multiply and write each answer in lowest terms.** (Toolbox, p. 598)

**9.** $\dfrac{2}{3} \cdot \dfrac{3}{7}$

**10.** $1\dfrac{3}{4} \cdot \dfrac{6}{7}$

**11.** $\dfrac{8}{11} \cdot 77$

**Write each fraction as a decimal and as a percent. Round to the nearest hundredth.** (Toolbox, p. 597)

**12.** $\dfrac{5}{8}$

**13.** $\dfrac{12}{36}$

**14.** $\dfrac{7}{9}$

**15.** $\dfrac{1}{5}$

**MODULE 2**                                           **LABSHEET** 1A

## Group Survey Results (Use with Question 1–3 on page 83, Question 12 on page 87, and Question 14 on page 88.)

| What kind of store do you think is most important at a mall? | Number of group members who chose the type of store | Ratio of the number of group members who chose that kind of store to the total number of group members | | |
| --- | --- | --- | --- | --- |
| | | Fraction form | Decimal form | Percent form |
| clothing | | | | |
| shoes | | | | |
| CD/tape/video/ music | | | | |
| sporting goods | | | | |
| department store | | | | |
| video arcade | | | | |

| How often do you go to a mall? | Number of group members who go that often | Ratio of the number of group members who go that often to the total number of group members | | |
| --- | --- | --- | --- | --- |
| | | Fraction form | Decimal form | Percent form |
| one or more times a week | | | | |
| once every 2 to 3 weeks | | | | |
| once a month | | | | |
| less than once a month | | | | |
| never | | | | |

**MODULE 2**                                            **LABSHEET**  **1B**

## Combined Group Survey Results (Use with Question 14 on page 88 and Questions 16–19 on pages 88–89.)

**Directions** Combine your group's data from Labsheet 1A with data from two other groups. First record the total number of people in the combined groups. Then use the tables below to record the combined group survey results.

**Total number of people in combined groups:** _____

| What kind of store do you think is most important at a mall? | Number of people who chose that type of store (combined group totals) |
|---|---|
| clothing | |
| shoes | |
| CD/tape/video/ music | |
| sporting goods | |
| department store | |
| video arcade | |

| How often do you go to a mall? | Number of people who go that often (combined group totals) |
|---|---|
| one or more times a week | |
| once every 2 to 3 weeks | |
| once a month | |
| less than once a month | |
| never | |

**MODULE 2**  **LABSHEET  A**

**Inventory List** (Use with the module project questions on pages 94, 104, 134, and 157.)

**Directions** The items for sale in your game, along with their lowest possible sale prices, are given below. You must use these items and the price information in your game in some way.

| Item | Maximum price | Minimum sale price |
|---|---|---|
| digital watch | $29.99 | $17.50 |
| jeans | $35.00 | $17.00 |
| basketball | $12.99 | $10.00 |
| backpack | $35.00 | $19.00 |
| sandals | $17.99 | $12.00 |
| athletic shoes | $45.00 | $25.00 |
| CD | $17.99 | $10.00 |
| T-shirt | $22.99 | $7.99 |
| movie video | $29.99 | $18.00 |
| fanny pack | $15.99 | $9.00 |
| CD player | $135.00 | $69.99 |
| purse | $24.99 | $15.00 |
| athletic socks | $2.99 | $0.99 |
| computer game | $69.99 | $40.00 |

Name _____     Date _____

**Game Board**  (Use with the module project questions on pages 94, 104, 134, and 157.)

**Directions**  Use the gameboard to make a game that imitates shopping at a mall.

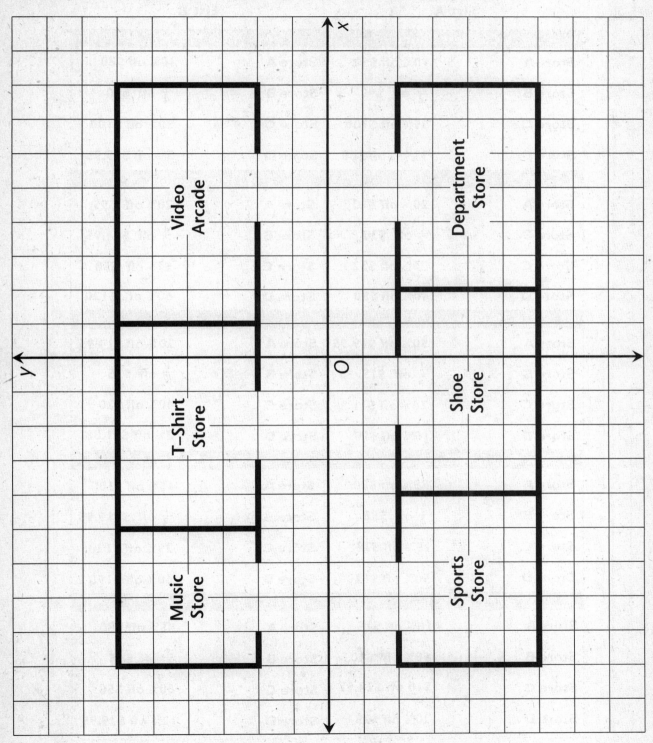

**MODULE 2**                                                                  LABSHEET **2A**

## Bargain Basement Game Cards (Use with Question 6 on page 97.)

**Directions**  You will need one photocopy for each group of students.

|  | **List A** |  |  | **List B** |  |
|---|---|---|---|---|---|
|  | **Cordless Phone** |  |  | **Tape Player** |  |
| Store A | | 10% off $50 | Store A | | 10% off $80 |
| Store B | | $\frac{1}{2}$ off $90 | Store B | | $\frac{1}{4}$ off $90 |
| Store C | | 55% off $100 | Store C | | 30% off $100 |
| Store D | | $33\frac{1}{3}$% off $60 | Store D | | 5% off $69.95 |
|  | **Jeans** |  |  | **35 mm Camera** |  |
| Store A | | 20% off $20 | Store A | | 20% off $55 |
| Store B | | $\frac{1}{3}$ off $30 | Store B | | $\frac{1}{2}$ off $94.95 |
| Store C | | 25% off $32 | Store C | | $15 off $58 |
| Store D | | 40% off $50 | Store D | | 60% off $120 |
|  | **Sunglasses** |  |  | **Compact Disc** |  |
| Store A | | 50% off $19.95 | Store A | | 20% off $14.95 |
| Store B | | $\frac{1}{3}$ off $15 | Store B | | $\frac{1}{5}$ off $15 |
| Store C | | 20% off $11 | Store C | | 40% off $20 |
| Store D | | 10% off $10 | Store D | | 7% off $21.88 |
|  | **Graphing Calculator** |  |  | **Roller Blades** |  |
| Store A | | 25% off $80 | Store A | | 15% off $100 |
| Store B | | $\frac{1}{4}$ off $88 | Store B | | $\frac{1}{3}$ off $119.95 |
| Store C | | 15% off $70 | Store C | | 25% off $120 |
| Store D | | 50% off $120 | Store D | | 60% off $190 |
|  | **Air Mattress** |  |  | **Bike Helmet** |  |
| Store A | | 10% off $15 | Store A | | 85% off $80 |
| Store B | | 60% off $40 | Store B | | $\frac{3}{5}$ off $45 |
| Store C | | $10 off $24.95 | Store C | | 60% off $50 |
| Store D | | 20% off $25 | Store D | | 12% off $29.95 |

# MODULE 2                                          LABSHEET 3A

## Group Drawings   (Use with Questions 11 and 12 on page 110.)

**Directions**   Your group will conduct three trials. For each trial, each
group member draws a single bean from the cup and keeps the bean
until the cup is empty. A trial is completed when all the beans have been
drawn from the cup. Follow the steps below for recording data during
each trial:

• Before each draw, record in the appropriate columns of the trial table
  the number of possible winning outcomes, the total number of possible
  outcomes, and the theoretical probability of winning.

• After each draw, record the actual outcome in the last column of the
  trial table.

| Trial 1 | Number of red beans (winning outcomes) | Total number of beans (total outcomes) | Probability of winning | Actual outcome (red or white) |
|---------|------------------------------------------|-----------------------------------------|------------------------|-------------------------------|
| Draw 1  |                                          |                                         |                        |                               |
| Draw 2  |                                          |                                         |                        |                               |
| Draw 3  |                                          |                                         |                        |                               |
| Draw 4  |                                          |                                         |                        |                               |

| Trial 2 | Number of red beans (winning outcomes) | Total number of beans (total outcomes) | Probability of winning | Actual outcome (red or white) |
|---------|------------------------------------------|-----------------------------------------|------------------------|-------------------------------|
| Draw 1  |                                          |                                         |                        |                               |
| Draw 2  |                                          |                                         |                        |                               |
| Draw 3  |                                          |                                         |                        |                               |
| Draw 4  |                                          |                                         |                        |                               |

| Trial 3 | Number of red beans (winning outcomes) | Total number of beans (total outcomes) | Probability of winning | Actual outcome (red or white) |
|---------|------------------------------------------|-----------------------------------------|------------------------|-------------------------------|
| Draw 1  |                                          |                                         |                        |                               |
| Draw 2  |                                          |                                         |                        |                               |
| Draw 3  |                                          |                                         |                        |                               |
| Draw 4  |                                          |                                         |                        |                               |

**MODULE 2**

# Grand Giveaway Experiment  (Use with Questions 16–18 on pages 111–112.)

**Directions**  With your group, complete 12 trials as described:

- Remove the red bean labeled *2* to represent the first draw.

- Each group member draws a single bean from the cup and keeps it until the cup is empty. Drawing a red bean is a winning outcome. A trial is completed when all the beans have been drawn from the cup.

- Record the outcomes in the *Trials* table.

**Example**

A trial consists of three draws.

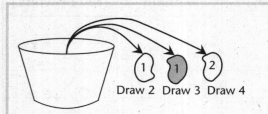

Draw 2  Draw 3  Draw 4

Record the outcomes of a trial in the Trials table.

| | Draw | | |
|---|---|---|---|
| | 2nd | 3rd | 4th |
| Trial 1 | W1 | R1 | W2 |

**Trials**

| | Draw | | |
|---|---|---|---|
| | 2nd | 3rd | 4th |
| Trial 1 | | | |
| Trial 2 | | | |
| Trial 3 | | | |
| Trial 4 | | | |
| Trial 5 | | | |
| Trial 6 | | | |
| Trial 7 | | | |
| Trial 8 | | | |
| Trial 9 | | | |
| Trial 10 | | | |
| Trial 11 | | | |
| Trial 12 | | | |

**Group Results**

| | Draw | | |
|---|---|---|---|
| | 2nd | 3rd | 4th |
| Number of times a winning bean is drawn on this draw | | | |
| Total number of trials | 12 | 12 | 12 |
| Experimental probability of winning on this draw | | | |

**Class Results**

| | Draw | | |
|---|---|---|---|
| | 2nd | 3rd | 4th |
| Number of times a winning bean is drawn on this draw | | | |
| Total number of trials | | | |
| Experimental probability of winning on this draw | | | |

**MODULE 2**

# Tree Diagram for the Grand Giveaway Experiment

(Use with Questions 23 and 24 on page 114.)

| 1st Draw | 2nd Draw | 3rd Draw | 4th Draw | Outcome |
|----------|----------|----------|----------|---------|
| | W2 | R1 | R2 | W1 W2 R1 R2 |
| | | R2 | R1 | W1 W2 R2 R1 |
| W1 | R1 | W2 | R2 | W1 R1 W2 R2 |
| | | R2 | W2 | W1 R1 R2 W2 |
| | R2 | W2 | R1 | W1 R2 W2 R1 |
| | | R1 | W2 | W1 R2 R1 W2 |
| | W1 | R1 | R2 | W2 W1 R1 R2 |
| | | R2 | R1 | W2 W1 R2 R1 |
| W2 | R1 | W1 | R2 | W2 R1 W1 R2 |
| | | R2 | W1 | W2 R1 R2 W1 |
| | R2 | W1 | R1 | W2 R2 W1 R1 |
| | | R1 | W1 | W2 R2 R1 W1 |
| | W1 | W2 | R2 | R1 W1 W2 R2 |
| | | R2 | W2 | R1 W1 R2 W2 |
| R1 | W2 | W1 | R2 | R1 W2 W1 R2 |
| | | R2 | W1 | R1 W2 R2 W1 |
| R2 | | | | |

## MODULE 2                                          LABSHEET **4A**

**Integer Speedway Rules** (Use with Questions 3 and 4 on page 122.)

### Getting Started:

- Play the game with a partner.

- Each player should choose one of the starting positions.

- Each of you should make a table like the one below to record your starting position, each move, and your position at the end of each turn.

- On your first turn, you may move one unit either vertically or horizontally, but not both. Be sure to record your move.

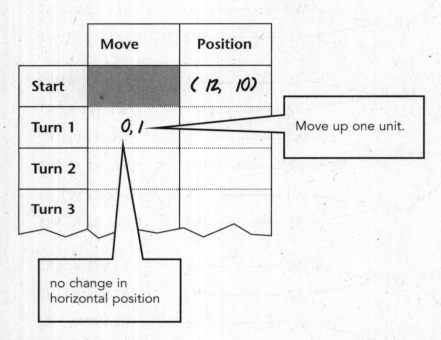

|        | Move | Position  |
|--------|------|-----------|
| Start  |      | ( 12, 10) |
| Turn 1 | 0, 1 | ← Move up one unit. |
| Turn 2 |      |           |
| Turn 3 |      |           |

no change in horizontal position

### Playing the Game:

- Players take turns moving along the track. On each turn a player may:

    1) use the same move as in the previous turn, or

    2) change the move by 1 unit, either horizontally or vertically, but not both.

- Players may cross each other's path, but they cannot occupy the same position at the same time.

- The arrow for a move must stay on the racetrack. If the arrow goes off the track, it is a CRASH and the player loses the race.

- You win the game when you cross the finish line first or when your opponent crashes.

**MODULE 2**                                                    **LABSHEET** **4B**

**Integer Speedway**  (Use with Questions 3 and 4 on page 122.)

**Directions**  Follow the instructions on Labsheet 4A to play *Integer Speedway*.

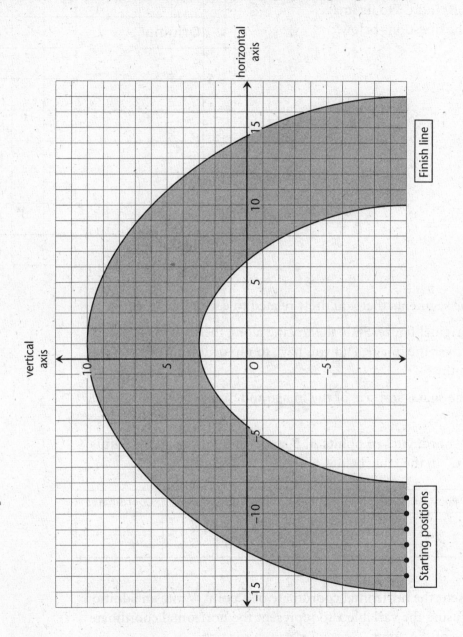

**MODULE 2**                                              LABSHEET **4C**

## Exploring Translations  (Use with Question 19 on page 125.)

**Directions** Draw a segment connecting each point (*A*, *B*, and *C*) to its image. Then answer the questions below.

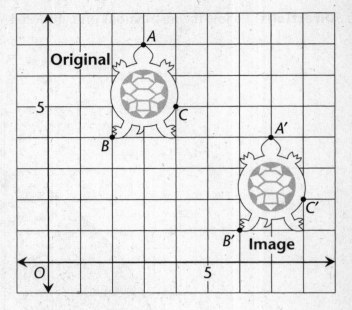

**a.** How are the segments that you drew related to each other?

**b.** Trace the original figure. Slide the tracing along the segments until it fits exactly over the image. Did you have to flip or turn the tracing in order to do this?

**c.** Compare the shape and size of the image and original figure. What do you notice?

**d.** Record the coordinates of points *A*, *B*, and *C* and of the image points *A′*, *B′*, and *C′* in the table below.

|          | Point | Coordinates | Point | Coordinates | Point | Coordinates |
|----------|-------|-------------|-------|-------------|-------|-------------|
| Original | *A*   | (3, 7)      | *B*   |             | *C*   |             |
| Image    | *A′*  |             | *B′*  |             | *C′*  |             |

**e.** Let *x* represent the horizontal coordinate of a point. Write an addition expression using the variable *x* to represent the horizontal coordinate of the image of the point.

**f.** Let *y* represent the vertical coordinate of a point. Write a subtraction expression using the variable *y* to represent the vertical coordinate of the image of the point.

**MODULE 2**                                    LABSHEET **4D**

## Exploring Multiplication  (Use with Questions 24–26 on pages 127–128.)

### Directions

• Plot the points below on the coordinate plane.

   $A(1, 1)$            $B(4, 3)$            $C(5, 2)$            $D(-1, -4)$

• Draw segments to connect the points in alphabetical order.
  Then connect point $D$ to point $A$ to form a four-sided polygon.

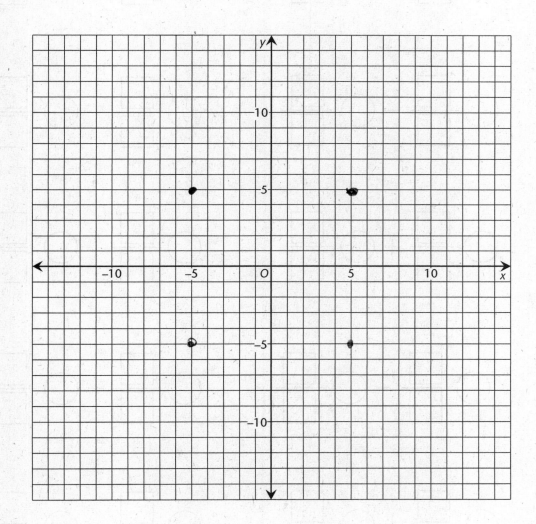

# Fraction Drop Game Boards

(Use with Questions 5 and 6 on page 138 and Question 8 on page 139.)

Player: _____    Player: _____

**Game 1**   ◯ □/□ + ◯ □/□         ◯ □/□ − ◯ □/□

**Game 2**   ◯ □/□ − ◯ □/□         ◯ □/□ + ◯ □/□

**Game 3**   ◯ □/□ + ◯ □/□         ◯ □/□ − ◯ □/□

**Game 4**   ◯ □/□ − ◯ □/□         ◯ □/□ + ◯ □/□

**Game 5**   ◯ □/□ + ◯ □/□         ◯ □/□ − ◯ □/□

**MODULE 2**                                    LABSHEET  6A

## T-Shirt Box-and-Whisker Plots (Use with Questions 23–25 on page 150.)

### Directions
- Find the lower extreme, lower quartile, median, upper quartile, and upper extreme of the T-shirt prices at a mall, listed below. Record these values in the table.

- Draw a box-and-whisker plot for the mall prices below the box-and-whisker plot for the Internet prices.

| T-shirt Prices at a Mall | | | | | | | |
|---|---|---|---|---|---|---|---|
| $8.00 | $9.00 | $10.00 | $12.00 | $12.00 | $13.00 | $14.00 | $15.00 |
| $15.00 | $15.00 | $15.00 | $16.00 | $16.00 | $16.00 | $16.00 | $16.00 |
| $16.00 | $16.50 | $17.00 | $17.00 | $17.00 | $17.00 | $17.00 | $18.00 |
| $18.00 | $18.00 | $18.00 | $18.00 | $19.50 | $20.00 | $20.00 | $20.00 |
| $20.00 | $21.00 | $22.00 | $24.00 | $25.00 | $25.00 | $28.00 | $30.00 |

| | |
|---|---|
| Lower Extreme | |
| Lower Quartile | |
| Median | |
| Upper Quartile | |
| Upper Extreme | |

### T-Shirt Prices on the Internet and at a Mall

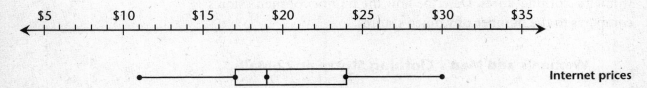

Internet prices

## MODULE 2                   REVIEW AND ASSESSMENT LABSHEET

### Cyber Spaceship Obstacle
(Use with Exercise 23 on page 159.)

**Directions** Draw the image of the triangle
after the translation $(x + 6, y + (-4))$.

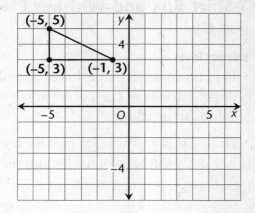

..................................................................................................................................................

### Clothing Stores at 22 Malls  (Use with Exercise 32 on page 159.)

**Directions** The table shows the number of men's clothing
stores at 22 malls. The box-and-whisker plot shows the
number of women's clothing stores at the same malls.

| Number of Men's Clothing Stores at 22 Malls | | | | |
|---|---|---|---|---|
| 9 | 25 | 33 | 7 | 41 |
| 23 | 25 | 17 | 10 | 19 |
| 14 | 9 | 18 | 7 | 7 |
| 16 | 10 | 20 | 20 | 12 |
| 6 | 7 | | | |

**a.** Estimate the median of the number of women's clothing
stores in the malls.

**b.** What was the greatest number of women's clothing stores
at any of the malls? Why is it marked with an asterisk?

**c.** About what percent of the malls had from 15 to 30
women's clothing stores?

**d.** Use the data in the table to make a box-and-whisker plot for the
number of men's clothing stores. Place your plot below the one for
women's clothing stores. Describe how the number of men's stores
compares to the number of women's stores.

### Women's and Men's Clothing Stores at 22 Malls

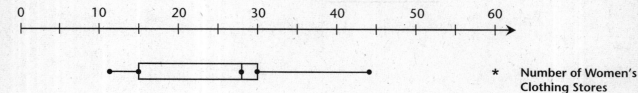

\*  **Number of Women's
Clothing Stores**

                    

Name _____          Problem _____

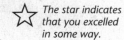
*The star indicates that you excelled in some way.*

 **Problem Solving**

❶    ❷    ❸    ❹    ❺

You did not understand the problem well enough to get started or you did not show any work.

You understood the problem well enough to make a plan and to work toward a solution.

You made a plan, you used it to solve the problem, and you verified your solution.

 **Mathematical Language**

❶    ❷    ❸    ❹    ❺

You did not use any mathematical vocabulary or symbols, or you did not use them correctly, or your use was not appropriate.

You used appropriate mathematical language, but the way it was used was not always correct or other terms and symbols were needed.

You used mathematical language that was correct and appropriate to make your meaning clear.

 **Representations**

❶    ❷    ❸    ❹    ❺

You did not use any representations such as equations, tables, graphs, or diagrams to help solve the problem or explain your solution.

You made appropriate representations to help solve the problem or help you explain your solution, but they were not always correct or other representations were needed.

You used appropriate and correct representations to solve the problem or explain your solution.

 **Connections**

❶    ❷    ❸    ❹    ❺

You attempted or solved the problem and then stopped.

You found patterns and used them to extend the solution to other cases, or you recognized that this problem relates to other problems, mathematical ideas, or applications.

You extended the ideas in the solution to the general case, or you showed how this problem relates to other problems, mathematical ideas, or applications.

 **Presentation**

❶    ❷    ❸    ❹    ❺

The presentation of your solution and reasoning is unclear to others.

The presentation of your solution and reasoning is clear in most places, but others may have trouble understanding parts of it.

The presentation of your solution and reasoning is clear and can be understood by others.

**Content Used:** _____          **Computational Errors:**  Yes ☐  No ☐

**Notes on Errors:** _____

_____

## STUDENT | SELF-ASSESSMENT SCALES

 *If your score is in the shaded area, explain why on the back of this sheet and stop.*

☆ *The star indicates that you excelled in some way.*

 ### Problem Solving

**❶**      **❷**      **❸**      **❹**      **❺**    ☆

**❶** I did not understand the problem well enough to get started or I did not show any work.

**❷** I understood the problem well enough to make a plan and to work toward a solution.

**❸** I made a plan, I used it to solve the problem, and I verified my solution.

 ### Mathematical Language

**❶**      **❷**      **❸**      **❹**      **❺**    ☆

**❶** I did not use any mathematical vocabulary or symbols, or I did not use them correctly, or my use was not appropriate.

**❸** I used appropriate mathematical language, but the way it was used was not always correct or other terms and symbols were needed.

**❺** I used mathematical language that was correct and appropriate to make my meaning clear.

 ### Representations

**❶**      **❷**      **❸**      **❹**      **❺**    ☆

**❶** I did not use any representations such as equations, tables, graphs, or diagrams to help solve the problem or explain my solution.

**❸** I made appropriate representations to help solve the problem or help me explain my solution, but they were not always correct or other representations were needed.

**❺** I used appropriate and correct representations to solve the problem or explain my solution.

 ### Connections

**❶**      **❷**      **❸**      **❹**      **❺**    ☆

**❶** I attempted or solved the problem and then stopped.

**❸** I found patterns and used them to extend the solution to other cases, or I recognized that this problem relates to other problems, mathematical ideas, or applications.

**❺** I extended the ideas in the solution to the general case, or I showed how this problem relates to other problems, mathematical ideas, or applications.

 ### Presentation

**❶**      **❷**      **❸**      **❹**      **❺**    ☆

**❶** The presentation of my solution and reasoning is unclear to others.

**❸** The presentation of my solution and reasoning is clear in most places, but others may have trouble understanding parts of it.

**❺** The presentation of my solution and reasoning is clear and can be understood by others.

**MODULE 2  SECTION 1**                          **PRACTICE AND APPLICATIONS**

## For use with Exploration 1

**Estimate each percent. Tell which method you used.**

**1.** 24% of 400          **2.** 56% of $200          **3.** 30% of 300

**Marketing Use the information at the right for Exercises 4 and 5. Round decimal answers to the nearest unit.**

In a survey of 800 teens:

56.2% listen to rock music radio stations

12% listen to new age music radio stations

33.8% listen to the radio at least once a day

**4. a.** Estimate how many of the teens listen to rock music radio stations. Then find the actual number.

    **b.** Estimate how many of the teens listen to new age music radio stations. Then find the actual number.

**5. a.** Estimate how many of the teens listen to the radio at least once a day.

    **b.** Use the "Undoing" method to find the actual number of students who listen to the radio once a day.

    **c.** Use the "Equivalent Fraction" method to find the number of students who listen to the radio once a day.

    **d.** Based on your answers to parts (b) and (c), which method do you prefer? Explain.

**Use a proportion to find each percent.**

**6.** 18% of 340         **7.** 175% of 92         **8.** 16.8% of 600

**9.** 62.4% of 430       **10.** 0.4% of 8000      **11.** 115% of 12

**12.** A top-grossing music concert was given by the Rolling Stones in March 1995, with a revenue of $27,600,000. If the Elton John/Billy Joel concert in April 1995, earned $4,400,000, use a percent to compare the revenue of the concerts.

*(continued)*

## MODULE 2  SECTION 1 | PRACTICE AND APPLICATIONS

### For use with Exploration 2

**Use an equation to find each number or percent.**

**13.** What is 60% of 90?

**14.** 0.8% of 20 is what number?

**15.** 45 is what percent of 225?

**16.** 6 is what percent of 300?

**17.** 6.3 is 9% of what number?

**18.** 42 is 175% of what number?

**19.** 84 is what percent of 56?

**20.** 8% of what number is 24?

**21.** Suppose a middle school survey is taken to find out if students should be allowed to eat their lunch outside during good weather. The survey is given only to eighth graders.

  **a.** What is the population? What is the sample?

  **b.** Is this a representative sample? Why or why not?

**22.** Use the information shown in the graph. Find what percent of music media are each type.

  **a.** music videos

  **b.** compact discs

  **c.** tapes

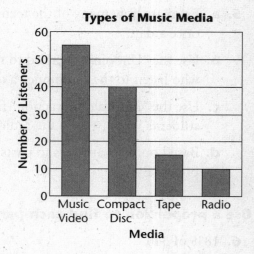

Types of Music Media

**23.** The average number of customers in a restaurant on a typical day in January is 28. To increase the number of customers the manager advertises that the second meal of equal or lesser cost will be free to the first 10 customers when the first meal is ordered. On the next night in January, the number of free meals served was 20% of the total number of customers.

  **a.** Write an equation and find the total number of meals ordered in the restaurant that day.

  **b.** Do you think the free meal giveaway helped increase the number of customers? Why or why not?

  **c.** Suppose the free meals averaged $15, and the price of a regular meal averages $21. Was the promotion a good idea? Explain your answer.

# MODULE 2  SECTION 2

## For use with Exploration 1

**1.** Find 51% of $39.99. Describe two different ways to find the number.

**For Exercises 2–7, estimate the answer. Then find the exact answer.**

**2.** 33% of 120

**3.** 60% of 48

**4.** 9% of 700

**5.** 41% of 250

**6.** 19% of 230

**7.** 49% of 200

**A store advertises that all prices are 25–50 percent off. The price tags below represent the tags used by a store to label its sale prices. The original price is crossed out on each sale tag, and the sale price is written above. Use estimation or mental math to check that each price is within the advertised range. Tell which tags are marked incorrectly and explain how you know.**

**8.**

$26.00
$~~49.95~~

**9.**

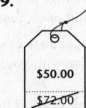

$50.00
$~~72.00~~

**10.**

$60.00
$~~79.95~~

**11.**

$64.00
$~~120.00~~

**12.**

$62.00
$~~89.95~~

**13.**

$2.50
$~~10.95~~

*(continued)*

## MODULE 2  SECTION 2                    PRACTICE AND APPLICATIONS

### For use with Exploration 2

**14.** Suppose a store's sales increased 8% from June to July and 8% from July to August.

    **a.** Sales were $8199 in June. Estimate the sales in July.

    **b.** Use your estimate in part (a) to estimate the sales in August.

    **c.** Find the actual sales in July. Then use your answer to find the actual sales in August. Compare the answers with your estimates.

    **d.** Harry thinks that since sales increased 8% in July and 8% in August, they increased by the same number of dollars each month. Is he correct? Explain why or why not.

**15.** In 1992, a typical starting salary for a college graduate with a degree in computer science was $30,890. In 1993, the typical starting salary was $31,600.

    **a.** Estimate the percent of change in starting salary from 1992 to 1993. Explain your method of estimating.

    **b.** Find the actual percent of change in starting salary from 1992 to 1993. How does it compare with your estimate?

**16.** In 1979, there were 90 million workers in the United States. In 1992, there were 108 million workers.

    **a.** Estimate the percent of change in the number of workers from 1979 to 1992. Explain your method of estimating.

    **b.** Find the actual percent of change in the number of workers from 1979 to 1992. How does it compare with your estimate?

**17.** The number of cars and light trucks sold in the United States is shown in the graph.

    **a.** Find the percent of increase from 1991 to 1993.

    **b.** Find the percent of decrease from 1990 to 1991.

Vehicle Sales in Millions

## MODULE 2 SECTION 3                          PRACTICE AND APPLICATIONS

### For use with Exploration 1

**For Exercises 1–4, a number cube with sides numbered
1 through 6 is rolled. Find each probability and plot the
number on a number line as on page 115 of the textbook.
Label each point.**

1. the theoretical probability of rolling a 5

2. the theoretical probability of rolling an 8

3. the theoretical probability of rolling a 2, 3, or 4

4. the theoretical probability of rolling a number less than 4

5. Which of the events in Exercises 1–4 are certain? Which ones are impossible?

**In Exercises 6–8, tell whether or not the outcomes of the
events described are equally likely.**

6. rolling an odd number on a cube with sides numbered 1 through 6
   and rolling a number that is evenly divisible by 3

7. rolling a number greater than 4 on a cube with sides numbered
   1 through 6 and rolling a number less than 2 on the same
   number cube

8. spinning an A on this spinner or spinning a B on this spinner

9. In a bag of 50 marbles, 20 are red and 30 are green.

   **a.** One marble is drawn from the bag. What is the probability that it
   is a red marble? that it is not a red marble?

   **b.** Suppose the red marble is drawn at the first draw and not
   replaced. What is the probability of drawing a red marble on the
   second draw?

   **c.** Suppose a green marble is drawn on the first draw and not
   replaced. What is the probability of drawing a red marble on the
   second draw?

   **d.** Is drawing a red marble on the second draw dependent on the
   first draw or independent of the first draw? Explain your answer.

   **e.** Suppose a red marble is drawn on the first draw and replaced.
   What is the probability that a red marble is drawn on the next
   draw? Compare your answer with your answer in part (d).

*(continued)*

**MODULE 2  SECTION 3**                    **PRACTICE AND APPLICATIONS**

## For use with Exploration 2

**10.** Suppose a number cube with sides numbered 1 through 6 is rolled. What is the theoretical probability that it will show the number 1?

**Suppose a game uses the spinner shown. Three players take turns spinning the spinner. If the spinner lands on A, Player 1 wins. If the spinner lands on B, Player 2 wins, and if the spinner lands on C, Player 3 wins. If the spinner lands on D, nobody wins.**

**11. a.** Play 20 rounds of the spinner game with two partners. After each round, record the results in the table like this one.

| Round number | Player 1 | Player 2 | Player 3 |
|:---:|:---:|:---:|:---:|
| 1 | W | L | L |
| 2 | L | W | L |
| 3 | L | L | L |

**b.** What is the theoretical probability of Player 1 winning? of Player 2 winning? of Player 3 winning? of no player winning?

**c.** Did any player win most often? Do your results agree with the theoretical probabilities in part (b)?

## For use with Exploration 3

**For Exercises 12–14, use the spinner game played in Ex. 11(a).**

**12. Writing** Is the spinner game a fair game? Explain.

**13. Writing** Suppose you notice that the spinner never lands on C. What are some possible explanations? How could you verify if your explanations are accurate?

**14.** Suppose Player 3 doesn't win the spinner game on the first two spins. Draw a tree diagram to show the possible outcomes.

**15.** Draw a tree diagram to show all possible outcomes when a coin is flipped four times.

Name _____ Date _____

## For use with Exploration 1

**Find each sum.**

**1.** $-19 + (-12)$           **2.** $82 + (-8)$           **3.** $-12 + 5$

**4.** $9 + (-9)$           **5.** $-72 + (-13)$           **6.** $3 + (-12) + 8$

**Find the opposite of each integer.**

**7.** $-14$           **8.** $-92$           **9.** $104$

**10.** $17$           **11.** $-18$           **12.** $3$

**Find each absolute value.**

**13.** $|14|$           **14.** $|-34|$           **15.** $|0.18|$

**16.** $|-0.31|$           **17.** $\left|-\frac{1}{4}\right|$           **18.** $\left|-2\frac{1}{8}\right|$

**19.** Find two different integers with an absolute value of 13.

**Solve each equation.**

**20.** $|y| = 17$           **21.** $-x = -4$

**22.** $|s| = 0$           **23.** $-y = 6$

**24.** Huy earned $12 one week and bought a radio for $8. The next week he earned $5. He went to the mall and spent $2 on lunch. Write an addition expression for his earnings and expenses. Simplify the expression.

*(continued)*

         

Name _____     Date _____

## For use with Exploration 2

**Find each difference.**

**25.** $9 - 12$

**26.** $12 - (-3)$

**27.** $3 - (-14)$

**28.** $-4 - (-4)$

**29.** $-18 - 3$

**30.** $-6 - (-21)$

**31.** The translation $(x - 3, y + 4)$ is applied to given figure SHAPE.

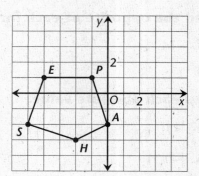

    **a.** Give the coordinates of the image points $S'$, $H'$, $A'$, $P'$, and $E'$.

    **b. Writing** Describe in words a translation that moves SHAPE to the opposite side of the vertical axis.

## For use with Exploration 3

**Find each product or quotient.**

**32.** $-36 \div 12$

**33.** $\dfrac{-18}{-9}$

**34.** $-56 \div (-8)$

**35.** $\dfrac{-28}{7}$

**36.** $12 \cdot (5)$

**37.** $-23(-2)(4)$

**Evaluate each expression when $a = -12$, $b = -4$, and $c = 32$.**

**38.** $ab$

**39.** $bc$

**40.** $abc$

**41.** $a \div b$

**42.** $c \div b$

**43.** $a - b$

**44. Weather** On each of three consecutive hours, the temperature dropped 4°F. If loss in temperature is represented by a negative number, write a multiplication expression that describes the total change in temperature, and find the total drop in temperature.

Name _____  Date _____

## For use with Exploration 1

**Find each sum or difference.**

**1.** $-\frac{6}{8} + \left(-\frac{5}{8}\right)$

**2.** $\frac{4}{9} - \frac{7}{9}$

**3.** $-\frac{9}{5} + \left(\frac{2}{5}\right)$

**4.** $\frac{3}{8} - \left(-\frac{3}{4}\right)$

**5.** $\frac{9}{15} + \left(-\frac{2}{5}\right)$

**6.** $-\frac{5}{16} - \left(-\frac{7}{8}\right)$

**7.** $-\frac{5}{6} + \left(-\frac{1}{2}\right)$

**8.** $-\frac{4}{3} - \frac{5}{9}$

**9.** $-\frac{4}{9} - \left(-\frac{1}{3}\right)$

**10. Cooking** A baker has $18\frac{1}{2}$ pounds of sugar and needs $1\frac{3}{4}$ pounds for cookies for the week.

   **a.** After the cookies are made, how much sugar is left for other recipes?

   **b.** Is there enough sugar to make seven batches of cookies?

**Find each sum or difference.**

**11.** $2\frac{3}{4} - 3\frac{1}{4}$

**12.** $-2\frac{7}{8} + 5\frac{3}{4}$

**13.** $-1\frac{7}{8} - 5\frac{1}{4}$

**14.** $4\frac{1}{8} + \left(-3\frac{1}{6}\right)$

**15.** $-4\frac{3}{5} - \left(3\frac{1}{4}\right)$

**16.** $6\frac{1}{2} - \left(-2\frac{1}{4}\right)$

**17. Challenge** The value of certain stock fluctuated 5 times during a single day from $-\frac{1}{2}$ point to $-6\frac{1}{4}$ points. Write a mathematical sentence using 5 fractions that could represent the fluctuations.

**18.** A fraction is between 0 and 1. If you add $\frac{1}{4}$ to it, the result is equivalent to $\frac{6}{16}$. Find the fraction.

| MODULE 2  SECTION 6 | PRACTICE AND APPLICATIONS |
|---|---|

## For use with Exploration 1

**Write an inequality to describe each situation. Then graph each inequality on a number line.**

1. The price of a pair of sneakers is more than $32 but less than $50.

2. The submarine was submerged no more than 100 feet in the ocean.

3. The temperature today ranged from − 4°F to 28°F.

4. The speed limit was over 55 mi/h but less than 70 mi/h.

5. The weight limit for the elevator was 2000 pounds.

6. The change in the stock price fluctuated from $-1\frac{3}{4}$ points to $3\frac{1}{4}$ points.

**Use the box-and-whisker plot below for Exercises 7– 9.**

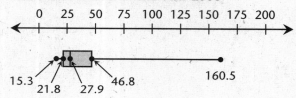

Projected Number of Computers in
Various Countries in the Year 2000

0   25   50   75   100   125   150   175   200

15.3   21.8   27.9   46.8   160.5

7. The box-and-whisker plot contains at least one outlier. Use the box-and-whisker plot and the data in the table to determine which countries are outliers.

| Country | Number of Computers (in millions) |
|---|---|
| United States | 160.5 |
| Japan | 46.8 |
| Germany | 29.8 |
| United Kingdom | 26.0 |
| France | 21.8 |
| Canada | 15.3 |

8. **Open-ended** Write and graph an inequality that shows the number of computers projected in the year 2000.

9. **Writing** Write a paragraph describing the data in the table.

*(continued)*

**MODULE 2  SECTION 6**                         **PRACTICE AND APPLICATIONS**

## For use with Exploration 2

**The heights of the girls 8th grade basketball team in 1996
and 1997 are given below.**

| Height (in inches) 1996 Girls Basketball Team | | | |
|----|----|----|----|
| 58 | 58 | 59 | 59 |
| 60 | 61 | 61 | 62 |
| 62 | 62 | 63 | 63 |
| 64 | 65 | 65 | 66 |

| Height (in inches) 1997 Girls Basketball Team | | | |
|----|----|----|----|
| 58 | 59 | 59 | 60 |
| 60 | 60 | 61 | 61 |
| 61 | 62 | 63 | 63 |
| 64 | 64 | 66 | 69 |

10. Make a box-and-whisker plot for the 1996 heights and one for the
    1997 heights. Label each box-and-whisker plot.

11. Does either of the data sets contain outliers? If so, redraw the
    box-and-whisker plot using asterisks to show the outliers.

12. What do the box-and-whisker plots show about the change of heights
    of the girls basketball team from 1996 to 1997? Explain.

**The number of computers (in millions) in use in 1994 and
1995 for 9 countries is given below.**

|      | U.S. | Japan | Germany | U.K. | France | Canada | Italy | Australia | S. Korea |
|------|------|-------|---------|------|--------|--------|-------|-----------|----------|
| 1994 | 85.8 | 14.9  | 12.3    | 10.9 | 8.6    | 6.2    | 5.9   | 4.0       | 2.6      |
| 1995 | 96.2 | 18.3  | 14.2    | 12.6 | 10.0   | 7.2    | 6.7   | 4.8       | 3.5      |

13. **Graphing Calculator** Make a box-and-whisker plot for each set
    of data.

14. Does either set of data contain outliers? Explain.

15. How does the number of computers in 1994 compare with the
    number of computers in 1995? Is this what you would expect?

# Your Opinion Counts!   Using Proportions and Percents

**GOAL**   **LEARN HOW TO:** • use proportional reasoning to estimate the percent of a number
• solve a proportion to find the percent of a number
• write equations to solve percent problems
• find a representative sample

**AS YOU:** • make predictions based on a sample
• analyze the results of the Mall Survey

## Exploration 1: Proportions and Percents

### Surveys

A **survey** is used to gather information about a group called a
**population**. When it is not practical to contact every member
of the population, a smaller group called a **sample** is surveyed.
When making a prediction based on observations or surveys,
usually only a sample of the population is used.

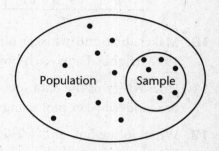

### Estimating Percents

You can use a "nice" fraction to estimate the percent of a
number, or you can use multiples of 10%.

---

**Example**

Estimate 27% of 600.

**■ Sample Response ■**

27% is close to both 25% and 30%.

**Using 25%:**

25% equals the "nice" fraction $\frac{1}{4}$.

$\frac{1}{4}$ of $600 = \frac{1}{4} \cdot 600 = 150$

**Using 30%:**

10% of 600 is 60, so 30% of 600 is
$3 \cdot 60 = 180$.

Since 25% < 27% < 30%, 27% of 600 is between 150 and 180.

---

### Finding Percents

To find the exact percent of a number, you can write and solve a
proportion. A **proportion** is a statement that two ratios are equal.
You can use cross products when solving a proportion. In a
proportion, the **cross products** are equal.

## MODULE 2 SECTION 1                                    STUDY GUIDE

### Example

Use a proportion to find 27% of 600.

### Sample Response

$$
\begin{array}{c}
\text{Percent} \quad \text{Number} \\
\text{part} \rightarrow \dfrac{27}{100} = \dfrac{x}{600} \leftarrow \text{part} \\
\text{whole} \rightarrow \phantom{\dfrac{27}{100} = \dfrac{x}{600}} \leftarrow \text{whole}
\end{array}
$$

$27 \cdot 600 = 100 \cdot x$  ← The cross products are equal.

$16{,}200 = 100x$  ← Divide both sides by 100.

$162 = x$

So, 27% of 600 is 162.

## Exploration 2: Samples and Percent

### Representative Samples

Care must be taken when choosing a sample. To make accurate predictions based on a sample, the sample must be a *representative sample* of the total population. A **representative sample** has the same characteristics as the entire population.

You can find an exact percent of a number by writing and solving an equation.

### Example

Write and solve an equation to find 27% of 600.

### Sample Response

Think: 27% of 600 is what number?

Now write this sentence as an equation and solve the equation.

$0.27 \cdot 600 = x$  ← Write 27% as a decimal.

$162 = x$

So, 27% of 600 is 162.

## MODULE 2 SECTION 1 | PRACTICE & APPLICATION EXERCISES | STUDY GUIDE

## Exploration 1

**Estimate each percent. Tell which method you used.**

**1.** 73% of 400

**2.** 39% of 250

**3.** 21% of $37

**4.** 32% of 9000

**5.** 59% of $350

**6.** 87% of 480

**Use a proportion to find each percent.**

**7.** 300% of 72

**8.** 35% of 112

**9.** 15% of 74

**10.** 24% of 350

**11.** 0.1% of 45,000

**12.** 43.8% of 1000

**Use an equation to find each number or percent.**

**13.** What is 20% of 38?

**14.** 16% of what number is 8?

**15.** 54 is what percent of 15?

**16.** What is 27% of 350?

**17.** 150% of what number is 540?

**18.** 117 is what percent of 234?

## Exploration 2

**19.** Suppose a manufacturer of baby food is conducting a survey to find the ages of babies who are most likely to eat their applesauce. The survey is sent to every household that mailed in the company's rebate offer during the previous year.

   **a.** What is the population? What is the sample?

   **b.** Is this a representative sample? Explain.

## Spiral Review

**20.** What is the least possible perimeter of a rectangle whose area is 49 in.$^2$? **(Module 1, p. 72)**

**Divide. Round each answer to the nearest tenth.** **(Toolbox, p. 594)**

**21.** 40 ÷ 2.3

**22.** 512 ÷ 1.5

**23.** 81 ÷ 1.6

**Find each product.** **(Toolbox, p. 592)**

**24.** 48 • 0.1

**25.** 7.2 • 0.01

**26.** 0.13 • 1000

**27.** 0.29 • 100

**MODULE 2  SECTION 2**                                          **STUDY GUIDE**

# The Price is Right, Isn't It?    Working with Percents

**GOAL**   **LEARN HOW TO:** • estimate percents
                          • use mental math to find percents
                          • use percents to solve problems
                          • estimate percents of change

       **AS YOU:** • play *Bargain Basement*
                 • analyze sale prices

## Exploration 1: Estimating with Percents

### Estimating Percents

You can use estimation or mental math to find a percent of a number.

---

**Example**

Find the amount of the discount and the sale price of a $28 watch on sale for 25% off.

---

**▪ Sample Response ▪**

First, find the amount of the discount.

**Method 1:** Use a decimal.

25% = 0.25
So, 25% of $28 is 0.25 • $28, or $7.

**Method 2:** Use a fraction.

$25\% = \frac{1}{4}$
So, 25% of $28 is $\frac{1}{4}$ • $28, or $7.

Now, find the sale price.

The sale price of an item is found by subtracting the amount of the discount from the original price.

So, the sale price of the watch is $28 − $7, or $21.

---

In the Example above, the sale price could have been found another way.
Since the watch is being sold for 25% off the original price, this means you
must pay 100% − 25%, or 75% of the original price. So the sale price can
be obtained by finding 75% of $28, or 0.75 • $28 = $21. The amount of
the discount can then be found by subtracting the sale price from the
original price: $28 − $21 = $7.

## MODULE 2  SECTION 2                                    STUDY GUIDE

### Exploration 2: Percent of Change

A percent discount is an example of a **percent of decrease**. You can find a percent of decrease by using a ratio.

$$\text{Percent of decrease} = \frac{\text{amount of decrease}}{\text{original amount}}$$

---

**Example**

What percent of decrease do you receive when you pay $40 for a $50 sweater?

**■ Sample Response ■**

To use the percent of decrease ratio, you need to find the amount of decrease and you need to identify the original amount.

The original price is $50. The decrease in price is $50 − $40, or $10.

$$\text{Percent of decrease} = \frac{\text{amount of decrease}}{\text{original amount}}$$
$$= \frac{\$10}{\$50} = 0.2, \text{ or } 20\%$$

So, there is a 20% discount on the sweater.

---

A **percent of increase** is also an example of percent of change. A percent of increase can be used to describe price markups and other increases.

$$\text{Percent of increase} = \frac{\text{amount of increase}}{\text{original amount}}$$

---

**Example**

A discount store paid $15 for each copy of a software program. If the store is selling the program for $20, what is the percent of increase?

**■ Sample Response ■**

To use the percent of increase ratio, you need to find the amount of increase and you need to identify the original amount.

The original amount is $15. The increase in price (*markup*) is $20 − $15, or $5.

$$\text{Percent of increase} = \frac{\text{amount of increase}}{\text{original amount}}$$
$$= \frac{\$5}{\$15} = 0.333..., \text{ or } 33\frac{1}{3}\%$$

So, there was a $33\frac{1}{3}\%$ markup on the computer program.

---

## MODULE 2 SECTION 2 | PRACTICE & APPLICATION EXERCISES | STUDY GUIDE

## Exploration 1

**1.** Describe two different ways to estimate 73% of $149.95.

**For Exercises 2–5, estimate the answer. Then find the exact answer.**

**2.** 49% of 36        **3.** 19% of 300        **4.** 60% of 13        **5.** 4% of 122

**6.** Find the amount of the discount and the sale price of a $75 jacket on sale for 30% off.

**7.** Find the amount of the discount and the sale price of a $15 book on sale for 40% off.

## Exploration 2

**8.** What percent of decrease do you get if you pay $29.25 for a $65 pair of pants?

**9.** What is the percent of increase on a paperback book selling for $5 that cost the bookstore $2?

**10.** What is the percent of increase on a box of cereal selling for $4.50 that cost the grocery store $1.50?

**11.** What percent of decrease do you get if you pay $18 for a 15 lb ham that normally sells for $32?

## Spiral Review

**Use a proportion to find each percent.** (Module 2, p. 90)

**12.** 19% of 340        **13.** 1% of 675        **14.** 51% of 30

**15.** 100% of 45        **16.** 2.5% of 1200        **17.** 24% of 365

**Find the greatest common factor and the least common multiple for each pair of numbers.** (Toolbox, p. 596)

**18.** 12, 15        **19.** 10, 14        **20.** 3, 15        **21.** 25, 35

**Replace each __?__ with <, >, or =.** (Toolbox, p. 597)

**22.** $\frac{3}{5}$ __?__ $\frac{2}{7}$        **23.** $\frac{5}{7}$ __?__ $\frac{1}{2}$        **24.** $\frac{2}{9}$ __?__ $\frac{1}{4}$

**25.** $\frac{4}{5}$ __?__ $\frac{8}{9}$        **26.** $\frac{3}{11}$ __?__ $\frac{3}{10}$        **27.** $\frac{1}{6}$ __?__ $\frac{2}{12}$

Name _____     Date _____

# The Grand Giveaway    Exploring Probability

**GOAL**   **LEARN HOW TO:** • find theoretical probabilities
• recognize dependent and independent events
• find experimental probabilities
• use a tree diagram to model and find theoretical probabilities

**AS YOU:** • examine a promotional drawing
• model a promotional drawing
• analyze a promotional drawing

## Exploration 1: Theoretical Probability

### Outcomes and Events

An **experiment** is an activity whose results can be observed and recorded.
The result of an experiment is an **outcome**. Outcomes are **equally likely** if
they have the same chance of occurring. An **event** is a set of outcomes of
an experiment.

---

### Example

Suppose an experiment involves rolling a cube
numbered 1 through 6.

**a.** Name the possible outcomes and tell if they are equally likely.

**b.** Name some possible events.

### ▤ Sample Response ▤

**a.** The possible outcomes are 1, 2, 3, 4, 5, and 6. The outcomes are equally likely
because they each have the same chance of occurring.

**b.** Some possible events are: rolling an even number; rolling an odd number; and
rolling a multiple of 3.

---

## Theoretical Probability

A **probability** is a number from 0 through 1 that tells how likely
something is to happen.

**Probability**

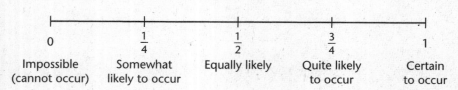

| 0 | $\frac{1}{4}$ | $\frac{1}{2}$ | $\frac{3}{4}$ | 1 |
|---|---|---|---|---|
| Impossible (cannot occur) | Somewhat likely to occur | Equally likely | Quite likely to occur | Certain to occur |

**MODULE 2  SECTION 3**                                    **STUDY GUIDE**

A **theoretical probability** is found without doing an experiment.

$$\text{Theoretical probability} = \frac{\text{number of outcomes that make up the event}}{\text{total number of possible outcomes}}$$

### Example

What is the theoretical probability of rolling a 1 on the number cube discussed in the Example on the previous page?

### ▪ Sample Response ▪

There are six possible outcomes, each of which is equally likely. Only one of these outcomes is a 1. So, the theoretical probability of rolling a 1 is

$$P(\text{rolling a 1}) = \frac{1}{6} \qquad \leftarrow \text{Read: "The probability of rolling a 1 is } \frac{1}{6}."$$

When the occurrence of one event affects the probability of the occurrence of another event, the events are **dependent**. Otherwise, they are **independent**.

## Exploration 2: Experimental Probability

A probability that is found by repeating an experiment several times and recording the results is an **experimental probability**.

$$\text{Experimental probability} = \frac{\text{number of times an event occurs}}{\text{number of times the experiment is done}}$$

## Exploration 3: Tree Diagrams

A **tree diagram** can be used to show all the possible outcomes of an experiment. You can follow a path along the "branches " of a tree diagram to examine a specific outcome. For example, the tree diagram below shows the possible outcomes of spinning the spinner at the right.

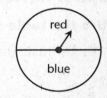

| First Spin | Second Spin | Outcome |
|---|---|---|
| r | r | rr |
|   | b | rb |
| b | r | br |
|   | b | bb |

The probability of spinning red once and blue once is $\frac{1}{2}$.

The probability of spinning the same color on both spins is also $\frac{1}{2}$.

## MODULE 2  SECTION 3 | PRACTICE & APPLICATION EXERCISES | STUDY GUIDE

## Exploration 1

**In Exercises 1–4, suppose you spin a spinner that has five equal sectors numbered 1 through 5. Find the theoretical probability of each event.**

**1.** spinning a 3

**2.** spinning a 1 or a 5

**3.** spinning a number greater than 5

**4.** spinning an odd number

**5.** In a box of 20 pencils, 10 pencils are red, 4 pencils are yellow, and the rest are blue.

    **a.** One pencil is taken from the box without looking. What is the probability that it is a red pencil? that it is not a yellow pencil?

    **b.** Suppose two pencils are drawn, one at a time. Are the two events below *dependent* or *independent*? Explain.

        Event 1: A blue pencil is drawn and is not put back in the box.

        Event 2: When a second pencil is drawn, it is also blue.

## Exploration 2

**6.** The table at the right shows the results of 30 flips of a coin. What is the experimental probability of the coin landing on heads?

| Heads | Tails |
|-------|-------|
| 18    | 12    |

## Exploration 3

**7.** Draw a tree diagram to show all the possible outcomes of two spins of the spinner at the right.

## Spiral Review

**Use the table for Exercise 8 and 9.** (Module 2, p. 100)

**8.** Estimate the percent of change in newspaper sales from June to July.

**9.** Estimate the percent of change in the cost of a newspaper from June to July.

| Newspaper Sales (in dollars) | | |
|-------|-------|-------|
| **Month** | **Total sales** | **Price per paper** |
| June | $530 | $1.00 |
| July | $450 | $1.25 |

**Tell whether each angle is *acute, obtuse, right*, or *straight*.** (Toolbox, p. 604)

**10.** 95°          **11.** 71°          **12.** 90°          **13.** 180°

**Write each group of integers in order from least to greatest.** (Toolbox, p. 601)

**14.** 10, −7, −11          **15.** − 4, − 6, 0          **16.** −5, −9, −17

**MODULE 2  SECTION 4**                                     **STUDY GUIDE**

# The Video Arcade    Operations with Integers

**GOAL**   **LEARN HOW TO:** • add, subtract, multiply, and divide integers
                         • find the opposite of an integer
                         • find absolute values

**AS YOU:** • simulate a video game
             • explore translations on a coordinate grid
             • explore a new visual effect

## Exploration 1: Adding Integers

The **integers** are the numbers ..., $-3, -2, -1, 0, 1, 2, 3, ...$ . The sum of two
integers may be positive, negative, or zero.

| **Example** |
| --- |
| Find each sum. |
| **a.** $-5 + 4$  **b.** $8 + (-8)$  **c.** $5 + 5$  **d.** $-5 + (-9)$ |
| **■ Sample Response ■** |
| **a.** $-5 + 4 = -1$  **b.** $8 + (-8) = 0$  **c.** $5 + 5 = 10$  **d.** $-5 + (-9) = -14$ |

The **absolute value** of a number tells you its distance from 0 on
a number line.

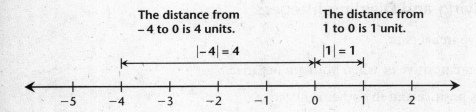

## Exploration 2: Subtracting Integers

Two numbers are **opposites** if their sum is 0. For example, 6 and $-6$ are
opposites.

To subtract an integer, add its opposite.

## MODULE 2  SECTION 4

### Example

Find each difference.

**a.** $4 - 6$　　　　　**b.** $-4 - 6$　　　　　**c.** $4 - (-6)$　　　　　**d.** $-4 - (-6)$

### ■ Sample Response ■

**a.** $4 - 6 = 4 + (-6)$　　　　　　　**b.** $-4 - 6 = -4 + (-6)$
　　　　$= -2$　　　　　　　　　　　　　　$= -10$

**c.** $4 - (-6) = 4 + 6$　　　　　　　**d.** $-4 - (-6) = -4 + 6$
　　　　　$= 10$　　　　　　　　　　　　　　$= 2$

A **translation**, or slide, moves each point of a figure the same distance in the same direction. A translation can be described by adding values to the coordinates of a point. The result of a translation is the **image**.

In the figure at the right, the vertices of the original triangle, $\triangle ABC$, are $A(-6, 2)$, $B(-4, 4)$, and $C(-2, 3)$.

The vertices of the image triangle, $\triangle A'B'C'$, are $A'(-2, -1)$, $B'(0, 1)$, and $C'(2, 0)$.

This translation can be described by $(x + 4, y + (-3))$.

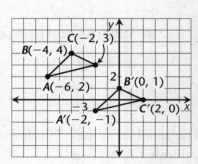

## Exploration 3: Multiplying and Dividing Integers

The product or quotient of two integers is:

• *positive* when both integers are positive or when both are negative.

• *negative* when one integer is positive and the other is negative.

### Example

Find each product or quotient.

**a.** $-4(-5)$　　　　　**b.** $4(-5)$　　　　　**c.** $-20 \div 5$　　　　　**d.** $-20 \div (-5)$

### ■ Sample Response ■

**a.** $-4(-5) = 20$　　　**b.** $4(-5) = -20$　　　**c.** $-20 \div 5 = -4$　　　**d.** $-20 \div (-5) = 4$

## MODULE 2  SECTION 4 | PRACTICE & APPLICATION EXERCISES | STUDY GUIDE

## Exploration 1

**Find each sum.**

**1.** $-13 + 25$ **2.** $35 + (-15)$ **3.** $-5 + 8 + (-9)$ **4.** $-255 + (-22)$

**Find each absolute value.**

**5.** $|45|$ **6.** $|-33|$ **7.** $\left|-1\frac{1}{2}\right|$ **8.** $|-3.5|$

## Exploration 2

**Find each difference.**

**9.** $-5 - 17$ **10.** $37 - (-6)$ **11.** $-27 - (-77)$ **12.** $-19 - 9$

## Exploration 3

**Find each product or quotient.**

**13.** $-6(-3)$ **14.** $6(-12)$ **15.** $-7 \cdot 8$ **16.** $-10 \cdot (-21)$

**17.** $-44 \div (-4)$ **18.** $-36 \div 9$ **19.** $\frac{45}{-5}$ **20.** $\frac{-220}{-10}$

## Spiral Review

**A box contains 3 red pens, 5 blue pens, and a green pen. Find the theoretical probability of each event.** (Module 2, p. 115)

**21.** pulling out a red pen on the first try

**22.** not pulling out a green pen on the first try

**23.** pulling out a blue pen after two red pens have been removed

**Find each quotient. Write each answer in lowest terms.**
(Toolbox, p. 598)

**24.** $\frac{4}{5} \div \frac{2}{3}$ **25.** $\frac{5}{12} \div \frac{3}{4}$ **26.** $\frac{24}{36} \div \frac{8}{9}$ **27.** $\frac{22}{33} \div \frac{10}{11}$

**Replace each ___?___ with the number that will make the fractions equivalent.** (Toolbox, p. 597)

**28.** $\frac{5}{7} = \frac{?}{63}$ **29.** $\frac{2}{3} = \frac{12}{?}$ **30.** $\frac{?}{96} = \frac{5}{8}$

## MODULE 2 SECTION 5

# A World Class Wonder    Operations with Fractions

**GOAL**    **LEARN HOW TO:** • add and subtract positive and negative fractions
**AS YOU:** • play a game with fractions

## Exploration 1: Working with Negative Fractions

### Adding and Subtracting Positive and Negative Fractions

To add and subtract positive and negative fractions, use the same rules as
for adding and subtracting integers. Remember that subtracting is the
same as adding the opposite. Make sure that the denominators of the
fractions are the same before adding or subtracting.

---

### Example

Find each sum or difference.

**a.** $-\dfrac{3}{7} + \left(-\dfrac{5}{6}\right)$     **b.** $-\dfrac{3}{7} - \left(-\dfrac{5}{6}\right)$

### Sample Response

Begin by rewriting the fractions using a common denominator. Choosing the least
common denominator will usually result in an answer that does not have to be
reduced to lowest terms.

**a.** $-\dfrac{3}{7} + \left(-\dfrac{5}{6}\right) = -\dfrac{18}{42} + \left(-\dfrac{35}{42}\right)$     ← The least common denominator is 42.

$\qquad = \dfrac{-18 + (-35)}{42}$     ← Assign the negative symbols to the numerators.

$\qquad = \dfrac{-53}{42}$

$\qquad = -1\dfrac{11}{42}$

**b.** $-\dfrac{3}{7} - \left(-\dfrac{5}{6}\right) = -\dfrac{18}{42} - \left(-\dfrac{35}{42}\right)$

$\qquad = -\dfrac{18}{42} + \dfrac{35}{42}$     ← Add the opposite of the second fraction.

$\qquad = \dfrac{-18 + 35}{42}$     ← Assign the negative symbol to the numerator.

$\qquad = \dfrac{17}{42}$

---

## MODULE 2  SECTION 5 | PRACTICE & APPLICATION EXERCISES | STUDY GUIDE

## Exploration 1

**For Exercises 1–12, find each sum or difference.**

**1.** $\dfrac{2}{3} - \dfrac{4}{5}$

**2.** $-\dfrac{1}{4} + \dfrac{1}{6}$

**3.** $\dfrac{6}{2} - \left(-\dfrac{3}{4}\right)$

**4.** $-1\dfrac{1}{3} - \left(-\dfrac{2}{9}\right)$

**5.** $-\dfrac{4}{5} + 2\dfrac{3}{10}$

**6.** $\dfrac{7}{8} + 1\dfrac{1}{2}$

**7.** $-\dfrac{6}{9} + \left(-\dfrac{5}{12}\right)$

**8.** $\dfrac{1}{9} - \dfrac{2}{3}$

**9.** $-1\dfrac{2}{5} - \left(-3\dfrac{4}{15}\right)$

**10.** $-\dfrac{2}{9} + \dfrac{4}{5} + \left(-\dfrac{5}{9}\right)$

**11.** $-\dfrac{1}{6} + \dfrac{3}{8} - \dfrac{1}{6}$

**12.** $\dfrac{9}{3} - \left(-2\dfrac{1}{2}\right)$

**13. a.** Use the numbers 2, 4, 8, and 9, the symbols + and –, and the part of the game board shown to create the greatest number you can.

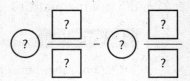

  **b.** How would your answer to part (a) be different if both symbols were – ?

## Spiral Review

**For Exercises 14–17, simplify each expression.** (Module 2, p. 130)

**14.** $35 + (-23)$

**15.** $-5 \cdot (-19)$

**16.** $88 \div (-11)$

**17.** $-9 - 25$

**18.** The box-and-whisker plot models survey data from 25 classrooms. Find the lower extreme, the upper extreme, and the lower quartile of the data. (Module 1, p. 21)

**Students per Classroom Who Would
Like to Study About Space**

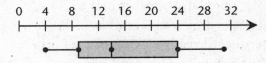

**MODULE 2  SECTION 6**                                    **STUDY GUIDE**

# Nice T-Shirt!    Inequalities and Box-and Whisker Plots

**GOAL**  **LEARN HOW TO:** • write and graph inequalities
• make a box-and-whisker plot
• use box-and-whisker plots to make comparisons

**AS YOU:** • examine bids for a charity auction
• compare T-shirt prices from different sources

## Exploration 1: Graphing Inequalities

### Inequalities and Outliers

Mathematical sentences that compare two quantities using the symbols ≤, ≥, <, and > are **inequalities**. Inequalities can be graphed on a number line.

---

**Example**

On a number line, graph the numbers that are less than 4 and greater than or equal to −3. Write the inequality for this word sentence.

**Sample Response**

On the graph below, a closed circle is used at −3 to indicate that −3 is part of the graph. The open circle at 4 indicates that 4 is *not* part of the graph.

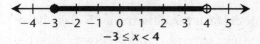

$$-3 \le x < 4$$

---

A data value that is significantly different from other values in a data set is called an **outlier**. An asterisk (*) is used on a box-and-whisker plot to show an outlier of the data set. Each whisker is drawn so it ends at the last data point that is not an outlier. The **interquartile range (IQR)** of a set of data is the range of the values modeled by the box in a box-and-whisker plot.

IQR = Upper Quartile − Lower Quartile

The interquartile range is used to tell whether a value in a data set is an outlier. If a data value is more than 1.5 × IQR units less than the lower quartile or greater than the upper quartile, then it is an outlier.

| MODULE 2  SECTION 6 | STUDY GUIDE |

## Exploration 2: Making Box-and-Whisker Plots

The steps for constructing a box-and-whisker plot are given below.

**Step 1** Put the data in order from least to greatest.

**Step 2** Find the upper and lower extremes of the data.

**Step 3** Find the median.

**Step 4** Find the lower quartile and the upper quartile.

**Step 5** Plot the lower extreme, lower quartile, median, upper quartile, and upper extreme below a number line. Use these values to draw the box and the whiskers.

| Example |

Make a box-and-whisker plot using the data: 3, 8, 9, 6, 7, 8, 8, 6, 12, 9, 11.

### ■ Sample Response ■

**Step 1** Put the data in order from least to greatest: 3, 6, 6, 7, 8, 8, 8, 9, 9, 11, 12

**Step 2** Find the upper and lower extremes of the data. The lower extreme is 3 and the upper extreme is 12.

**Step 3** Find the median. There are 11 data values, so the median is the 6th value from either end of the ordered list in Step 1. Therefore, the median is 8.

**Step 4** Find the lower quartile and the upper quartile. There are five data values in the ordered list that are to the left of the median and five others that are to its right. The lower quartile is the median of the lower five values and the upper quartile is the median of the upper five values. So, the lower quartile is 6 and the upper quartile is 9.

**Step 5** Plot the lower extreme, lower quartile, median, upper quartile, and upper extreme below a number line. Use these values to draw the box and whiskers.

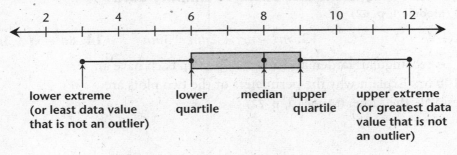

## MODULE 2  SECTION 6 | PRACTICE & APPLICATION EXERCISES | STUDY GUIDE

### Exploration 1

**Write an inequality to describe each situation. Then graph each inequality on a number line.**

1. The cost of getting a haircut was greater than $15.

2. The depth of the swimming pool ranged from 3 ft to 12 ft.

3. The game is recommended for ages 9 years and up.

4. The breathing apparatus was good for ocean depths up to 300 ft below sea level.

### Exploration 2

**The data values below are the speeds (in miles per hour) of ten cars traveling on Interstate 75.**

**55, 55, 65, 60, 68, 65, 54, 75, 35, 65**

5. Find the lower extreme, lower quartile, median, upper quartile, and upper extreme.

6. Find the interquartile range.

7. Which, if any, of the speeds in the list are outliers?

8. If speeds of 45 mi/h and 40 mi/h were added to the data set, would there be any outliers? Explain.

### Spiral Review

**Find each sum or difference.** (Module 2, p. 139)

9. $-\frac{2}{3} + \left(-\frac{2}{3}\right)$

10. $\frac{5}{6} - \left(-\frac{7}{20}\right)$

11. $-5\frac{1}{4} - \frac{3}{8}$

**For Exercises 12–14, combine like terms to simplify each expression.** (Module 1, p. 62)

12. $15x - 3x + 9$

13. $m^3 - m^2 + 2mn + 3mn$

14. $8d - 5d + 3dr$

15. **Writing**  A rectangular garden and a square garden each have an area of 100 ft$^2$. Explain why the perimeters of the two plots are not necessarily the same. (Module 1, p. 72)

**MODULE 3**                                    LABSHEET **2A**

## Nomogram   (Use with Questions 3–6 on page 176, Question 11 on page 178, Question 18(d) on page 181, and Exercise 34(b) on page 186.)

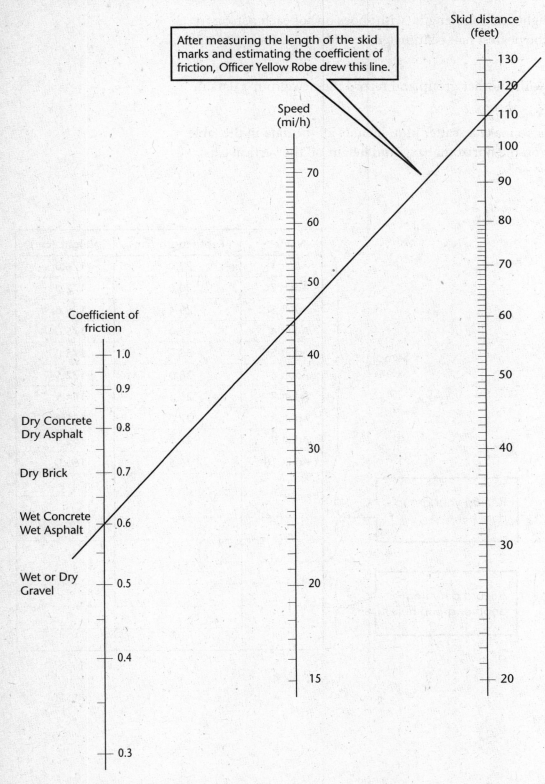

After measuring the length of the skid marks and estimating the coefficient of friction, Officer Yellow Robe drew this line.

Skid distance (feet)

Speed (mi/h)

Coefficient of friction

Dry Concrete
Dry Asphalt

Dry Brick

Wet Concrete
Wet Asphalt

Wet or Dry
Gravel

**MODULE 3**                    LABSHEET  **3A**

## Foot Length and Height Table   (Use with Questions 12–14 on page 193.)

### Directions

• Measure the height and foot length (with shoes on) of each person in your group to the nearest half centimeter. Record your data in the table below.

• Exchange data with another group and record the new group's data in the table below.

• Use graph paper to make a scatter plot. Include all the data in the table. Put foot length on the horizontal axis and height on the vertical axis.

• Draw a fitted line.

| Name | Foot length (cm) | Height (cm) |
|------|------------------|-------------|
| Adult 1 | 29.0 | 178.0 |
| Adult 2 | 30.0 | 177.0 |
| Adult 3 | 29.4 | 175.0 |
| Adult 4 | 29.0 | 175.0 |
| Adult 5 | 30.0 | 178.0 |
| Adult 6 | 28.0 | 172.5 |
| Adult 7 | 26.5 | 164.5 |
| Adult 8 | 27.0 | 165.5 |
| Adult 9 | 27.0 | 169.0 |
| Adult 10 | 26.5 | 160.0 |
| | | |
| | | |
| | | |
| | | |
| | | |
| | | |
| | | |
| | | |

Sample data

Record your group's data here.

Record data from another group here.

**MODULE 3**                                                    LABSHEET **4A**

## Two Right Triangles   (Use with Question 6 on page 203.)

**Directions**  The large triangle below can be divided into two similar triangles. Use the two triangles to answer the questions below. You'll need a protractor and a centimeter ruler.

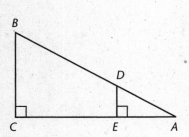
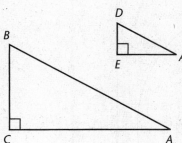

**a.** Complete the table below. Find each given side length for $\triangle ABC$ to the nearest tenth of a centimeter. Then name each corresponding side length for $\triangle ADE$, and find its measure. Then find the ratio of the corresponding sides. Round decimals to the nearest tenth.

| $\triangle ABC$ | $\triangle ADE$ | Ratio of corresponding sides |
|---|---|---|
| $AB =$ | | |
| $BC =$ | | |
| $AC =$ | | |

**b.** Complete the table below. For $\triangle ABC$, find each given angle measure. Then name each corresponding angle for $\triangle ADE$ and find its measure.

| $\triangle ABC$ | $\triangle ADE$ |
|---|---|
| $m\angle A =$ | |
| $m\angle B =$ | |
| $m\angle C =$ | |

**c.** In part (b), how did you find the measures of the angles? Describe any "shortcuts" you used.

**d.** Explain why $\triangle ABC \sim \triangle ADE$.

**MODULE 3**                                                    LABSHEET **4B**

## Circle 1  (Use with Question 13 on page 205.)

**Directions**  Follow the directions in your book for cutting and folding the circle.

## Circle 2  (Use with Question 13 on page 205.)

**Directions**  Follow the directions in your book for cutting and folding the circle.

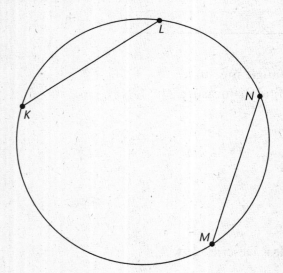

**MODULE 3**

## Circular Platter (Use with Question 17 on page 206.)

**Directions** The sketch below represents a pottery fragment from a circular platter. Use what you know about perpendicular bisectors of chords to estimate the original diameter of the platter. You will need a compass and ruler.

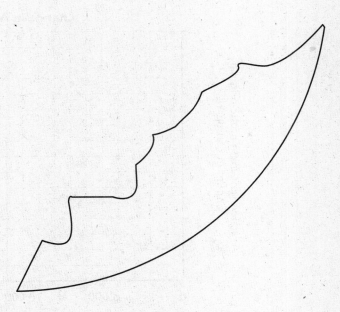

**MODULE 3**                                                                    LABSHEET **5A**

## Half-Life of Carbon-14   (Use with Question 3 on page 213 and with Question 11 on page 216.)

**Directions**

• Complete the table below.

• Use the data in the table to make a scatter plot on the grid. Draw a smooth curve through the points.

• Describe any patterns you see in the table and graph.

| Decay Pattern of Carbon-14 | | | |
|---|---|---|---|
| Number of years | Number of half-lives | Fraction remaining of the original amount of carbon-14 | Visual model |
| 0 | 0 | all | |
| 5,730 | 1 | $\frac{1}{2}$ | |
| 11,460 | 2 | $\frac{1}{2}$ of $\frac{1}{2} = \frac{1}{2} \cdot \frac{1}{2} = \frac{1}{4}$ | |
| | 3 | $\frac{1}{2}$ of $\frac{1}{4} =$ | |
| | | | |
| | | | |

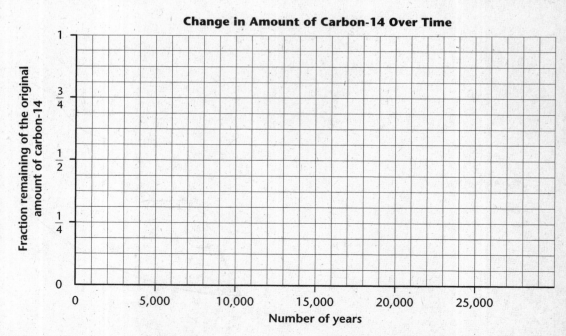

**Change in Amount of Carbon-14 Over Time**

Fraction remaining of the original amount of carbon-14

Number of years

# MODULE 3  LABSHEET 6A

**Suspect List**  (Use with Question 3 on page 225.)

| Suspect name | Condensed alibi | Absent from field trip? | Blood type |
|---|---|---|---|
| Alvarado, Winona | On the field trip. | No | O |
| Blanco, Gloria | Went to the movies. | Yes | A |
| Chan, Da-wei | Went grocery shopping. | Yes | O |
| Chee, LeVerle | At the Crownpoint minimall. | Yes | A |
| Cordero, Carl | On the field trip. | No | O |
| Foley, Bridget | At home. | Yes | A |
| Fuentes, Robert | On the field trip. | No | O |
| Kelley, Pat | On the field trip. | No | A |
| Martinez, Perry | At the Crownpoint rodeo. | Yes | A |
| Mendoza, Luis | On the field trip. | No | O |
| Nordquist, Karin | On the field trip. | No | AB |
| Pappas, Sophie | Ran errands in Crownpoint. | Yes | A |
| Perlman, Morris | On the field trip. | No | A |
| Puente, Rita | On the field trip. | No | O |
| Sakiestewa, Willie | Drove to Crownpoint. | Yes | O |
| Seowtewa, Teresa | At the Crownpoint library. | Yes | A |
| Stein, Nate | On the field trip. | No | AB |
| Suarez, Maria Elena | Worked out at a Crownpoint gym. | Yes | A |
| Sullivan, Michael | Catered a wedding. | Yes | A |
| Valenzuela, Martina | On the field trip. | No | O |
| Valenzuela, Pedro | At home. | Yes | O |
| Weatherwax, Alice | At a conference in Crownpoint. | Yes | A |

**MODULE 3**                                    **PROJECT LABSHEET** (5A)

## Suspect List  (Use with Project Question 15 on page 231.)

| Suspect name | Condensed alibi | Absent from field trip? | Blood type | Height (cm) |
|---|---|---|---|---|
| Alvarado, Winona | On the field trip. | No | O | 168 |
| Blanco, Gloria | Went to the movies. | Yes | A | 160 |
| Chan, Da-wei | Went grocery shopping. | Yes | O | 175 |
| Chee, LeVerle | At the Crownpoint minimall. | Yes | A | 182 |
| Cordero, Carl | On the field trip. | No | O | 185 |
| Foley, Bridget | At home. | Yes | A | 188 |
| Fuentes, Robert | On the field trip. | No | O | 187 |
| Kelley, Pat | On the field trip. | No | A | 158 |
| Martinez, Perry | At the Crownpoint rodeo. | Yes | A | |
| Mendoza, Luis | On the field trip. | No | O | 175 |
| Nordquist, Karin | On the field trip. | No | AB | 170 |
| Pappas, Sophie | Ran errands in Crownpoint. | Yes | A | 190 |
| Perlman, Morris | On the field trip. | No | A | 182 |
| Puente, Rita | On the field trip. | No | O | 174 |
| Sakiestewa, Willie | Drove to Crownpoint. | Yes | O | 180 |
| Seowtewa, Teresa | At the Crownpoint library. | Yes | A | 175 |
| Stein, Nate | On the field trip. | No | AB | 190 |
| Suarez, Maria Elena | Worked out at a Crownpoint gym. | Yes | A | 160 |
| Sullivan, Michael | Catered a wedding. | Yes | A | 182 |
| Valenzuela, Martina | On the field trip. | No | O | 170 |
| Valenzuela, Pedro | At home. | Yes | O | 173 |
| Weatherwax, Alice | At a conference in Crownpoint. | Yes | A | |

## MODULE 3                    REVIEW AND ASSESSMENT LABSHEET

## Diameter of a Tree Trunk   (Use with Exercise 18 on page 235.)

### Directions
• Use paper folding and the outer tree trunk section shown below to determine the approximate length of the diameter of the tree trunk.

• Mark a radius and a chord.

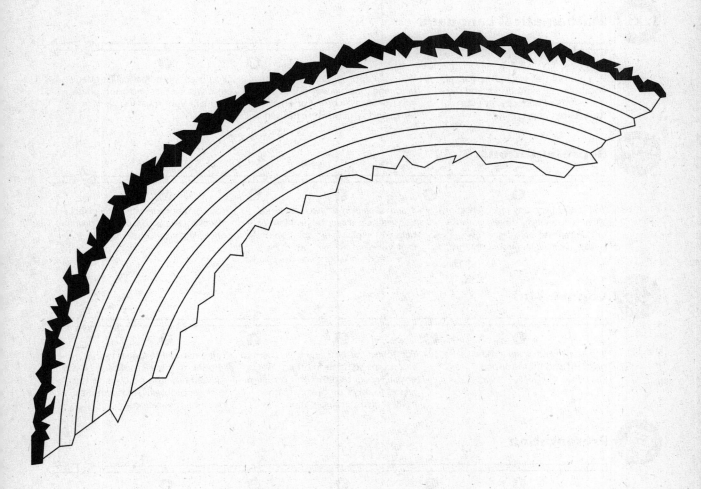

## TEACHER  ASSESSMENT SCALES

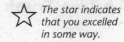
*The star indicates that you excelled in some way.*

 **Problem Solving**

**①**  **②**  **③**  **④**  **⑤**

**①** You did not understand the problem well enough to get started or you did not show any work.

**③** You understood the problem well enough to make a plan and to work toward a solution.

**⑤** You made a plan, you used it to solve the problem, and you verified your solution.

 **Mathematical Language**

**①**  **②**  **③**  **④**  **⑤**

**①** You did not use any mathematical vocabulary or symbols, or you did not use them correctly, or your use was not appropriate.

**③** You used appropriate mathematical language, but the way it was used was not always correct or other terms and symbols were needed.

**⑤** You used mathematical language that was correct and appropriate to make your meaning clear.

 **Representations**

**①**  **②**  **③**  **④**  **⑤**

**①** You did not use any representations such as equations, tables, graphs, or diagrams to help solve the problem or explain your solution.

**③** You made appropriate representations to help solve the problem or help you explain your solution, but they were not always correct or other representations were needed.

**⑤** You used appropriate and correct representations to solve the problem or explain your solution.

 **Connections**

**①**  **②**  **③**  **④**  **⑤**

**①** You attempted or solved the problem and then stopped.

**③** You found patterns and used them to extend the solution to other cases, or you recognized that this problem relates to other problems, mathematical ideas, or applications.

**⑤** You extended the ideas in the solution to the general case, or you showed how this problem relates to other problems, mathematical ideas, or applications.

## Presentation

**①**  **②**  **③**  **④**  **⑤**

**①** The presentation of your solution and reasoning is unclear to others.

**③** The presentation of your solution and reasoning is clear in most places, but others may have trouble understanding parts of it.

**⑤** The presentation of your solution and reasoning is clear and can be understood by others.

**Content Used:** _____  **Computational Errors:** Yes ☐ No ☐

**Notes on Errors:** _____

**STUDENT**  **SELF-ASSESSMENT SCALES**

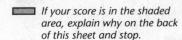 *If your score is in the shaded area, explain why on the back of this sheet and stop.*

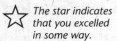 *The star indicates that you excelled in some way.*

 ## Problem Solving

**①**     **②**     **③**     **④**     **⑤**

**①** I did not understand the problem well enough to get started or I did not show any work.

**③** I understood the problem well enough to make a plan and to work toward a solution.

**⑤** I made a plan, I used it to solve the problem, and I verified my solution.

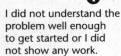 ## Mathematical Language

**①**     **②**     **③**     **④**     **⑤**

**①** I did not use any mathematical vocabulary or symbols, or I did not use them correctly, or my use was not appropriate.

**③** I used appropriate mathematical language, but the way it was used was not always correct or other terms and symbols were needed.

**⑤** I used mathematical language that was correct and appropriate to make my meaning clear.

 ## Representations

**①**     **②**     **③**     **④**     **⑤**

**①** I did not use any representations such as equations, tables, graphs, or diagrams to help solve the problem or explain my solution.

**③** I made appropriate representations to help solve the problem or help me explain my solution, but they were not always correct or other representations were needed.

**⑤** I used appropriate and correct representations to solve the problem or explain my solution.

 ## Connections

**①**     **②**     **③**     **④**     **⑤**

**①** I attempted or solved the problem and then stopped.

**③** I found patterns and used them to extend the solution to other cases, or I recognized that this problem relates to other problems, mathematical ideas, or applications.

**⑤** I extended the ideas in the solution to the general case, or I showed how this problem relates to other problems, mathematical ideas, or applications.

 ## Presentation

**①**     **②**     **③**     **④**     **⑤**

**①** The presentation of my solution and reasoning is unclear to others.

**③** The presentation of my solution and reasoning is clear in most places, but others may have trouble understanding parts of it.

**⑤** The presentation of my solution and reasoning is clear and can be understood by others.

**MODULE 3  SECTION 1**                    **PRACTICE AND APPLICATIONS**

## For use with Exploration 1

**Use mental math to find each value.**

**1.** $\sqrt{64}$

**2.** $-\sqrt{81}$

**3.** $\sqrt{2500}$

**4.** $\sqrt{0.01}$

**5.** $\sqrt{\dfrac{36}{49}}$

**6.** $-\sqrt{16,000,000}$

**7.** The dimensions of a typical front page newspaper screen is 34 cm by 56 cm.

  **a.** What is the area of the front page?

  **b.** Suppose a square piece of paper has the same area. Estimate the dimensions of the paper to the nearest centimeter.

**8.** Use the sketch of the building plan for each of the following.

  **a.** Find the perimeter of the storage building.

  **b.** Find the area of the storage building.

  **c.** Find the area surrounding the storage building.

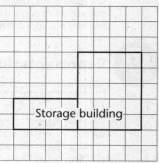

1 unit of length = 3 yd

**Estimate each square root to the nearest tenth.**

**9.** $\sqrt{42}$

**10.** $\sqrt{71}$

**11.** $\sqrt{8}$

**12.** $\sqrt{150}$

**13.** A square television screen covers an area of about 41 in.² Estimate the length of a side of the screen.

**14.** What whole numbers can you substitute for $n$ to make the statement $12 < \sqrt{n} < 13$ true?

**15. Probability** A lottery game includes numbers 1–54. What is the probability that a number picked at random for the game is a perfect square?

**16. Fill in the Blank** If the square of a number is between 25 and 49, then the number is between __?__ and __?__.

*(continued)*

**MODULE 3 SECTION 1** ␣ **PRACTICE AND APPLICATIONS**

## For use with Exploration 2

**17. Writing** Refer to the figure in Exercise 8. A home-owner estimates that the cost of installing sod on his lot is $4 per square yard less than installing a floor in his storage building. Explain why you think this is true or not true.

**For Exercises 18–19, use the equation $C = 10a + 3000$, where $C$ is the cooling capacity in Btu's of an air conditioner and $a$ is the area in square feet of the room it is cooling.**

**18.** A two-room apartment has rooms with dimensions 12 ft × 16 ft and 10 ft × 14 ft. Chris bought an air conditioner rated at 10,000 Btu.

   **a.** Sketch each room. Label the dimensions. Then find the required Btu's needed for each room.

   **b.** Determine if Chris bought the correct size air conditioner.

**19.** One room in Jorge's house is 18 ft × 26 ft, and another room is 9 ft × 13 ft. Jorge estimates that the larger room needs twice as much cooling capacity as the smaller room.

   **a.** Sketch each room. Label the dimensions.

   **b.** Do you think Jorge is correct? Explain.

**20. a.** Find the volume of the box at the right.

   **b.** Give the dimensions of another box with the same volume.

   **c. Challenge** Give the dimensions of a cube with the same volume.

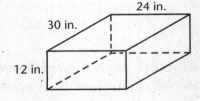

**21. a.** Find the volume of a cube with sides 16 in. and of a rectangular prism with sides 8 in. × 16 in. × 32 in.

   **b.** Compare the amount of cardboard needed to make each box in part (a).

   **c.** What can be said about the amount of cardboard needed to make a cubical box compared to the amount of cardboard needed to make a second box with the same volume?

## MODULE 3  SECTION 2                    PRACTICE AND APPLICATIONS

### For use with Exploration 1

**Evaluate each expression. Round decimals to the nearest hundredth.**

**1.** $\dfrac{2 \cdot 9}{6 - 3}$

**2.** $\dfrac{3(8 - 2)}{2}$

**3.** $\dfrac{(-6)^2}{14 - 2 - (3 \cdot 2)}$

**4.** $5\sqrt{3 \cdot 7}$

**5.** $-\sqrt{12 \cdot 3} + 5$

**6** $\dfrac{\sqrt{8 + 2} + 1}{3}$

**For Exercises 7–10, evaluate each expression.**

**7.** $3\sqrt{4^2 - 12}$

**8.** $\dfrac{12 - 7}{-4(2)^3}$

**9.** $6\sqrt{\dfrac{25}{3^2 - 4}}$

**10.** $8 + 3\sqrt{4 \cdot 2}$

**11.** The length of the shoreline of Keeler Lake is about 32 miles, and its surface area is about 14 mi$^2$.

   **a.** Evaluate the expression $\dfrac{L}{2\sqrt{\pi A}}$, where $L$ is the length of the shoreline in miles and $A$ is the surface area of the lake in square miles.

   **b.** Compare your value in part (a) with the value 1. The closer the value is to 1, the more circular the lake. Do you think Keeler Lake is circular? Explain.

   **c.** Suppose a lake is perfectly circular and has a diameter of 18 miles. Evaluate the expression for this lake. Will the value be the same for any circular lake? Explain.

**Evaluate each expression when $m = 4$ and $n = -3$. Round decimal answers to the nearest hundredth.**

**12.** $5\sqrt{m + n}$

**13.** $\dfrac{6m + n}{3}$

**14.** $\dfrac{m^3}{n}$

**15.** $\dfrac{m^2 + mn}{2mn}$

**16.** $\dfrac{25n}{2 \cdot 3}$

**17.** $\dfrac{\sqrt{m^2 - 4mn}}{2n}$

**18.** Write an expression that equals 6. Your expression should include a fraction bar, a $\sqrt{\phantom{x}}$ symbol, and at least three different numerical operations.

*(continued)*

**MODULE 3   SECTION 2**                    **PRACTICE AND APPLICATIONS**

## For use with Exploration 2

**19.** The recommended "following distance" for a car is given by $d = 1.5s$, where $d$ is the recommended following distance in feet and $s$ is the speed of the car in miles per hour.

   **a.** Find the recommended following distance for a car traveling at 25 mi/h.

   **b.** If the recommended following distance is 80 ft, how fast is the car traveling?

**20. a.** Estimate the speed of a car that leaves a 20 ft skid mark on a road with a coefficient of friction 0.81. Use the formula $s = 5.5\sqrt{d \cdot f}$, where $d$ is the length of the skid mark in feet.

   **b.** Use a graphing calculator to graph the equation $y = 5.5\sqrt{0.81x}$, where 0.81 is the coefficient of friction for dry concrete.

   **c.** Use your answer to part (b) to estimate the speed of a car that leaves a 50 ft skid mark.

**Graph each equation.**

**21.** $y = 3x - 1$          **22.** $y = -4x$          **23.** $y = 2x - 4$

**24.** $y = 6$              **25.** $y = 20 + x$       **26.** $y = 30 - x$

**Graphing Calculator Graph each equation. Tell whether the graph is *linear* or *nonlinear*.**

**27.** $y = \sqrt{x}$        **28.** $y = -0.2x$        **29.** $y = 2x^2$

**30.** $y = \dfrac{1}{x}$    **31.** $y = \sqrt{5} + x$  **32.** $y = x^3$

## MODULE 3  SECTION 3                          PRACTICE AND APPLICATIONS

### For use with Exploration 1

**Find the slope of each line.**

1.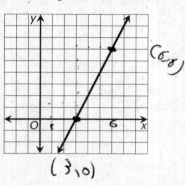

(6,8)

(3,0)

2.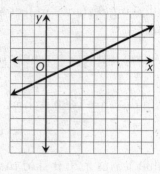

3.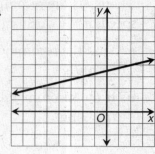

**For Exercises 4 and 5, use the graph at the right. The graph models Juan's average Calorie usage while jogging.**

4. **a.** Find the slope of the line.

   **b.** Find the average number of Calories used per minute.

   **c.** Write an equation that you can use to find the average number of Calories used per minute.

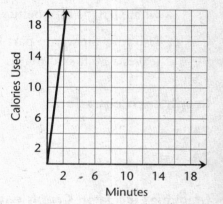

5. **a.** For Exercise (4), suppose Juan increases the number of Calories he uses while jogging by 10%. Write a new equation to model the number of Calories he uses.

   **b.** Graph the new equation. Find the slope of the graph.

6. **a.** On a coordinate grid, graph the points $(-4, 2)$ and $(4, 6)$.

   **b.** Draw a line connecting the points.

   **c.** Find the slope of the line.

   **d.** Explain how to find the slope of the line connecting two points.

7. **Challenge** Find the slope of a line that passes through the points $(-3, 6)$ and $(0, 4)$ without graphing.

*(continued)*

## MODULE 3  SECTION 3                    PRACTICE AND APPLICATIONS

### For use with Exploration 2

**Match each equation with its graph. State where the graph of each line crosses the y-axis.**

**8.** $y = 0.6x$

**9.** $y = 0.6x - 4$

**10.** $y = 0.6x + 4$

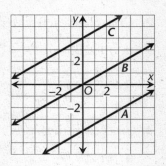

**Health** **The average remaining life expectancy for 11–17-year-old males (for their age in 1991) is given in the table shown. Use the table for Exercises 11–12.**

| Age | Years |
|-----|-------|
| 11  | 62.0  |
| 12  | 61.0  |
| 13  | 60.0  |
| 14  | 59.0  |
| 15  | 58.1  |
| 16  | 57.1  |
| 17  | 56.2  |

**11. Interpreting Data** On the average, how does the remaining life expectancy for males change as males get older?

**12. a.** Use the data in Exercise 11 to make a scatter plot.

    **b.** Draw a fitted line for the graph. Then find its slope.

    **c.** Suppose that you guess that the equation for your fitted line follows this pattern:
        Remaining years = 73 – slope × current age
    Write an equation for your fitted data based on this pattern.

    **d.** Use your equation in part (c) to predict the remaining life expectancy for a 21-year-old male.

    **e.** The actual answer to part (d) is 52.5 years. How does your answer in part (d) compare?

| MODULE 3  SECTION 4 | PRACTICE AND APPLICATIONS |

## For use with Exploration 1

**For Exercises 1–3, use similar figures *ABCD* and *RSTU*.**

1. Find the ratio of the corresponding side lengths.

2. Complete each statement.

   a. $m \angle B = m \angle$ ___?___

   b. $\dfrac{AB}{RS} = \dfrac{BC}{?}$

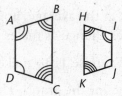

3. Find each measure.

   a. $m \angle R$          b. $m \angle D$          c. $BC$

**For each pair of figures, write a mathematical statement saying the figures are similar.**

4.
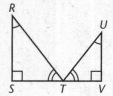

5.
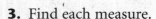

6. **Open-ended** Draw two figures to show why you may need to check more than angle measures to determine if 2 figures are similar. Explain.

7. a. The Sears Tower is 1454 ft high. How far is the flagpole from the building?

   b. Explain how you know the triangles in the diagram are similar.

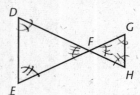

8. Label the angles so that $\triangle EDF$ is similar to $\triangle GHF$.

*(continued)*

**MODULE 3  SECTION 4**                          **PRACTICE AND APPLICATIONS**

## For use with Exploration 2

9. **a.** Draw a circle. Then draw two perpendicular diameters. Connect the endpoints to form a rectangle.

   **b.** What kind of special rectangle did you draw? How could you verify this?

10. **a.** Draw a circle with a chord perpendicular to a diameter. Connect the endpoints to form a four-sided figure.

   **b.** Is the figure a parallelogram? Explain.

   **c.** Label the vertices on the circle in part (a). The diameter divides the figure into two triangles. Measure each angle of both triangles. What do you know about each triangle?

   **d.** Name one pair of angles in the four-sided figure that are equal.

11. Repeat Exercise 10 using different chords perpendicular to different diameters. Verify that you get the same results.

12. The name for the figure formed in Exercises 10 and 11 is a "kite." Based on your results, name some properties of kites.

13. **a.** Draw a rectangle. Then draw the two diagonals.

   **b.** What do you notice about the diagonals?

   **c.** How would you verify your answer in part (b)?

   **d.** Do the diagonals of a rectangle bisect the angles?

   **e.** Are the triangles that are formed similar?

   **f.** Draw a rectangle whose diagonals bisect the angles. What kind of rectangle does it appear to be?

14. **a.** Draw a parallelogram that is not a rectangle. Then draw the diagonals.

   **b.** What do you notice about the diagonals?

   **c.** How would you verify your answer in part (b)?

   **d.** Do the diagonals of a parallelogram bisect the angles?

   **e.** Are the triangles similar?

   **f.** Draw a parallelogram whose diagonals bisect the angles. What kind of parallelogram does it appear to be?

15. **a.** Draw a circle. Then draw three equal chords that form a triangle.

   **b.** What kind of triangle is formed?

   **c.** Draw a circle inside the triangle so that each side of the triangle touches the circle at exactly 1 point. What do you think is true of the two resulting circles?

**MODULE 3  SECTION 5**          **PRACTICE AND APPLICATIONS**

## For use with Exploration 1

**For Exercises 1–4, write each product in decimal notation.**

1. approximate consumption of natural gas in the U.S.:
   $1.86 \cdot 10^{10}$ cubic feet

2. approximate average distance from Jupiter to the sun:
   $7.8 \cdot 10^{8}$ kilometers

3. approximate time the dinosaurs became extinct: $6.5 \cdot 10^{7}$ years ago

4. approximate number of atoms in a molecular unit of a substance:
   $6.02 \cdot 10^{23}$

5. Which numbers below are written in scientific notation?

   **a.** $3.4 \cdot 10^{4}$          **b.** $62.75 \cdot 10^{8}$          **c.** $5 \cdot 10^{9}$

**Astronomy  Use 1 light-year = $5.88 \times 10^{12}$ miles and the bar graph below for Exercises 6 – 8. Note: A light-year is the distance that light travels in a vacuum in one year.**

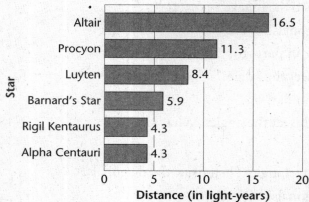

Distance to the Stars in Light Years

| Star | Distance (in light-years) |
|---|---|
| Altair | 16.5 |
| Procyon | 11.3 |
| Luyten | 8.4 |
| Barnard's Star | 5.9 |
| Rigil Kentaurus | 4.3 |
| Alpha Centauri | 4.3 |

6. Which star(s) is the closest to Earth? Write the distance(s) in miles.

7. Which star is approximately four times further from Earth than Rigil Kentaurus? Write the distance in miles.

8. In 1990, the population of China was about $1.2 \cdot 10^{9}$ people.

   **a.** Write the population in decimal notation.

   **b.** **Challenge**  By 2020, the population is projected to increase to $1.4 \cdot 10^{9}$ people. About how many times greater is this?

*(continued)*

## MODULE 3  SECTION 5                    PRACTICE AND APPLICATIONS

### For use with Exploration 2

**Solve each equation. Round decimal answers to the nearest hundredth.**

**9.** $22.5 = 1.5x$

**10.** $0.8y - 3 = 24$

**11.** $\dfrac{n}{0.4} = 3.2$

**12.** $8 = 0.5z + 3.5$

**13.** $6.4 = \dfrac{n}{3.2} - 0.4$

**14.** $\dfrac{n}{0.05} + 0.75 = 15.5$

**15.** $-9.5 + 0.75h = -9.5$

**16.** $0.15s + 13.45 = 13.6$

**17.** $0.34 - 1.15x = 8.39$

**18.** $5.5 + 6.5k = -7.5$

**19.** $-0.5s + 6.5 = 10.8$

**20.** $1.4x - 0.6 = -25.8$

**The number of Calories burned per hour playing tennis is $c = 2.9w$, where $c$ is the number of Calories and $w$ is the weight in pounds.**

**21. a.** Jonathan weighs 145 pounds and plays tennis for one hour. How many Calories does he burn?

    **b.** Estimate the total number of Calories Jonathan burns if he plays tennis for an additional half hour.

    **c.** Ellen wants to burn 1000 Calories playing tennis. How long would she have to play if she weighs 105 pounds?

**The formulas below relate the amount of money Carol and Mary Beth have saved, where $w$ is the number of weeks and $a$ is the amount saved. Each girl saves $4 per week.**

**Carol**
**$a = 4w + 105.50$**

**Mary Beth**
**$a = 4w + 85.25$**

**22.** Carol saves for 6 weeks. Estimate her savings.

**23.** Mary Beth saves for 9 weeks. Estimate her savings.

**24.** Carol wants to save for a bicycle which costs $153.50. How long will it take her to save the money?

**25.** Will Carol and Mary Beth ever have the same amount saved? Explain.

# MODULE 3  SECTION 6                          PRACTICE AND APPLICATIONS

## For use with Exploration 1

**For Exercises 1–3, tell whether the *inclusive or* or the *exclusive or* is used.**

1. Jerome uses his allowance to go to the movies or to buy some popcorn. Jerome has enough money to do both.

2. Juanita wears her hat or her gloves or both.

3. Caroline will read a book or watch television.

**For Exercises 4 –7, use the Venn diagram at the right.**

4. How many students have a morning math class but not a morning science class?

5. How many students have both math and science classes in the morning?

6. What is the total number of students taking math or science classes in the morning?

7. Marya is a new student and is scheduled to take math and science in the morning. Describe how to include her in the Venn diagram.

Morning math class — 18 students   6   Morning science class — 16 students

**For Exercises 8 –9, use the Venn diagram at the right.**

8. Which species listed are classified as both threatened and endangered?

9. **Challenge** There are 1525 species that are either endangered, threatened, or both. Estimate what percent is represented by this Venn diagram.

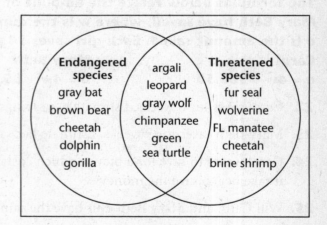

Endangered species: gray bat, brown bear, cheetah, dolphin, gorilla
argali, leopard, gray wolf, chimpanzee, green sea turtle
Threatened species: fur seal, wolverine, FL manatee, cheetah, brine shrimp

| MODULE 3 SECTION 1 | STUDY GUIDE |
|---|---|

# Ancient Sites of Mystery    Square Roots and Measurements

**GOAL**   **LEARN HOW TO:** • find and estimate square roots
                 • describe patterns related to length, area, and volume

**As you:** • find dimensions of a room at an archaeological site
            • compare dimensions of rooms at an archaeological site

## Exploration 1: Finding Square Roots

### Squares and Square Roots

One of two equal factors of a number is a **square root** of that number.
If $A = s^2$, then $s$ is a square root of $A$. Every positive number has both a
positive and a negative square root. The **principal square root**, indicated
by $\sqrt{\phantom{x}}$, is the positive square root. The negative square root is indicated
by $-\sqrt{\phantom{x}}$. A number is a **perfect square** if its principal square root is a
whole number.

| **Example** |
|---|
| Find the square roots of 225. |

| **Sample Response** |
|---|
| Since $(-15)^2 = 225$ and $15^2 = 225$, $-15$ and $15$ are the square roots of 225. |

| **Example** |
|---|
| Is 220 a perfect square? Explain. |

| **Sample Response** |
|---|
| No; $14^2 = 196$ and $15^2 = 225$, so 220 is not a perfect square because its square root is not a whole number. |

| **Example** |
|---|
| Find $-\sqrt{100}$ and $\sqrt{100}$. |

| **Sample Response** |
|---|
| $-\sqrt{100} = -10$ and $\sqrt{100} = 10$ |

**MODULE 3  SECTION 1**                              **STUDY GUIDE**

## Estimating Square Roots

You can estimate a square root by using a calculator, or by looking for the closest perfect squares less than and greater than the number.

---
**Example**

Estimate $\sqrt{20}$.

---
■ **Sample Response** ■

The closest perfect squares less than 20 and greater than 20 are 16 and 25.

$$\sqrt{16} < \sqrt{20} < \sqrt{25}, \text{ or } 4 < \sqrt{20} < 5$$

So, $\sqrt{20} \approx 4.5$.

---

## Exploration 2: Length, Area, and Volume

### Changing Dimensions

A **cube** is a rectangular prism with six square **faces**. It also has 12 **edges**.

When you compare sizes of objects, you need to know whether you are comparing lengths, areas, or volumes.

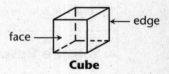

**Cube**

---
**Example**

Suppose the length, width, and height of the prism at the right are each multiplied by 2. Describe how this changes the areas of the faces and the volume of the prism.

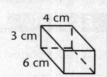

---
■ **Sample Response** ■

The areas of faces of the given prism are 12 cm$^2$, 12 cm$^2$, 18 cm$^2$, 18 cm$^2$, 24 cm$^2$, and 24 cm$^2$.

The areas of faces of the new prism are 48 cm$^2$, 48 cm$^2$, 72 cm$^2$, 72 cm$^2$, 96 cm$^2$, and 96 cm$^2$.

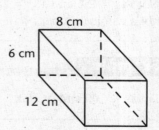

The volume of the given prism is 72 cm$^2$. The volume of this new prism is 576 cm$^2$.

So, the area of each of the faces of the new prism is 4 times the area of the faces of the given prism, and the volume of the new prism is 8 times the volume of the given prism.

---

| MODULE 3  SECTION 1 | PRACTICE & APPLICATION EXERCISES | STUDY GUIDE |

## Exploration 1

**Use mental math to find each value.**

**1.** $\sqrt{360,000}$      **2.** $-\sqrt{64}$      **3.** $\sqrt{\dfrac{1}{25}}$      **4.** $\sqrt{0.04}$

**5.** $\sqrt{0.000081}$      **6.** $\sqrt{4900}$      **7.** $\sqrt{0.0009}$      **8.** $\sqrt{\dfrac{9}{16}}$

**Estimate each square root to the nearest tenth.**

**9.** $\sqrt{37}$      **10.** $\sqrt{24}$      **11.** $\sqrt{143}$      **12.** $\sqrt{133}$

**13.** $\sqrt{103}$      **14.** $\sqrt{228}$      **15.** $\sqrt{35}$      **16.** $\sqrt{2}$

**Find each value. Tell whether your answer is *exact* or an *estimate*.**

**17.** $\sqrt{0.0025}$      **18.** $\sqrt{36.4}$      **19.** $-\sqrt{900}$

## Exploration 2

**20.** The volume of a cube is 27 cm$^3$. What will its volume be if each of its edge lengths are multiplied by 3?

## Spiral Review

**21.** Use the data to create a box-and-whisker plot. Identify any outliers.
(Module 2, p. 152)

| Distances Run by Students on the Cross Country Team (kilometers) |
|---|
| 30, 51, 51, 60, 64, 67, 71, 71, 71, 85, 85, 87, 90, 90, 102 |

**Solve each equation.** (Module 2, p. 130)

**22.** $|x| = 5$      **23.** $|y| = 12$      **24.** $-t = 22$      **25.** $-m = -3$

**Use the figure shown.** (Module 2, p. 130)

**26. a.** Give the coordinates of points $A$, $B$, and $C$.

  **b.** Give the coordinates of the image points $A'$, $B'$, and $C'$ after a translation of $(x - 1, y + 2)$.

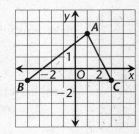

## MODULE 3 SECTION 2      STUDY GUIDE

# On the Road    Equations and Graphs

**GOAL**   **LEARN HOW TO:** • evaluate expressions with square roots and fraction bars
                    • graph equations
      **AS YOU:** • estimate speeds of cars involved in accidents
               • investigate highway safety issues

## Exploration 1: Order of Operations

The order of operations is a set of rules for evaluating an expression
so that the expression has only one value.

**First**   Perform all calculations inside grouping symbols. Grouping
symbols include parentheses, fraction bars, and square root
symbols.

**Next**   Perform multiplications and divisions in order from left to right.
Simplify exponents before other multiplications.

**Then**   Perform additions and subtractions in order from left to right.

---

### Example

Simplify $\dfrac{\sqrt{6+3}}{6+3 \cdot 4^2}$ .

---

### ■ Sample Response ■

When an expression has a fraction bar, simplify the numerator and the denominator
as much as possible.

**First**   Do the addition inside the square root symbol,
and evaluate the square root.

$$\frac{\sqrt{6+3}}{6+3 \cdot 4^2} = \frac{\sqrt{9}}{6+3 \cdot 4^2}$$

$$= \frac{3}{6+3 \cdot 4^2}$$

**Next**   Simplify the power, $4^2$, and evaluate the product.

$$= \frac{3}{6+3 \cdot 16}$$

$$= \frac{3}{6+48}$$

**Then**   Find the sum in the denominator, and simplify
the resulting fraction.

$$= \frac{3}{54}$$

$$= \frac{1}{18}$$

---

        

## MODULE 3  SECTION 2 | STUDY GUIDE

### Exploration 2: Graphing Equations

An ordered pair of numbers that make an equation with two variables true is a **solution of the equation**. The graph of an equation includes all possible solutions of the equation. When the graph of an equation is a *straight line*, the graph and the equation are called **linear**. Graphs and equations that do not make a straight line are called **nonlinear**.

---

**Example**

Graph the equation $y = 2x - 1$. Tell whether the graph is *linear* or *nonlinear*.

■ **Sample Response** ■

**First** Make a table of values (solutions). Include several values so the pattern in the plotted points can be seen. Be sure to include both positive and negative values for $x$.

| $x$ | $y$ | $(x, y)$ |
|---|---|---|
| $-1$ | $-3$ | $(-1, -3)$ |
| $0$ | $-1$ | $(0, -1)$ |
| $1$ | $1$ | $(1, 1)$ |
| $2$ | $3$ | $(2, 3)$ |

**Then** Plot the ordered pairs on a coordinate grid. The points lie along a line. Draw a line to show the pattern. Use arrowheads to show that the graph extends.

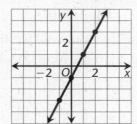

The equation is linear because its graph is a straight line.

---

## MODULE 3  SECTION 2 | PRACTICE & APPLICATION EXERCISES

### Exploration 1

**Evaluate each expression. Round decimal answers to the nearest hundredth.**

**1.** $\dfrac{4 \cdot 2}{3 + 7 - 3(2)}$

**2.** $2 + 3\sqrt{2 \cdot 8}$

**3.** $\dfrac{\sqrt{12 + 6}}{5}$

**4.** $(4 + 6)\sqrt{4(13)}$

**5.** $24 - 3(2)$

**6.** $\sqrt{\dfrac{8}{19 - 3}}$

## MODULE 3  SECTION 2 | PRACTICE & APPLICATION EXERCISES | STUDY GUIDE

**Evaluate each expression when $f = -2$ and $g = 5$. Round decimal answers to the nearest hundredth.**

**7.** $\dfrac{3 - 5f}{2g}$

**8.** $\dfrac{\sqrt{g^2 - 3}}{g - f}$

**9.** $\dfrac{-4f}{9 + g} - g$

## Exploration 2

**For Exercises 10 –12, graph each equation.**

**10.** $y = 5x$

**11.** $y = -2x - 3$

**12.** $y = x - 3$

**13.** For which equations in Exercises 10 –12 is $(0, -3)$ a solution?

**Graphing Calculator Graph each equation. Tell whether the graph is *linear* or *nonlinear*.**

**14.** $y = x^2$

**15.** $y = 2.5x + 1$

**16.** $y = |x|$

## Spiral Review

**For Exercises 17– 20, estimate each value.** (Module 3, p. 170)

**17.** $-\sqrt{27}$

**18.** $\sqrt{20}$

**19.** $\sqrt{0.4}$

**20.** $-\sqrt{37}$

**21.** Use the coordinate plane shown. List the ordered pairs for the points labeled on the lines. **(Module 1, p. 29)**

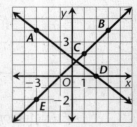

**For each rate, write a unit rate.** (Module 1, p. 9)

**22.** $1.36 for 8 oz

**23.** 7.5 mi in 30 s

**24.** $45 for 2.25 h

## MODULE 3  SECTION 3                                          STUDY GUIDE

# Big Foot    Slope and Equations

**GOAL**   **LEARN HOW TO:** • find the slope of a line
                              • use equations and graphs to model situations
                              • use an equation to make a prediction

   **AS YOU:** • compare walking rates
                • estimate heights from foot lengths

## Exploration 1: Finding Slope

### Slope

The **slope** of a line is the ratio of its vertical change, **rise**, to its horizontal
change, **run**. Slope is a ratio that measures the steepness of a line.

$$\text{slope} = \frac{\text{rise}}{\text{run}}$$

### ■ Example

Find the slope of the line in the graph below.

### ■ Sample Response ■

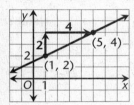

The vertical change (rise) is $4 - 2$, or **2**.

The horizontal change (run) is $5 - 1$, or **4**.

Therefore, the slope is $\frac{2}{4}$, or $\frac{1}{2}$.

## Exploration 2: Using Equations

### Equations for Predictions

You can use an equation of a fitted line to make predictions.

### ■ Example

An equation of the fitted line on a scatter plot is $t = c + 40$, where $t$ = temperature in
degrees Fahrenheit and $c$ = number of chirps a cricket makes in 15 s. What can you
predict about the temperature if you hear a cricket chirp 10 times in 15 s?

### ■ Sample Response ■

Evaluate the equation when $c = 10$.

   $t = c + 40 = 10 + 40 = 50$

If you hear a cricket chirp 10 times in 15 s, the temperature is about 50° F.

Name _____  Date _____

## MODULE 3  SECTION 3 | PRACTICE & APPLICATION EXERCISES | STUDY GUIDE

## Exploration 1

**Find the slope of each line.**

**1.**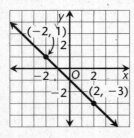

**2.**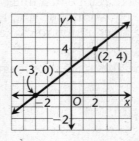

## Exploration 2

**The scatter plot at the right shows the number of hits and the number of times at bat for members of a baseball team. Use the scatter plot for Exercises 3 –5.**

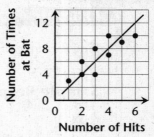

Batting Statistics for a Baseball Team

**3.** Predict the number of times a batter will get a hit in 6 times at bat.

**4.** Find the slope of the fitted line.

**5.** Let $t$ = the number of times at bat and let $h$ = the number of hits. Which equation can you use to predict the number of hits if you know the number of times at bat?

**A.** $t = 2h + 1$    **B.** $t = \frac{1}{2}h$    **C.** $t = 2h$    **D.** $t = \frac{1}{2}h - 1$

## Spiral Review

**For Exercises 6 –9, evaluate each expression.** (Module 3, p. 183)

**6.** $\dfrac{7(-5)}{-6 + 3}$

**7.** $4\sqrt{5 - (-20)}$

**8.** $\dfrac{\sqrt{7 \cdot 7}}{3}$

**9.** $\dfrac{(-5)^2}{3 + 2}$

**10.** Tell what inverse operation you would use to solve $x + (-5) = 9$. Then solve the equation. (Module 1, p. 62)

**Use a proportion to find each percent.** (Module 2, p. 90)

**11.** 12% of 50

**12.** 13.5% of 28

**13.** 0.3% of 8

# Cliff Dwellers   Similar Figures and Constructions

**GOAL**   **LEARN HOW TO:** • tell whether triangles are similar
                              • make indirect measurements
                              • find a perpendicular bisector of a chord

   **As you:** • estimate the height of a cliff
              • estimate dimensions of artifacts

## Exploration 1: Similar Figures

Two figures are **similar** if they have the same shape, but not necessarily
the same size. The symbol $\sim$ means "is similar to." If two figures are
similar, the measures of their **corresponding angles** are equal, and the
ratios of their **corresponding side** lengths are in proportion.

### Similar Triangles and Indirect Measurement

Two triangles are similar if two angles of one triangle have the same
measures as two angles of the other triangle. You can use similar triangles
to make indirect measurements and to find missing side lengths.

---

**Example**

In the figures at the right, $\triangle ABC$ and $\triangle DEF$
are similar.
**a.** Find the measures of $\angle D$, $\angle E$, and $\angle F$.
**b.** Find the lengths of $\overline{DF}$ and $\overline{EF}$.

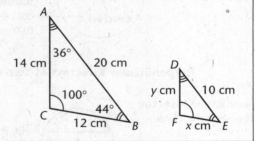

**▪ Sample Response ▪**

**a.** Since $\angle D$ corresponds to $\angle A$, then $m\angle D = 36°$.
   Since $\angle E$ corresponds to $\angle B$, then $m\angle E = 44°$.
   Since $\angle F$ corresponds to $\angle C$, then $m\angle F = 100°$.

**b.** Since $\overline{DE}$ corresponds to $\overline{AB}$, $\overline{EF}$ corresponds to $\overline{BC}$, and $\overline{DF}$ corresponds to $\overline{AC}$, the
   following proportions can be written.

   $$\frac{AB}{DE} = \frac{BC}{EF} \qquad \frac{AB}{DE} = \frac{AC}{DF}$$

   Inserting the known values gives these proportions:

   $$\frac{20}{10} = \frac{12}{x} \qquad \frac{20}{10} = \frac{14}{y}$$

   *(Continues on next page.)*

---

**MODULE 3  SECTION 4**                               **STUDY GUIDE**

---

### Sample Response (continued)

The cross products of these proportions form equations that can be solved to find the values of $x$ and $y$.

| | | |
|---|---|---|
| $20x = 10(12)$ | ← Cross products are equal. → | $20y = 10(14)$ |
| $20x = 120$ | ← Divide both sides by 20. | $20y = 140$ |
| $x = 6$ | | $y = 7$ |

So, $EF = 6$ cm and $DF = 7$ cm.

---

## Exploration 2: Bisecting Chords

### Circles and Chords

A **circle** is the set of all points in a plane that are a given distance (the *radius*) from a point (the *center* of the circle).

**Parts of a Circle**

**Chord**  A segment that joins two points on a circle.

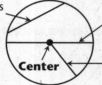

**Diameter**  A chord that passes through the center of a circle.

**Radius**  Any segment that connects a point on the circle to the center.

**Center**

**Perpendicular Bisectors of Two Chords**

The **perpendicular bisector** of a chord bisects the chord (divides it into two equal segments), intersecting the chord at a right angle.

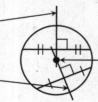

The **perpendicular bisectors** of any two chords on a circle intersect at the center of the circle.

Name _____ Date _____

## Exploration 1

**For Exercises 1–3, use the similar triangles *ABC* and *EDC*.**

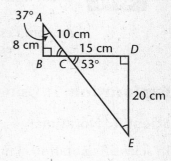

**1.** Find the ratio of the corresponding side lengths.

**2.** Copy and complete each statement.

   **a.** $\dfrac{AB}{ED} = \dfrac{AC}{?}$   **b.** $\dfrac{BC}{?} = \dfrac{?}{EC}$

**3.** Find each measure.

   **a.** $m\angle E$   **b.** $BC$   **c.** $EC$

## Exploration 2

**4.** Draw a large circle. Label its center, a diameter, a radius, and two chords. Then draw the perpendicular bisectors of the two chords. Measure and label the two halves of each chord to the nearest centimeter.

## Spiral Review

**Plot each pair of points on a coordinate plane and draw a line through them. Find the slope of the line.** (Module 3, p. 195)

**5.** $(2, 2)$ and $(-4, 3)$   **6.** $(0, 7)$ and $(4, 1)$

**Find each percent of change.** (Module 2, p. 100)

**7.** A $23.00 books sells for $13.80.

**8.** A child grows from 150 cm tall to 162 cm tall.

**Find each product.** (Toolbox, p. 600)

**9.** $2.7 \cdot 10^3$   **10.** $267 \cdot 10^5$   **11.** $0.0085 \cdot 10^4$

**12.** $20.99 \cdot 10^7$   **13.** $0.3 \cdot 10^2$   **14.** $0.99 \cdot 10^6$

# Forgotten Bones   Scientific Notation and Decimal Equations

**GOAL**  **LEARN HOW TO:** • write very large numbers in scientific notation
• solve equations involving decimals

**AS YOU:** • estimate ages of bones
• estimate heights

## Exploration 1: Using Scientific Notation

### Scientific Notation

In **scientific notation**, a number is written as the product of a decimal greater than or equal to 1 and less than 10, and a power of 10. You can change between **decimal notation** and scientific notation.

---

**Example**

**a.** Change the *decimal notation* 42,000 to *scientific notation*.

**b.** Change the *scientific notation* $5.46 \cdot 10^5$ to *decimal notation*.

---

**Sample Response**

**a.** $42,000 = 4.2 \cdot 10,000 = 4.2 \cdot 10^4$

**b.** $5.46 \cdot 10^5 = 5.46 \cdot 100,000 = 546,000$

---

## Exploration 2: Equations with Decimals

### Solving Equations with Decimals

You can use inverse operations to solve an equation with decimals.

---

**Example**

Solve $2.4x - 3.5 = 1.9$.

---

**Sample Response**

$$2.4x - 3.5 = 1.9$$
$$2.4x - 3.5 + 3.5 = 1.9 + 3.5 \qquad \leftarrow \text{Add 3.5 to both sides to undo the subtraction.}$$
$$2.4x = 5.4$$
$$\frac{2.4x}{2.4} = \frac{5.4}{2.4} \qquad \leftarrow \text{Divide both sides by 2.4 to undo the multiplication.}$$
$$x = 2.25$$

---

## MODULE 3   SECTION 5   PRACTICE & APPLICATION EXERCISES   STUDY GUIDE

## Exploration 1

**Write each number in scientific notation.**

**1.** 4,870,000                **2.** 300                **3.** 102,000,000,000

**4.** 1,200,000,000            **5.** 890,230,000        **6.** 16,000,000,000,000

**Write each number in decimal notation.**

**7.** $1.9 \cdot 10^4$         **8.** $3.098 \cdot 10^5$       **9.** $8 \cdot 10^3$

**10.** $7.1 \cdot 10^3$        **11.** $3.52 \cdot 10^8$       **12.** $1.58 \cdot 10^6$

## Exploration 2

**Solve each equation. Round decimal answers to the nearest hundredth.**

**13.** $4.1 = 1.1m - (-1.02)$                **14.** $\dfrac{y}{6.7} + 10.8 = 2.3$

**15.** $0.32w + 9.12 = 15.04$                **16.** $\dfrac{t}{0.04} - 0.13 = 5.12$

## Spiral Review

**17.** $\triangle RGT \sim \triangle SGM$. Find the length of $\overline{MG}$. **(Module 3, p. 207)**

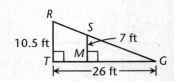

**Find each sum or difference.** (Module 2, p. 130)

**18.** $-4 + 6$        **19.** $8 - (-15)$        **20.** $72 + (-1)$        **21.** $-12 - (-11)$

**Use the box-and-whisker plot.** (Module 1, p. 21)

**10-Day High Temperatures (°F)**

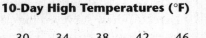
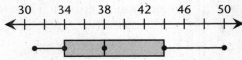

**22.** Estimate the lowest high temperature for the 10-day period.

**23.** Estimate the median high temperature for the 10-day period.

## MODULE 3  SECTION 6                                      STUDY GUIDE

# Whodunit?    Logical Thinking

**GOAL**   **LEARN HOW TO:** • interpret statements with *and*, *or*, and *not*
                              • organize information in a Venn diagram
          **AS YOU:** • analyze clues in a mystery

## Exploration 1: Using *And, Or, Not*

### Venn Diagram

A **Venn diagram** is used to model relationships among groups. It can help
you interpret statements that use the words *and*, *or*, and *not*.

The Venn diagrams below describe the recycling programs of eight
communities (identified by the letters A through H).

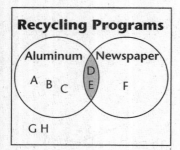

Communities D and E have
newspaper *and* aluminum
recycling programs.

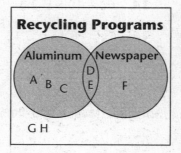

Communities A through F
offer newspaper *or* aluminum
recycling programs (*or both*).

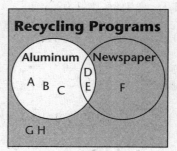

Communities F, G, and H
do *not* offer an aluminum
recycling program.

### Example

Derek Andrew surveyed his class to determine how many of his classmates could speak
French and/or Spanish. He made the Venn diagram below.

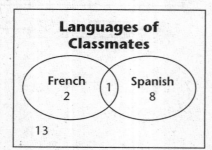

Number of students surveyed: 24
Number of students who speak French but not
Spanish: 2
Number of students who speak Spanish but not
French: 8
Number of students who speak French *and*
Spanish: 1
Number of students that speak French *or*
Spanish: 2 + 8 + 1 = 11
Number of students that do *not* speak French
and do *not* speak Spanish: 13

## MODULE 3  SECTION 6 | PRACTICE & APPLICATION EXERCISES | STUDY GUIDE

## Exploration 1

**For Exercises 1–5, use the Venn diagram at the right. It shows the results of a survey of students' preferences in flavors of ice cream.**

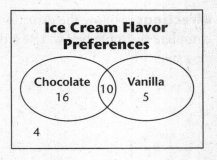

**Ice Cream Flavor Preferences**

Chocolate 16   10   Vanilla 5

4

1. Which ice cream flavor was favored by more students, vanilla or chocolate?

2. How many students prefer only chocolate?

3. How many students do *not* prefer chocolate?

4. How many students prefer both chocolate and vanilla ice cream?

5. How many students were surveyed?

## Spiral Review

**For Exercises 6 – 8, solve each equation. Round decimal answers to the nearest hundredth.** (Module 3, p. 218)

6. $20.5 = 0.2x + 8$

7. $\dfrac{y}{0.16} = 9$

8. $-14.5 = 62 + 0.3m$

9. A bus driver is asked to choose the order in which she will pick up three students: Agnes, Bill, and Clara.

   a. Draw a tree diagram to show all the possible orders in which the students could be picked up.

   b. Find the probability that the bus driver will choose an order in which Clara will be picked up before Bill.

**Tell whether each triangle is *isosceles*, *equilateral*, or *scalene*.**
(Toolbox, p. 604)

10.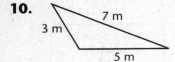
3 m   7 m   5 m

11.   8 ft
6 ft   6 ft

12.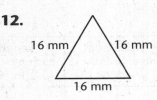
16 mm   16 mm   16 mm

**Use a compass to draw a circle with the given radius or diameter.** (Module 3, p. 206)

13. $r = 2.5$ cm

14. $d = 4$ cm

15. $r = 3$ cm

**MODULE 4**                                      **LABSHEET** **1A**

## Fractal Tree (Use with Questions 3–5 and Question 7 on pages 239–240.)

**Directions** Follow the directions in your book to create a fractal tree and complete the table below. Use a different color for the branches at each new step.

| Step | Number of new branches added | Length of each new branch (inches) | Height of tree (inches) | Total length of new branches (inches) | Total length of all branches (inches) |
|------|------|------|------|------|------|
| 1 | 1 | 2 | 2 | 2 | 2 |
| 2 | 3 | 1 | 3 | 3 | 5 |
| 3 | | | | | |
| 4 | | | | | |
| 5 | | | | | |
| 6 | | | | | |
| 7 | | | | | |

**MODULE 4**                    **LABSHEET** **1B**

## Sierpinski Triangle Table   (Use with Question 25 on page 246.)

| Steps | Number of unshaded triangles | Area of each unshaded triangle (in square units) | Total area of unshaded triangles (in square units) |
|---|---|---|---|
|  | 1 | 1 | 1 |
|  | 3 | $\frac{1}{4} = 0.25$ | $\frac{3}{4} = 0.75$ |
|  |  |  |  |
|  |  |  |  |
|  |  |  |  |
|  |  |  |  |
|  |  |  |  |

**MODULE 4**                                          **LABSHEET** **1C**

## Star Fractal   (Use with Exercise 1 on page 248.)

**Directions**   Use the star fractal to complete parts (a) and (b) below.

**a.** Find at least three parts of the fractal that are similar to the whole
fractal. Circle those parts.

**b.** How do the numbers in the table below relate to the pattern in the star
fractal? Write a rule for finding the next term in the sequence when
you know the previous term. Then complete the table.

| Term number | 1 | 2 | 3 | 4 | 5 | 6 | 7 | 8 |
|---|---|---|---|---|---|---|---|---|
| Term | 6 | 36 | 216 | | | | | |

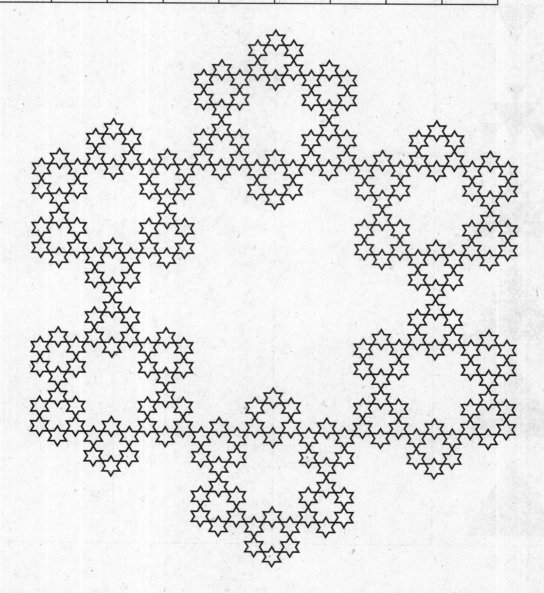

**Plant's Phyllotaxis**   (Use with Question 3 on page 258.)

**Directions**  Use the diagram to complete the table below. Then answer
parts (a)–(c).

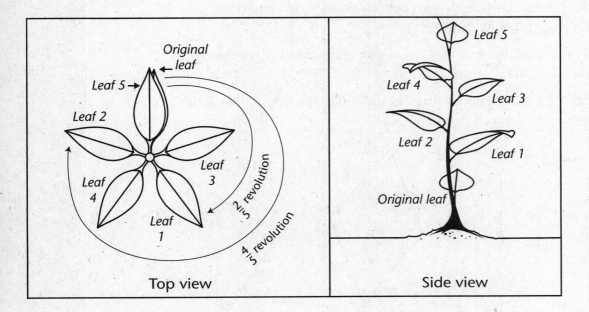

Top view

Side view

| Leaf | 1 | is produced after | $\frac{2}{5}$ | of a revolution around the stem from the original leaf. |
|------|---|-------------------|---------------|---------------------------------------------------------|
| Leaf | 2 | is produced after | $\frac{4}{5}$ | of a revolution around the stem from the original leaf. |
| Leaf | 3 | is produced after |               | of a revolution around the stem from the original leaf. |
| Leaf | 4 | is produced after |               | of a revolution around the stem from the original leaf. |
| Leaf | 5 | is produced after |               | of a revolution around the stem from the original leaf. |

**a.** Which leaf is exactly 2 revolutions from the original leaf?

**b.** How is the position of the leaf from part (a) related to the position of
the original leaf?

**c.** Is Leaf 3 *more* or *less* than one full revolution around the stem from the
original leaf? Explain.

**MODULE 4**                                    LABSHEET **3A**

# Characteristics of Quadrilaterals

(Use with Questions 14–16 on page 274 and Question 19 on page 275.)

**Directions**  For the quadrilaterals below:

• Find each of the quadrilaterals with opposite sides that are parallel.
  Mark each pair of parallel sides.

• Find all of the quadrilaterals that have right angles. Mark all of the right
  angles on each figure.

• Find each of the quadrilaterals that has any equal side lengths. Mark the
  equal side lengths on each figure.

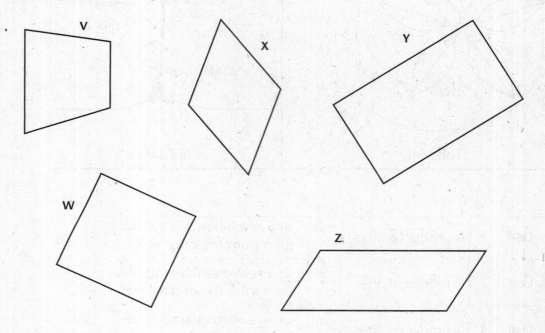

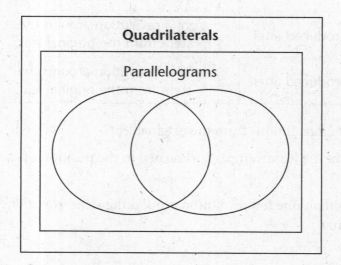

## Quadrilaterals (Use with Exercise 13 on page 277.)

**Directions** List as many names as possible for each figure. Tell which name is most precise.

A
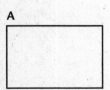

B
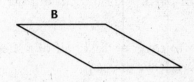

C
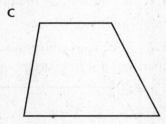

D
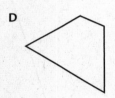

E
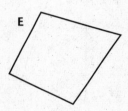

F
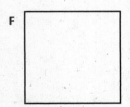

G
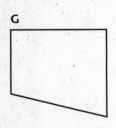

H
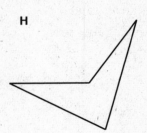

I
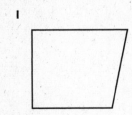

## Pentagons and Hexagons  (Use with Question 10(c) on page 283 and with Question 14 on page 284.)

**Directions**  Follow the steps below. Then answer parts (a) and (b).

**Step 1**  Cut out one of the polygons. Your partner should cut out the other polygon.

**Step 2**  Trace your polygon several times to cover at least half of a sheet of paper. Try not to overlap any polygons or leave any gaps.

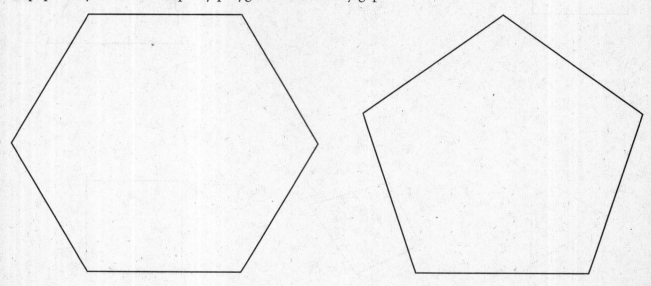

**a.** Which polygon can be copied to fit together without gaps or overlaps?

**b.** Can you explain why copies of one polygon fit together without gaps or overlaps and copies of the other polygon do not?

**MODULE 4**                                          **LABSHEET** **4B**

## Patterns in Polygons   (Use with Question 11 on page 283.)

**Directions**   Complete parts (a)–(i). Use the table below to record answers, as appropriate.

| Name of polygon | Number of sides | Number of triangles | Sum of the measures of the interior angles |
|---|---|---|---|
| triangle | 3 | 1 | |
| quadrilateral | 4 | | |
| pentagon | | | |
| hexagon | | | |

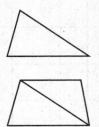

**a.** Draw a triangle on a sheet of paper. What is the sum of the measures of the interior angles?

**b.** Add another triangle to your original triangle to create a quadrilateral. The new triangle must share a side with the original triangle and the quadrilateral should be convex.

**c.** How many triangles is the quadrilateral divided into? What is the sum of the measures of the interior angles of the quadrilateral?

**d.** Add a triangle to your quadrilateral to create a convex pentagon. The new triangle must share a side with the quadrilateral.

**e.** How many triangles is the pentagon divided into? What is the sum of the measures of the interior angles of the pentagon?

**f.** Add a triangle to your pentagon to create a convex hexagon. The new triangle must share a side with the pentagon.

**g.** How many triangles is the hexagon divided into? What is the sum of the measures of the interior angles of the hexagon?

**h.** How is the number of triangles in each polygon related to the number of sides of the polygon?

**i.** How can you find the sum of the measures of the interior angles of any convex polygon?

**MODULE 4**                    **GRAPH PAPER FOR SECTION 5**

**MODULE 4**                                    **LABSHEET** (5A)

## Triangle Table   (Use with Questions 4 and 5 on pages 292 and 293.)

**Directions**   For each triangle you formed:

- Label the shorter sides *a* and *b* and the longest side *c*.

- Complete columns 1, 2, and 3 of the table.

- Put a >, <, or = symbol in column 4 to show how the sum of the areas of the smaller squares compares with the area of the largest square.

- Classify each triangle as *acute*, *right*, or *obtuse* in column 5. You can use a protractor or the corner of a piece of paper to tell whether an angle is acute, right, or obtuse.

| Column 1 | | | Column 2 | | | Column 3 | Column 4 | Column 5 |
|---|---|---|---|---|---|---|---|---|
| Side lengths (cm) | | | Areas of squares (cm$^2$) | | | Sum of areas of smaller squares (cm$^2$) | Sum of areas of smaller squares compared with area of largest square | Type of triangle |
| *a* | *b* | *c* | $a^2$ | $b^2$ | $c^2$ | $a^2 + b^2$ | $a^2 + b^2$ __?__ $c^2$ (>, <, = ) | acute, right, or obtuse |
| | | | | | | | | |
| | | | | | | | | |
| | | | | | | | | |
| | | | | | | | | |
| | | | | | | | | |
| | | | | | | | | |
| | | | | | | | | |
| | | | | | | | | |
| | | | | | | | | |
| | | | | | | | | |
| | | | | | | | | |
| | | | | | | | | |

## Searching for the *Titanic* (Use with Question 5 on page 304 and with Question 6 on page 305.)

**Directions** Use the map below to estimate the probability that the *Titanic* is in your search region.

**a.** Estimate the area in kilometers of the predicted shipwreck region.

**b.** Estimate the area in kilometers of your search region. (*Hint:* Try dividing your search region into triangles.)

**c.** Assume that the *Titanic* is in the predicted shipwreck region. Use your answers to parts (a) and (b) to estimate the probability that the *Titanic* is in your search region.

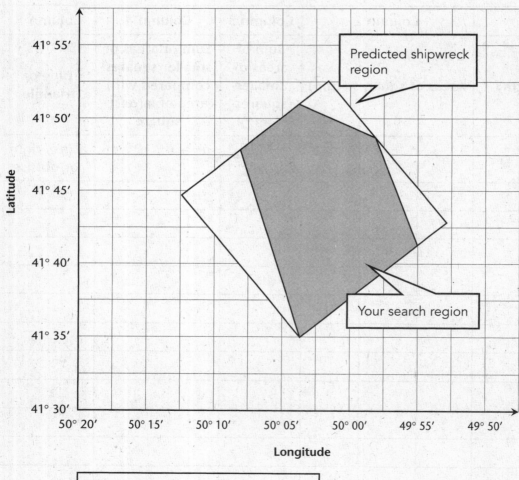

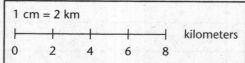

**MODULE 4**                                                    LABSHEET **6B**

**Tree Diagram**  (Use with Questions 9 and 11 on page 306 and with Questions 13 and 14 on page 307.)

**Directions**  Complete the tree diagram below. Fill in the missing probabilities, outcomes, and events.

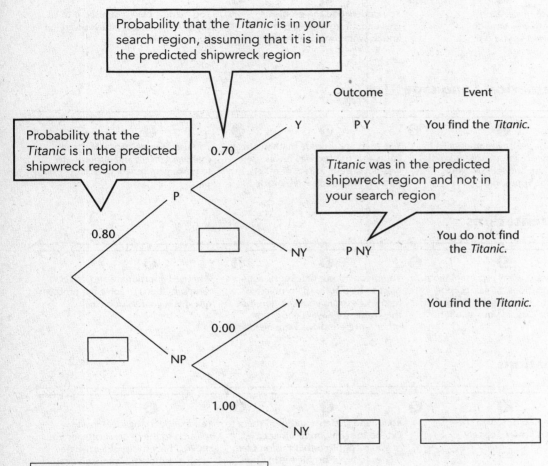

Probability that the *Titanic* is in your search region, assuming that it is in the predicted shipwreck region

Probability that the *Titanic* is in the predicted shipwreck region

*Titanic* was in the predicted shipwreck region and not in your search region

Outcome          Event

Y      P Y        You find the *Titanic*.

0.70

P

0.80

NY      P NY       You do not find the *Titanic*.

Y                  You find the *Titanic*.

0.00

NP

1.00

NY

**Key**
P = In Predicted shipwreck region
NP = Not in Predicted shipwreck region
Y = In Your search region
NY = Not in Your search region

Math Thematics, Book 3  **129**

Name _____ Problem _____

☆ *The star indicates that you excelled in some way.*

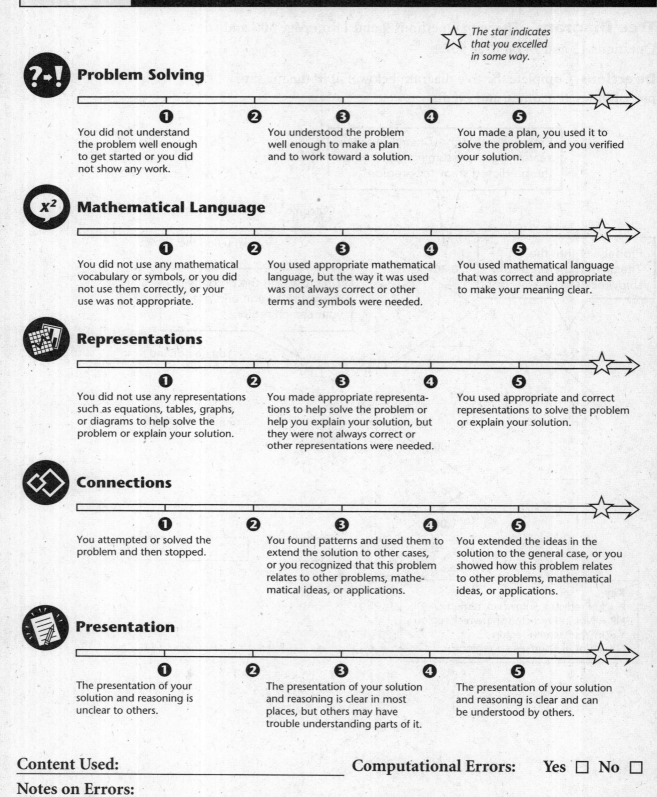

## Problem Solving

**①** **②** **③** **④** **⑤**

**①** You did not understand the problem well enough to get started or you did not show any work.

**③** You understood the problem well enough to make a plan and to work toward a solution.

**⑤** You made a plan, you used it to solve the problem, and you verified your solution.

## Mathematical Language

**①** **②** **③** **④** **⑤**

**①** You did not use any mathematical vocabulary or symbols, or you did not use them correctly, or your use was not appropriate.

**③** You used appropriate mathematical language, but the way it was used was not always correct or other terms and symbols were needed.

**⑤** You used mathematical language that was correct and appropriate to make your meaning clear.

## Representations

**①** **②** **③** **④** **⑤**

**①** You did not use any representations such as equations, tables, graphs, or diagrams to help solve the problem or explain your solution.

**③** You made appropriate representations to help solve the problem or help you explain your solution, but they were not always correct or other representations were needed.

**⑤** You used appropriate and correct representations to solve the problem or explain your solution.

## Connections

**①** **②** **③** **④** **⑤**

**①** You attempted or solved the problem and then stopped.

**③** You found patterns and used them to extend the solution to other cases, or you recognized that this problem relates to other problems, mathematical ideas, or applications.

**⑤** You extended the ideas in the solution to the general case, or you showed how this problem relates to other problems, mathematical ideas, or applications.

## Presentation

**①** **②** **③** **④** **⑤**

**①** The presentation of your solution and reasoning is unclear to others.

**③** The presentation of your solution and reasoning is clear in most places, but others may have trouble understanding parts of it.

**⑤** The presentation of your solution and reasoning is clear and can be understood by others.

**Content Used:** _____ **Computational Errors:** Yes ☐ No ☐

**Notes on Errors:** _____

_____

Name _____                Problem _____

 *If your score is in the shaded area, explain why on the back of this sheet and stop.*

☆ *The star indicates that you excelled in some way.*

 **Problem Solving**

**①**     **②**     **③**     **④**     **⑤**     ☆

I did not understand the problem well enough to get started or I did not show any work.

I understood the problem well enough to make a plan and to work toward a solution.

I made a plan, I used it to solve the problem, and I verified my solution.

 **Mathematical Language**

**①**     **②**     **③**     **④**     **⑤**     ☆

I did not use any mathematical vocabulary or symbols, or I did not use them correctly, or my use was not appropriate.

I used appropriate mathematical language, but the way it was used was not always correct or other terms and symbols were needed.

I used mathematical language that was correct and appropriate to make my meaning clear.

 **Representations**

**①**     **②**     **③**     **④**     **⑤**     ☆

I did not use any representations such as equations, tables, graphs, or diagrams to help solve the problem or explain my solution.

I made appropriate representations to help solve the problem or help me explain my solution, but they were not always correct or other representations were needed.

I used appropriate and correct representations to solve the problem or explain my solution.

 **Connections**

**①**     **②**     **③**     **④**     **⑤**     ☆

I attempted or solved the problem and then stopped.

I found patterns and used them to extend the solution to other cases, or I recognized that this problem relates to other problems, mathematical ideas, or applications.

I extended the ideas in the solution to the general case, or I showed how this problem relates to other problems, mathematical ideas, or applications.

 **Presentation**

**①**     **②**     **③**     **④**     **⑤**     ☆

The presentation of my solution and reasoning is unclear to others.

The presentation of my solution and reasoning is clear in most places, but others may have trouble understanding parts of it.

The presentation of my solution and reasoning is clear and can be understood by others.

## MODULE 4  SECTION 1                    PRACTICE AND APPLICATIONS

### For use with Exploration 1

**Write a rule for finding a term of each sequence when you know the previous term.**

**1.** 3, 7, 11, 15, …

**2.** 125, 25, 5, 1, …

**3.** −8, 24, −72, 216, …

**4.** $\dfrac{1}{2}, \dfrac{1}{8}, \dfrac{1}{32}, \dfrac{1}{128}, \ldots$

**5.** $3x, 15x^2, 75x^3, \ldots$

**6.** $-9, -1, -\dfrac{1}{9}, \ldots$

**7.** $\dfrac{x}{3}, \dfrac{x}{9}, \dfrac{x}{27}, \ldots$

**8.** 4.4, 2.2, 1.1, …

**9.** 0.1, 0.01, 0.001, 0.0001, …

**10.** 100, 50, 25, 12.5, …

**11.** In a sequence, the first term is 100. The rule is to multiply the previous term by 2 and add 1. What is the fifth term of the sequence?

**12.** In a sequence, the first term is 6. The rule is to multiply the previous term by 4 and then subtract 2. What is the fifth term of the sequence?

**13.** Use the sequences below.

| Term number | 1 | 2 | 3 | 4 | 5 | … | n |
|---|---|---|---|---|---|---|---|
| Sequence | 5 | 10 | 15 | 20 | 25 | … | |

| Term number | 1 | 2 | 3 | 4 | 5 | … | n |
|---|---|---|---|---|---|---|---|
| Sequence | 11 | 16 | 21 | 26 | 31 | … | |

| Term number | 1 | 2 | 3 | 4 | 5 | … | n |
|---|---|---|---|---|---|---|---|
| Sequence | 6 | 11 | 16 | 21 | 26 | … | |

**a.** For each sequence, write a rule. Write your rule as an expression.

**b.** How are the sequences above different from each other?

*(continued)*

## MODULE 4  SECTION 1 | PRACTICE AND APPLICATIONS

### For use with Exploration 2

**14.** **Visual Thinking** Without measuring or making any drawings, decide whether each set of segments could form the sides of a triangle.

a. _____     b. _____     c. _____

**15.** Use the triangles shown. Write an inequality to describe all possible values of *x*.

a.

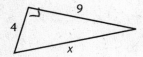

b.

c.

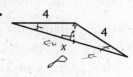

d.

### For use with Exploration 3

**16.** Compare the triangles below. Which appear to be similar? Which appear to be congruent? Explain how you can check.

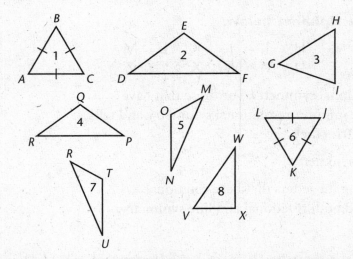

**Tell whether it is possible to construct a triangle from the given side lengths. If it is possible, construct the triangle.**

**17.** **a.** 6 in., 8 in., 1 in.     **b.** 4 in., 2 in., $2\frac{1}{2}$ in.     **c.** $1\frac{1}{2}$ in., $1\frac{3}{4}$ in., 2 in.

## MODULE 4 SECTION 2             PRACTICE AND APPLICATIONS

## For use with Exploration 1

**For Exercises 1–5, refer to the table you created to solve the Fibonacci rabbit problem on page 257.**

1. How is the total number of adult rabbit pairs in a month related to the number of growing rabbits?

2. How is the total number of rabbit pairs in a month related to the number of newborn rabbit pairs?

3. Which columns of your Fibonacci rabbit chart show the Fibonacci sequence?

4. How is the number of newborn rabbit pairs in any month related to the total number of rabbit pairs two months earlier?

5. Find the first 15 terms of the Fibonacci sequence.

6. **Books** A publishing company may refer to the number of pages that can be obtained from a large sheet of paper by folding it as "folio," or 2 pages; "quarto," or 4 pages; and "octavo," or 8 pages.

    a. Fold sheets of paper into 2, 4, and 8 congruent rectangles.

    b. List the numbers in this sequence.

    c. Write the next three numbers in the sequence.

**For Exercises 7–9, refer to the alphabet below.**

A B C D E F G H I J K L M
N O P Q R S T U V W X Y Z

7. List the letters that have rotational symmetry. For those that have rotational symmetry, give the minimum rotational symmetry and tell what other rotational symmetries they have.

8. List the letters that have line symmetry.

9. Draw a Venn diagram showing the letters that have rotational symmetry, line symmetry, and both rotational and line symmetry.

*(continued)*

    

## MODULE 4  SECTION 2 — PRACTICE AND APPLICATIONS

### For use with Exploration 2

**Write each rational number as the quotient of two integers.**

**10.** $0.20$

**11.** $\sqrt{49}$

**12.** $\sqrt{\dfrac{25}{64}}$

**13.** $3.5$

**14.** $8\dfrac{1}{2}$

**15.** $\sqrt{0.25}$

**Write each rational number as a repeating or a terminating decimal.**

**16.** $\dfrac{7}{12}$

**17.** $\dfrac{2}{3}$

**18.** $\sqrt{100}$

**19.** $\dfrac{2}{9}$

**20.** $7\dfrac{3}{4}$

**21.** $\sqrt{\dfrac{36}{64}}$

**Tell whether each number is *rational* or *irrational*.**

**22.** $2\dfrac{3}{5}$

**23.** $\sqrt{26}$

**24.** $\dfrac{\sqrt{12}}{4}$

**25.** $18.\overline{18}$

**26.** $0$

**27.** $\dfrac{23}{3}$

**28. Challenge** $\dfrac{2}{7}$ is a rational number because it can be written as the quotient of two integers.

  **a.** How many decimal places repeat?

  **b.** Give another rational number with a large number of decimal places that repeat.

**29.** Write the repeating decimals below in order from greatest to least. Explain your thinking.

  **a.** $0.15\overline{4}$          $0.1\overline{54}$          $0.\overline{154}$          $0.\overline{15}$

  **b.** $2.\overline{3}$          $2.3\overline{2}$          $2.\overline{32}$          $2.33\overline{2}$

**MODULE 4  SECTION 3**                    **PRACTICE AND APPLICATIONS**

## For use with Exploration 1

**Solve each equation.**

**1.** $\frac{2}{3}n = 18$

**2.** $12 = \frac{3}{4}y$

**3.** $1\frac{3}{5}x = 100$

**4.** $\frac{3}{4}x + 12 = 20$

**5.** $32 = \frac{2}{5}k - 16$

**6.** $3\frac{2}{3}r - 2 = 30$

**7.** $\frac{6}{7}m + \frac{2}{7} = \frac{8}{7}$

**8.** $\frac{4}{9}n + \frac{2}{3} = \frac{2}{3}$

**9.** $1\frac{4}{5}y - \frac{1}{8} = \frac{7}{8}$

**In Exercises 10–13, each triangle has an area of 200 ft². Find the length of the base of the triangle.**

**10.**

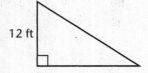

12 ft

**11.**

7.5 ft

**12.**

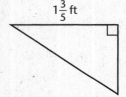

$1\frac{3}{5}$ ft

**13.**

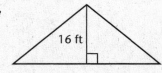

16 ft

**14. Challenge** When a normal ball bounces, it never bounces back to its original height because of friction. Suppose a ball is dropped from 8 feet, and each time it bounces, it bounces back to 70% of its original height.

**a.** Write a sequence listing the height of the ball.

**b.** How many times can it bounce before its height is not measurable?

*(continued)*

## MODULE 4 SECTION 3            PRACTICE AND APPLICATIONS

**For use with Exploration 2**

**For Exercises 15–18, tell whether each statement is *true* or *false*. Explain.**

**15.** A quadrilateral is sometimes a parallelogram.

**16.** A square is always a rhombus.

**17.** A rectangle is sometimes a rhombus.

**18.** A trapezoid is always a rhombus.

**For Exercises 19–23, use the description to draw and label each quadrilateral. Then give the most specific name for the quadrilateral that you sketched.**

**19.** a quadrilateral with opposite angles congruent but no 90° angles

**20.** a quadrilateral with exactly one pair of opposite sides parallel

**21.** a quadrilateral with four sides congruent that is not a square

**22.** a quadrilateral with four right angles that is not a square

**23.** a quadrilateral with exactly one pair of opposite sides parallel and one 90° angle

**24.** **Visual** Draw a "quadrilateral tree" to classify quadrilaterals like the one shown on page 275. Add statements to each branch that will make the quadrilateral more specific.

**25.** Use the diagram from Exercise 24 to fill in the blanks in the following statements. Use words *always*, *sometimes*, or *never*.

  **a.** A square is ___?___ a rhombus.

  **b.** A rectangle is ___?___ a rhombus.

  **c.** A rhombus is ___?___ a trapezoid.

  **d.** A trapezoid is ___?___ a quadrilateral.

  **e.** A parallelogram is ___?___ a quadrilateral.

  **f.** A rhombus is ___?___ a parallelogram.

  **g.** A quadrilateral is ___?___ a rectangle.

| MODULE 4  SECTION 4 | PRACTICE AND APPLICATIONS |

## For use with Exploration 1

1. Which sequences below use the rule *divide the previous number by* $-\frac{1}{3}$ *and then subtract* $\frac{1}{6}$ *to get the next number?*

   **a.** $0, -\frac{1}{6}, \frac{1}{3}$                              **b.** $8\frac{1}{3}, -25\frac{1}{6}, 75\frac{1}{3}$

   **c.** $8\frac{1}{3}, -24\frac{5}{6}, 74\frac{2}{3}$               **d.** $1, -3\frac{1}{6}, -2\frac{5}{6}$

2. Write a sequence of at least three numbers using the rule in Exercise 1. Use 1 for the first number in the sequence.

### Solve each equation.

3. $4x - 8 = 32$

4. $-0.5x - 1.75 = 8.25$

5. $\frac{5}{8}x = -\frac{3}{4}$

6. $-\frac{3}{4}x + \frac{1}{4} = \frac{11}{8}$

7. $3.75x + 7 = -26.75$

8. $\frac{3}{4}x + 8 = \frac{15}{16}$

9. To quickly convert from kilograms to pounds, multiply the number of kilograms by 2.2 to get an estimate of the number of pounds.

   **a.** Write an equation to convert from kilograms to pounds.

   **b.** 18 kilograms is about how many pounds?

   **c.** 14 pounds is about how many kilograms?

10. The equation $Y = 1.308M$ can be used to convert from cubic meters to cubic yards, where $Y$ is the number of cubic yards and $M$ is the number of cubic meters.

    **a.** What is the number of cubic yards for 18 cubic meters?

    **b.** What is the number of cubic meters for 20 cubic yards?

*(continued)*

## MODULE 4  SECTION 4

PRACTICE AND APPLICATIONS

### For use with Exploration 2

The sum of the measures of the interior angles of a polygon is given by the formula $s = 180(n - 2)$, where $n$ is the number of sides and $s$ is the sum. Find the sum of the measures of the interior angles of each polygon. Then draw each polygon.

**11.** 4 sides           **12.** 5 sides           **13.** 6 sides

**14.** 8 sides           **15.** 10 sides          **16.** 12 sides

**Find the unknown angle measure in each polygon.**

**17.**

360

120

**18.**

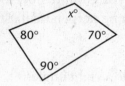

**19.**

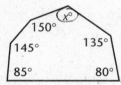

**20.**

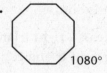

**21.** Find the measure of one interior angle of each regular polygon. Round answers to the nearest hundredth.

a.

720°

b.

1080°

## MODULE 4 SECTION 5       PRACTICE AND APPLICATIONS

## For use with Exploration 1

**Tell whether the triangle is *acute, obtuse,* or *right*.**

**1.** 5 cm, 12 cm, 13 cm

**2.** 5 cm, 14 cm, 14 cm

**3.** 6 mm, 8 mm, 12 mm

**4.** 7 in., 24 in., 25 in.

**5.** 8 in., 19 in., 20 in.

**6.** 10.5 mm, 15.5 mm, 20 mm

**7.** 18 cm, 24 cm, 30 cm

**8.** 8 mm, 15 mm, 18 mm

**9.** A cellular phone antenna needs to be supported by two wires as shown in the diagram. If the antenna is 40 ft high and is anchored along a 30 ft stretch of ground, how long should the support wires be if the antenna must be perpendicular to the ground?

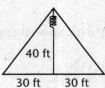

**10.** Is each labeled angle a right angle?

**a.**

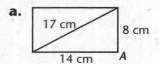

**b.**

**11. a.** Draw an example of an acute triangle. Then measure the sides and verify that it is acute.

    **b.** Draw an example of an obtuse triangle. Then measure the sides and verify that it is obtuse.

    **c.** Draw an example of a right triangle. Then measure the sides and verify that it is a right triangle.

*(continued)*

    

Name _____  Date _____

## For use with Exploration 2

**For each triangle, find the unknown side length. Give your answer to the nearest tenth.**

**12.**

8 in.   x

5 in.

**13.**

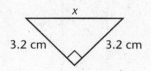

x

3.2 cm   3.2 cm

**14.**

14 ft   12 ft

x

**15.**

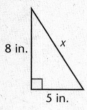

5.5 cm

12.8 cm   x

**16.**

x   12 in.

9 in.

**17.**

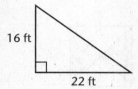

16 ft

22 ft

**18. Leisure**  A square television screen measures 20 inches on the diagonal.

**a.**  Explain how to find the length of a side using the methods in this section.

**b. Challenge**  If the square television screen increases to 40 inches on the diagonal, how does the length of the side of the television change?

**19.**  Find the missing length in each of the rectangles below. Round answers to the nearest tenth.

**a.**

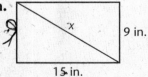

x   9 in.

15 in.

**b.**

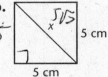

$5\sqrt{5}$

5   x   5 cm

5 cm

**c.**

25 in.

x   x

$\sqrt{2}$   x   x

$\sqrt{2}$   45   1   45   1

$x\sqrt{2} = 25$   x   $x\sqrt{2}$   x

**MODULE 4 SECTION 6**  **PRACTICE AND APPLICATIONS**

## For use with Exploration 1

**For each region, find the probability that an object falling randomly on each figure will land in the shaded area. Use π = 3.14.**

**1.**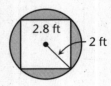

**2.**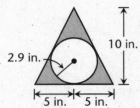

**3.**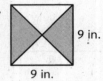

**4.**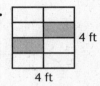

**5.**

**6.**

**7.** A 4 inch diameter circle is drawn in the middle of an 8.5 in. × 11 in. sheet of paper. What is the probability that an object falling randomly on the paper will hit the paper outside the circle?

**8. Writing** For Exercises 1, 2, and 4, describe a method for finding the probability that an object falling randomly on the paper will land in the shaded area.

*(continued)*

## MODULE 4  SECTION 6 — PRACTICE AND APPLICATIONS

### For use with Exploration 2

9. Suppose the weather forecast is a 60% chance of rain. What is the probability that it doesn't rain?

10. Suppose each of two plants have a gene combination called G1G2. Crossing the plants produces offspring according to the chart to the right.

   a. Find the probability of the offspring inheriting the G1G1 gene combination.

   b. Find the probability of the offspring inheriting the G2G2 combination.

   c. Suppose G2 is the dominant characteristic of curly leaves, where "dominant" means that characteristic will show in the offspring. Find the probability of curly leaves in the offspring.

|        |    | Plant 1 |       |
|--------|----|---------|-------|
|        |    | G1      | G2    |
| Plant 2 | G1 | G1G1    | G1G2  |
|        | G2 | G2G1    | G2G2  |

11. Suppose a coin is tossed and a six-sided die is rolled.

   a. Draw a grid representing both events.

   b. Shade the grid to represent the event of rolling a six and tossing a head. Find the probability of this event.

   c. Shade the grid to represent the event of rolling a 5 or a 6 and tossing a head. Find the probability of this event.

12. Suppose a card is drawn from a standard 52-card deck.

   a. If one card is drawn, find the probability that it is a spade.

   b. Suppose the card drawn is not a spade, and it is not replaced. If another card is drawn, find the probability that it is not the ace of spades.

13. Suppose two dice are rolled.

   a. Draw a grid representing both events.

   b. Shade the grid to represent the event of rolling a "double", or two matching numbers. Find the probability of this event.

   c. Find the probability of not rolling a double.

# New Patterns for an Old World

**Fractals, Sequences, and, Triangles**

 **GOAL**  **LEARN HOW TO:** • write rules for sequences
• name congruent figures
• apply the triangle inequality
• use a compass and ruler to construct a perpendicular bisector

**AS YOU:** • explore fractals
• construct triangles
• make a Sierpinski triangle

## Exploration 1: Fractals and Sequences

Two figures are **similar** if they are the same shape. A **fractal** is an object that contains smaller and smaller copies of itself. A fractal is **self-similar** if it is made up of pieces that are similar to the whole fractal. You can use sequences to describe some of the patterns in fractals. A **sequence** is an ordered list of numbers or objects called **terms**. You can write rules to describe some sequences.

**Example**

Write a rule to describe the pattern of shaded triangles in this fractal.

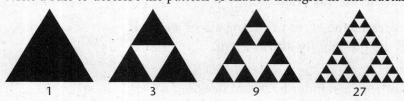

1          3          9          27

**Sample Response**

To get each term after the first term, multiply the previous term by 3.

## Exploration 2: Constructing Triangles

### Congruent Figures

Two figures are **congruent** if they are the same shape and size. Corresponding angles of congruent figures have the same measure, and corresponding sides are the same length. For example, if $\triangle ABC \cong \triangle DEF$, then $m\angle A = m\angle D = 30°$, $m\angle B = m\angle E = 60°$, $m\angle C = m\angle F = 90°$, $AB = DE = 2$, $BC = EF = 1$, and $AC = DF = \sqrt{3}$. If two triangles have corresponding sides that are the same length, then they are congruent.

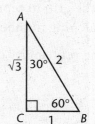

**MODULE 4  SECTION 1**                                   **STUDY GUIDE**

## Triangle Inequality

The **triangle inequality** states that the sum of the lengths of any two sides
of a triangle is greater than the length of the third side.

**Example**

Without measuring or making any drawings, decide whether each set of line segments
could form the sides of a triangle. Explain your thinking.

a. _____  ____                b. __  _____                c. _____  _____

**■ Sample Response ■**

**a.** Yes; the sum of the lengths of any two segments is greater than the length of the
third segment.

**b.** No; the sum of the lengths of the two shorter segments is less than the length of the
longest segment.

**c.** No; the sum of the lengths of the two shorter segments equals the length of the
longest segment.

# Exploration 3:  The Sierpinski Triangle

## Perpendicular Bisectors

The midpoint of a segment divides it into two congruent segments. You
can find the midpoint by constructing a perpendicular bisector.

**Example**

Find the midpoint of $\overline{AB}$.

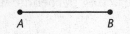

**■ Sample Response ■**

Set your compass to a radius that is equal
to the length of the segment.

Place the compass point on point A and
draw an arc above and below the segment.

Place the compass point on point B and
draw an arc above and below the segment.

The two sets of arcs should form an X above and
below the segment as shown in the figure at the right.

Draw the line through the points where the arcs intersect.
M is the midpoint.

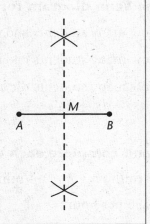

**MODULE 4  SECTION 1** | **PRACTICE & APPLICATION EXERCISES** | **STUDY GUIDE**

## Exploration 1

**Write a rule for finding a term of each sequence. Then find the next three terms of the sequence.**

**1.** 2, 5, 8, 11, ...

**2.** $x, -x, x, -x, x, ...$

**3.** 90, $89\frac{1}{2}$, 89, $88\frac{1}{2}$, ...

**4.** $34, \frac{34}{5}, \frac{34}{25}, ...$

## Exploration 2

**For Exercises 5–7, tell whether it is possible to construct a triangle with the given side lengths. If it is possible, construct the triangle.**

**5.** 8 ft, 4 ft, 1 ft

**6.** 2 in., 5 in., 3 in.

**7.** 5 cm, 4 cm, 8 cm

**8.** Compare the triangles at the right. Which appear to be similar? Which appear to be congruent? Write mathematical statements telling which triangles are congruent.

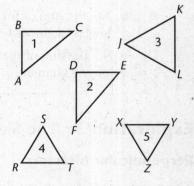

## Exploration 3

**9.** Construct a triangle with sides 6 cm, 7 cm, and 8 cm. Use a compass and ruler to find the midpoints of the sides of the triangle by constructing perpendicular bisectors.

## Spiral Review

**Use the Venn diagram for Exercises 10–12.** (Module 3, p. 227)

**10.** How many students had only toast for breakfast?

**11.** How many students had both cereal and toast for breakfast?

**12.** How many students did not have cereal for breakfast?

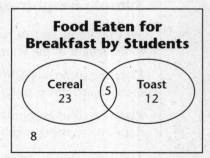

**Food Eaten for Breakfast by Students**

**Copy and complete each equation.** (Module 1, p. 9)

**13.** 18 mi/h = ___?___ mi/min

**14.** 2 ft/s = ___?___ ft/h

**15.** $2.35 per hour = ___?___ per day

**16.** $.09 per mL = ___?___ per L

**MODULE 4  SECTION 2**                                                    **STUDY GUIDE**

# Nature's Sequences    Rotations and Rational Numbers

**GOAL**  **LEARN HOW TO:** • describe rotational symmetry
                          • recognize rational and irrational numbers
                          • use notation for repeating decimals

**AS YOU:** • discover patterns in nature
            • explore ratios

## Exploration 1: Rotational Symmetry

### Fibonacci Sequence

In a **Fibonacci sequence**, each term after the first two terms is the sum of
the two previous numbers.

   1, 1, 2, 3, 5, 8, 13, 21, 34, ...

### Rotational Symmetry

A figure or an object has **rotational symmetry** if it fits exactly on itself
after being rotated less than 360° around a center point. You can find
the minimum rotational symmetry of an object by measuring the
rotation angle with a protractor or by dividing 360° by the number of
congruent angles.

---

**Example**

Does the figure appear to have rotational symmetry? If the figure does have rotational
symmetry, give the minimum rotational symmetry.

**a.**     **b.** 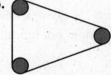    **c.**

---

■ **Sample Response** ■

**a.** 90° rotational symmetry    **b.** no rotational symmetry   **c.** 180° rotational symmetry

---

# MODULE 4 SECTION 2                                    STUDY GUIDE

## Exploration 2: Rational and Irrational Numbers

A **rational number** is a number that can be written in the form $\frac{a}{b}$, where $a$ and $b$ are integers and $b \neq 0$. When written as a decimal, a rational number is either a **terminating decimal** (a decimal containing a limited number of digits) or a **repeating decimal** (a decimal containing a digit or group of digits that repeats forever).

An **irrational number** cannot be written as the quotient of two integers. When written as a decimal, an irrational number does not terminate or repeat. The square root of a whole number that is not a perfect square is an irrational number. The constant $\pi$ is also irrational.

---

### Example

Tell whether each number is a *rational* or an *irrational* number. Then write each number as a decimal and describe that decimal.

**a.** $\frac{12}{25}$          **b.** $\frac{3}{9}$          **c.** $\sqrt{2}$

---

### Sample Response

**a.** This is a rational number. When written as a decimal, it is a terminating decimal:
$\frac{12}{25} = 0.48$.

**b.** This is a rational number. When written as a decimal, it is a repeating decimal:
$\frac{3}{9} = 0.3333\ldots$ or $0.\overline{3}$.

**c.** This is an irrational number because 2 is not a perfect square. When written as a decimal, it does not terminate and it does not repeat:
$\sqrt{2} = 1.414213\ldots$ .

---

In part (b) of the Example above, notice how the repeating digit in the decimal number is shown using an *overbar*.

**MODULE 4  SECTION 2** | PRACTICE & APPLICATION EXERCISES | **STUDY GUIDE**

## Exploration 1

**For Exercises 1–4, tell whether each figure appears to have rotational symmetry. If the figure has rotational symmetry, give the minimum rotational symmetry and tell what other rotational symmetries it has.**

**1.**

**2.**

**3.**

**4.**

**5.** Create your own design that involves rotational symmetry. Tell its minimum rotational symmetry and list all its rotational symmetries.

## Exploration 2

**Tell whether each number is a *rational* or an *irrational* number.**

**6.** $\frac{10}{18}$

**7.** $\sqrt{0.04}$

**8.** $\sqrt{49}$

**9.** $\frac{7}{11}$

**10.** $\frac{\pi}{3}$

**11.** $\sqrt{8}$

**12.** $\frac{3}{4}$

**13.** $\frac{28}{19}$

## Spiral Review

**Tell whether it is possible to construct a triangle with the given side lengths. If it is possible, construct the triangle.**
(Module 4, p. 247)

**14.** 7 cm, 1 cm, 5 cm

**15.** 3 in., 2 in., 3 in.

**16.** 1 cm, 1 cm, 1 cm

**Find each sum or difference.** (Module 2, p. 139)

**17.** $-3\frac{1}{5} + 2\frac{2}{5}$

**18.** $-1\frac{1}{2} - \left(-2\frac{1}{8}\right)$

**19.** $4\frac{5}{7} + \left(-3\frac{2}{9}\right)$

**20.** In the diagram, $\triangle XYZ \sim \triangle PQR$. Find the length of $\overline{PQ}$.
(Module 3, p. 207)

## MODULE 4  SECTION 3                                    STUDY GUIDE

# Music to Your Ears    Equations with Fractions and Quadrilaterals

**GOAL**  **LEARN HOW TO:** • solve equations with fractional coefficients
• classify quadrilaterals

**AS YOU:** • discover patterns in music
• look at different musical instruments

## Exploration 1: Equations with Fractions

### Reciprocals and Equations

You can use inverse operations to solve an equation with a fraction for a coefficient. Two numbers are **reciprocals** if their product is 1.

### Example

Solve $\frac{3}{4}x = 9$.

### ■ Sample Response ■

$$\frac{3}{4}x = 9$$

$$\frac{3}{4}x \div \frac{3}{4} = 9 \div \frac{3}{4} \qquad \leftarrow \text{The inverse of multiplication is division.}$$

$$\frac{3}{4}x \cdot \frac{4}{3} = 9 \cdot \frac{4}{3} \qquad \leftarrow \text{To divide by } \frac{3}{4}, \text{ multiply by its reciprocal, } \frac{4}{3}.$$

$$x = 12$$

## Exploration 2: Classifying Quadrilaterals

A **quadrilateral** is a polygon with four sides. Quadrilaterals are classified by their angle measures, parallel sides, and side lengths. Each type of quadrilateral has the characteristics of the quadrilateral(s) linked above it in the diagram.

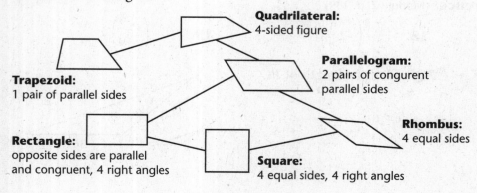

**Quadrilateral:**
4-sided figure

**Parallelogram:**
2 pairs of congruent parallel sides

**Trapezoid:**
1 pair of parallel sides

**Rhombus:**
4 equal sides

**Rectangle:**
opposite sides are parallel and congruent, 4 right angles

**Square:**
4 equal sides, 4 right angles

## MODULE 4  SECTION 3 | PRACTICE & APPLICATION EXERCISES | STUDY GUIDE

### Exploration 1

Solve each equation.

**1.** $\frac{1}{3}x = -5$

**2.** $4 = 8 + \frac{3}{4}m$

**3.** $\frac{4}{5}y - \frac{3}{10} = \frac{2}{10}$

**4.** $\frac{4}{9} + \frac{7}{18}t = \frac{5}{9}$

**5.** $\frac{3}{8}r = 39$

**6.** $11 = \frac{4}{11}f - 44$

### Exploration 2

List as many names as possible for each figure.

**7.**

**8.**

**9.**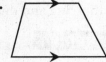

Tell whether each statement is *true* of *false*. Explain your answer.

**10.** A quadrilateral is *always* four sided.

**11.** A trapezoid is *sometimes* a parallelogram.

**12.** A rhombus is *never* a trapezoid.

### Spiral Review

Tell whether each number is a *rational* or an *irrational* number. (Module 4, p. 260)

**13.** $\frac{24}{5}$

**14.** $34.\overline{12}$

**15.** $\sqrt{121}$

**16.** $\sqrt{11}$

Tell whether each ordered pair is a solution of the equation $y = -2x + 3$. (Module 3, p. 183)

**17.** $(3, 4)$

**18.** $(1, 5)$

**19.** $(1, 1)$

**20.** $(3, 3)$

Solve each equation. Round decimal solutions to the nearest hundredth. (Module 3, p. 218)

**21.** $20 = 1.3x + (-12.5)$

**22.** $\frac{f}{2.4} - 32 = -0.9$

**23.** $5.6 + 0.4g = -1.9$

**24.** $\frac{y}{6} + 66.6 = 0.6$

## MODULE 4  SECTION 4

# Patterns in Art   Rational Numbers and Polygons

**GOAL**  **LEARN HOW TO:** • solve equations containing rational numbers
                               • find the sum of the measures of the interior angles of a polygon

    **AS YOU:** • create an abstract design
               • look for patterns in polygons

## Exploration 1: Multiplying and Dividing Rational Numbers

You can solve equations that contain rational numbers. The rules for
multiplying and dividing negative rational numbers are the same as the
rules for multiplying and dividing negative integers.

### Example

Solve $-\dfrac{2}{3}x + 8 = 22$.

### ■ Sample Response ■

$$-\frac{2}{3}x + 8 = 22$$

$$-\frac{2}{3}x + 8 - 8 = 22 - 8 \qquad \leftarrow \text{Subtract 8 from both sides.}$$

$$-\frac{2}{3}x = 14$$

$$-\frac{2}{3}x \div \left(-\frac{2}{3}\right) = 14 \div \left(-\frac{2}{3}\right) \qquad \leftarrow \text{Divide both sides by } -\frac{2}{3}.$$

$$-\frac{2}{3}x \cdot \left(-\frac{3}{2}\right) = 14 \cdot \left(-\frac{3}{2}\right) \qquad \leftarrow \text{Multiply both sides by } -\frac{3}{2}, \text{ the reciprocal of } -\frac{2}{3}.$$

$$x = -21$$

**Check:** $-\dfrac{2}{3}x + 8 = 22$

$$-\frac{2}{3}(-21) + 8 \stackrel{?}{=} 22 \qquad \leftarrow \text{Replace } x \text{ with } -21.$$

$$14 + 8 \stackrel{?}{=} 22$$

$$22 = 22 \checkmark$$

| Name | Date |
|------|------|

## MODULE 4  SECTION 4 STUDY GUIDE

## Exploration 2: Angles of Polygons

### Interior Angles of Polygons

The sum of the measures of the interior angles of a convex polygon depends on the number of sides. The equation $s = 180°(n - 2)$ gives the sum $s$ of the measures of the interior angles of a convex polygon with $n$ sides.

> ### Example
>
> **a.** Find the sum of the measures of the interior angles of a convex pentagon.
>
> **b.** What is the measure of one interior angle if the pentagon is regular?
>
> ### ■ Sample Response ■
>
> **a.** Use the formula $s = 180°(n - 2)$.
>
> $s = 180°(n - 2)$
> $\quad = 180°(5 - 2) \quad \leftarrow$ A pentagon has 5 sides, so $n = 5$.
> $\quad = 180°(3)$
> $\quad = 540°$
>
> **b.** If the pentagon is regular, then all five interior angles have the same measure. So, each interior angle measures $540° \div 5$, or $108°$.

## MODULE 4  SECTION 4 | PRACTICE & APPLICATION EXERCISES

## Exploration 1

**For each sequence in Exercises 1 and 2, write a rule that can be used to find a term. Then find the next term. (*Hint*: Each rule uses only multiplication.)**

**1.** 2.4, −4.8, 9.6, −19.2, …

**2.** $2\frac{2}{5}, 1\frac{1}{5}, \frac{3}{5}, …$

**3.** For which of the sequences below can you use the rule *multiply the previous term by −0.6 and then subtract 0.8* to find the next number?

   **A.** 1, 0.14, −0.72, …      **B.** 2, −2, 0.4, …      **C.** 3, −1, 1.4, …

**Solve each equation.**

**4.** $2.6x - 1.3 = 22.1$     **5.** $-7.3x + 8 = -0.03$     **6.** $8\frac{3}{4} = -\frac{7}{9}x$

**MODULE 4  SECTION 4** | **PRACTICE & APPLICATION EXERCISES** | **STUDY GUIDE**

## Exploration 2

**For Exercises 7–9, find the sum of the measures of the interior angles of each convex polygon.**

**7.** a 20-sided polygon  **8.** a 15-sided polygon  **9.** a 12-sided polygon

**10.** If the polygon in Exercise 9 is regular, what is the measure of each of its interior angles?

**Find the unknown angle measure in each polygon.**

**11.**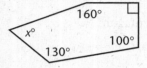

**12.**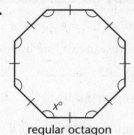

regular octagon

## Spiral Review

**Solve each equation.** (Module 4, p. 274)

**13.** $\dfrac{3}{4}x = 21$  **14.** $50 = \dfrac{2}{5}g - 5$  **15.** $22 = \dfrac{3}{2}y + \dfrac{1}{2}y$

**Find the unknown angle measure of each triangle. Tell whether each triangle is *acute, obtuse,* or *right*.** (Toolbox, p. 604)

**16.** 35°, 78°  **17.** 135°, 18°  **18.** 30°, 90°

**Evaluate each expression. Round decimal answers to the nearest hundredth.** (Module 3, p. 183)

**19.** $\dfrac{18 + 12}{8}$  **20.** $(5 + 4)\dfrac{8}{3}$  **21.** $\dfrac{5}{16 - 7}$

**MODULE 4  SECTION 5**                                    **STUDY GUIDE**

# Right On!   Working with Triangles

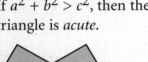 **LEARN HOW TO:** • identify different types of triangles by looking at their side lengths
• use the Pythagorean theorem to find an unknown side length of a right triangle

**AS YOU:** • work with paper squares
• explore the dimensions of the I.M. Pei pyramid

## Exploration 1: Triangle Side Length Relationships

### Sides Lengths of a Triangle

If you know the side lengths of a triangle, you can identify it as obtuse, acute, or right. Let $a$ and $b$ represent the lengths of the two shorter sides and let $c$ represent the length of the longest side.

| | | |
|---|---|---|
| If $a^2 + b^2 > c^2$, then the triangle is *acute*. | If $a^2 + b^2 = c^2$, then the triangle is *right*. | If $a^2 + b^2 < c^2$, then the triangle is *obtuse*. |

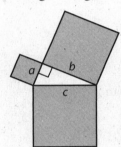
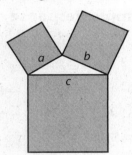

---

**Example**

Tell whether a triangle with side lengths of 5 m, 4 m, and 8 m is *acute*, *right*, or *obtuse*.

**Sample Response**

Let $a = 5$, $b = 4$, and $c = 8$.

Then $a^2 = 5^2$, or 25; $b^2 = 4^2$, or 16; and $c^2 = 8^2$, or 64.

So $a^2 + b^2 = 25 + 16$, or 41.

Since $41 < 64$, $a^2 + b^2 < c^2$.

Therefore, the triangle is obtuse.

---

## Exploration 2: The Pythagorean Theorem

A right triangle has a **hypotenuse**, the side opposite the right angle, and two **legs**, the two shorter sides. In a right triangle, the sum of the squares of the lengths of the legs is equal to the square of the length of the hypotenuse. This relationship, usually written as $a^2 + b^2 = c^2$, is known as the **Pythagorean Theorem**.

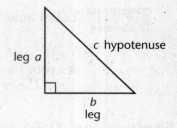

### Example

Find the unknown side length. Give the length to the nearest tenth.

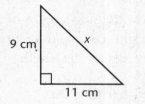

### ■ Sample Response ■

Use the formula $a^2 + b^2 = c^2$.

$a^2 + b^2 = c^2$

$9^2 + 11^2 = c^2$  ← Replace $a$ with 9 and $b$ with 11.

$81 + 121 = c^2$  ← Simplify.

$202 = c^2$

$\sqrt{202} = \sqrt{c^2}$  ← Take the square root of both sides since $\sqrt{c^2} = c$.

$14.2 \approx c$  ← Round to the nearest tenth.

The unknown side length is about 14.2 cm.

Name _____ Date _____

## Exploration 1

**Tell whether each triangle is *acute*, *obtuse*, or *right*.**

**1.**
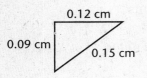
0.12 cm
0.09 cm
0.15 cm

**2.**
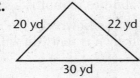
20 yd
22 yd
30 yd

**3.**
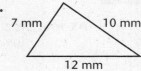
7 mm
10 mm
12 mm

**4.** a triangle with side lengths of 16 ft, 10 ft, and 13 ft

## Exploration 2

**For each triangle, find the unknown side length. Give each answer to the nearest tenth.**

**5.**
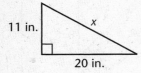
11 in.
x
20 in.

**6.**
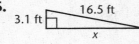
16.5 ft
3.1 ft
x

**7.**
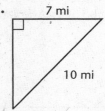
7 mi
10 mi

**Tell whether the given side lengths could be the side lengths of a right triangle. Explain why or why not.**

**8.** 12 cm, 13 cm, 5 cm

**9.** 5 m, 5 m, 8 m

**10.** 2.4 in., 1 in., 2.6 in.

## Spiral Review

**Find the unknown angle measure for each polygon.** (Module 4, p. 285)

**11.**

x°

**12.**
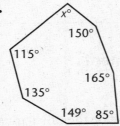
x°
150°
115°
165°
135°
149° 85°

**13.**
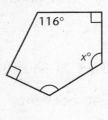
116°
x°

**14.** Find the volume of a rectangular prism when the length is 8.5 in., the width is 4.6 in., and the height is 10.2 in. (Module 1, p. 47)

**15.** There are 5 black socks and 4 brown socks in a drawer. (Module 2, p. 115)

   **a.** What is the probability of drawing a black sock?

   **b.** Suppose a brown sock was drawn first and not replaced. What is the probability of getting a brown sock on the second draw?

**MODULE 4  SECTION 6**                                    **STUDY GUIDE**

# Discoveries in the Deep   Geometry and Probability

**GOAL**  **LEARN HOW TO:** • find probabilities using areas
                                         • find probabilities in multistage experiments

 **AS YOU:** • examine the area of a shipwreck
                   • investigate how likely it is that you will find the *Titanic*

## Exploration 1: Geometric Probability

Probabilities that are based on length, area, or volume are **geometric probabilities**.

> **Example**
>
> Find the probability that an object falling randomly on the figure will land in the shaded region.
>
>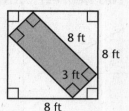
>
> **Sample Response**
>
> $P$ (landing in the shaded region) $= \dfrac{\text{area of shaded region}}{\text{area of square}}$
>
> $= \dfrac{24\ \text{ft}^2}{64\ \text{ft}^2}$
>
> $= 0.375$
>
> The probability of landing in the shaded region is 37.5%.

## Exploration 2: Multistage Experiments

### Complementary Events

Two events are **complementary events** if one or the other must occur but they cannot both occur. The sum of the probabilities of complementary events is 1.

 $P$ (the event occurs) $= 1 - P$ (the event does not occur)

Name _____    Date _____

### Example

If the probability of rain today is 30%, then the probability that it will not rain can be found using the formula for complementary events.

$$P \text{ (will not rain)} = 1 - P \text{ (will rain)}$$
$$= 1 - 0.3$$
$$= 0.7$$

There is 70% chance that it will not rain today.

## Multistage Experiments

A **multistage experiment** involves two or more events happening one after another. These are sometimes called *compound events*. You can use multiplication to find the probabilities of the outcomes in a multistage experiment.

$$P \text{ (1st event happening)} \cdot P \text{ (2nd event happening)} = P \text{ (both events happening)}$$

### Example

Suppose two objects fall onto the figure shown and have an equal chance of landing anywhere on the figure. What is the probability that the first object will land in the unshaded region and the second will land in the shaded region?

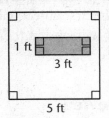

### Sample Response

The total area of the large square is $5^2$, or 25 ft$^2$.

The area of the shaded region is 3 ft$^2$.

Then the area of the unshaded region is $25 - 3$, or 22 ft$^2$.

| Probability of the 1st object landing in the unshaded region. | Probability of the 2nd object landing in the shaded region. | Probability that the 1st lands in the unshaded region and the 2nd lands in the shaded region. |
|:---:|:---:|:---:|
| $\dfrac{22}{25}$ | $\dfrac{3}{25}$ | $\dfrac{66}{625}$ |

So, the probability that the first object will land in the unshaded region and the second will land in the shaded region is $\dfrac{66}{625}$.

## MODULE 4 SECTION 6 | PRACTICE & APPLICATION EXERCISES | STUDY GUIDE

### Exploration 1

**Jenny's earring is somewhere in her bedroom, which is diagrammed at the right. Assume that the earring is equally likely to be anywhere in the entire room.**

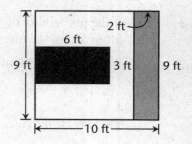

1. What is the probability that the earring is in the unshaded region?

2. What is the probability that the earring is in the region shaded black?

3. What is the probability that the earring is in the region shaded gray?

### Exploration 2

**For Exercises 4 – 6, suppose A and B are independent events. The probability that event A will occur is 0.35 and the probability that event B will not occur is 0.67. Find each probability.**

4. $P(\text{not } A)$

5. $P(B)$

6. $P(A \text{ and } B)$

7. Suppose two objects fall onto the figure shown and have an equal chance of landing anywhere on the figure. What is the probability that the first object will land in the unshaded region and the second object will land in the shaded region?

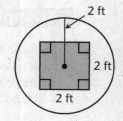

### Spiral Review

**Tell whether each triangle with the given side lengths is *acute*, *right*, or *obtuse*. (Module 4, p. 297)**

8. 11.2 cm, 8 cm, 10.3 cm

9. 6 mm, 10 mm, 14 mm

**Graph each equation. Tell whether the graph is *linear* or *nonlinear*. (Module 3, p. 183)**

10. $y = \frac{3}{4}x + 1$

11. $y = -2x^2$

12. $y = 3x$

**Find the volume of each cylinder. Round your answers to the nearest hundredth. (Module 1, p. 47)**

13. $r = 5$ mm
    $h = 6$ mm

14. $d = 2.4$ in.
    $h = 8.9$ in.

15. $r = 3$ ft
    $h = 12$ ft

# MODULE 5

## Cylinders (Use with Questions 13 and 14 on page 322.)

**Directions** Find the surface area, S.A., and the volume, V, of each cylinder.

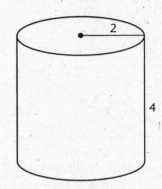

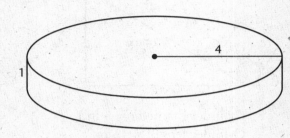

S.A. = _____

V = _____

S.A. = _____

V = _____

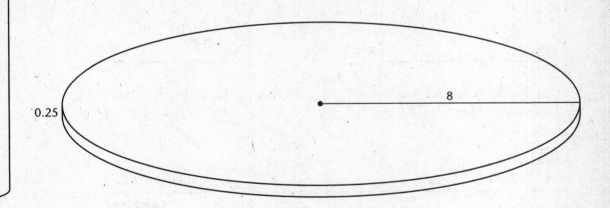

S.A. = _____

V = _____

S.A. = _____

V = _____

**MODULE 5**

## Ramp and Cylinders (Use with Project Questions 1–4 on page 328.)

**Directions** The diagrams below show a ramp and cylinders supporting a block. The diameter of the cylinders decreases from one diagram to the next. Use the diagrams to complete the table at the bottom of the page.

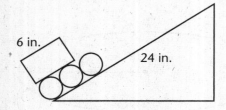

Cylinder diameter = 3 in.
Cylinder length = 12 in.

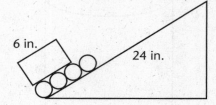

Cylinder diameter = 2 in.
Cylinder length = 12 in.

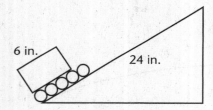

Cylinder diameter = 1.5 in.
Cylinder length = 12 in.

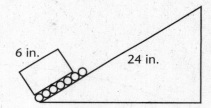

Cylinder diameter = 1 in.
Cylinder length = 12 in.

| Cylinder diameter (in.) | Number of cylinders needed | Volume of each cylinder (in.$^3$) | Combined volume of all cylinders (in.$^3$) |
|:---:|:---:|:---:|:---:|
| 3 | | | |
| 2 | | | |
| 1.5 | | | |
| 1 | | | |

**MODULE 5**                                           LABSHEET **2A**

# Graph of Black-and-White TV Sales
(Use with Questions 5–9 on pages 332–333.)

**Directions** Use the graph to complete the table.

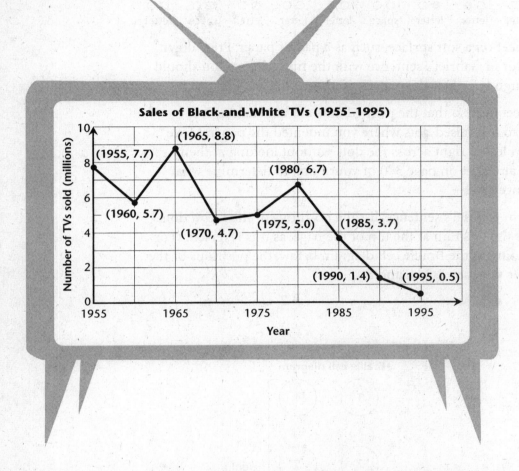

**Sales of Black-and-White TVs (1955–1995)**

(1955, 7.7)
(1965, 8.8)
(1980, 6.7)
(1960, 5.7)
(1970, 4.7)
(1975, 5.0)
(1985, 3.7)
(1990, 1.4)
(1995, 0.5)

Number of TVs sold (millions)

Year

| Period | Rise | Run | Slope of graph | Does graph slant *up* or *down* from left to right? | Are TV sales *increasing* or *decreasing*? |
|--------|------|-----|----------------|------------------------------------------------------|---------------------------------------------|
| 1955–1960 | –2 | 5 | –0.4 | down | decreasing |
| 1960–1965 | | | | | |
| 1965–1970 | | | | | |
| 1970–1975 | | | | | |
| 1975–1980 | | | | | |
| 1980–1985 | | | | | |
| 1985–1990 | | | | | |
| 1990–1995 | | | | | |

**MODULE 5**

## Gabriel's Sentence  (Use with Question 1 on page 370.)

**Directions**  Gabriel's Braille sentence is shown below. The sentence has been reversed.

| ○● | ●○ | ●○ | ○● | ●○ | ○○ | ●● | ○● | ●● | ○○ | ●○ |
|----|----|----|----|----|----|----|----|----|----|----|
| ●○ | ●● | ○● | ●● | ●● | ○○ | ●○ | ○○ | ○○ | ○○ | ○● |
| ○○ | ○● | ○○ | ○● | ●○ | ○○ | ○● | ○○ | ○○ | ○○ | ○○ |
| letter | letter | letter | letter | letter | space | letter | letter | letter | space | letter |

- Place this labsheet on a soft surface, such as a pad of paper. Press down on each solid dot in Gabriel's sentence with the tip of a pen. You should press hard enough to indent the paper without tearing it.

- Turn the labsheet over so that the printed dots are not shown. You should be able to feel raised dots where you indented the paper. Move your hand from left to right across the dots without looking at them. Use the Braille alphabet on page 370 of your book to determine what Gabriel's sentence says.

- For each letter in Gabriel's sentence, list the positions of the *raised* dots. Do not just use the diagram at the top of the page, as it is reversed. (For example, according to the Braille cell diagram below, the positions of the dots in the letter ●● are 1, 3, 4, and 5.)
  ○●
  ●○

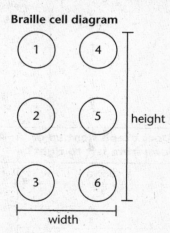

**Braille cell diagram**

## MODULE 5                                    LABSHEET 5B

### Tree Diagram   (Use with Question 10 on page 374.)

**Directions**  Use the Braille cell diagram below to complete the tree diagram.

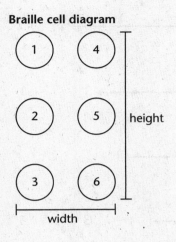

**Braille cell diagram**

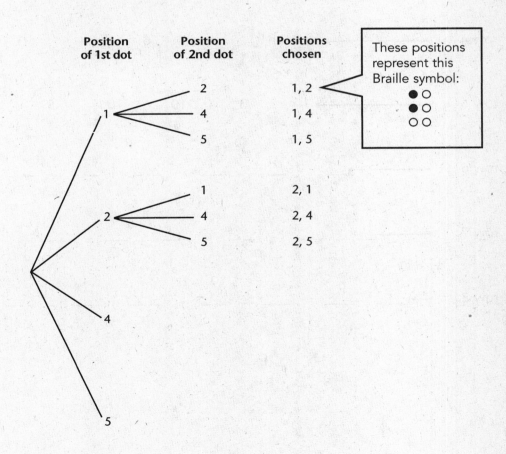

| Position of 1st dot | Position of 2nd dot | Positions chosen |
|---|---|---|

**MODULE 5**                                        LABSHEET **5C**

## Pascal's Triangle   (Use with Exercise 28 on page 380.)

**Directions** Complete rows 6–8 of Pascal's triangle.

row 0  ————————————————→  1

row 1  ——————————————→  1      1

row 2  ——————————————→  1       2       1

row 3  ————————————→  1       3        3        1

row 4  ————————————→  1      4      6      4      1

row 5  ——————————→  1      5      10      10      5      1

row 6  ——————→  __     __     __     __     __     __     __

row 7  ——→  __     __     __     __     __     __     __     __

row 8  →  __     __     __     __     __     __     __     __     __

Name _____  Problem _____

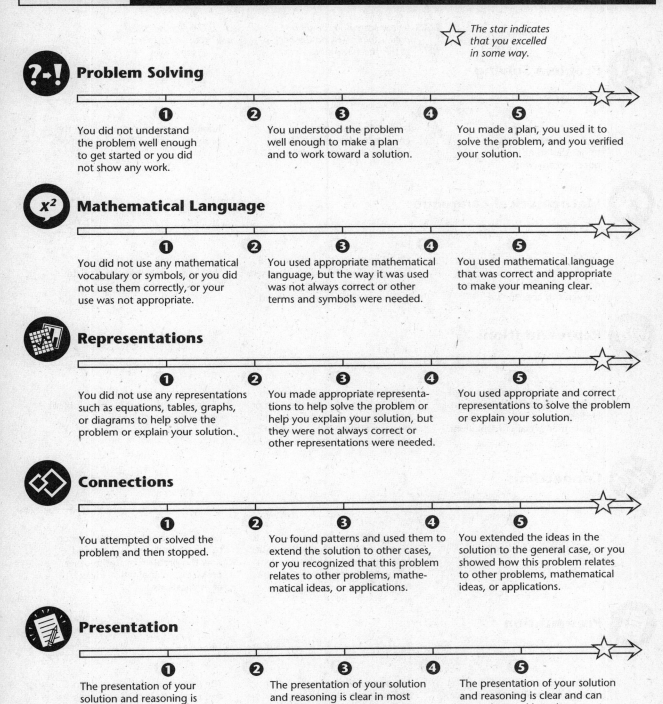

## TEACHER — ASSESSMENT SCALES

☆ *The star indicates that you excelled in some way.*

### Problem Solving

**❶** You did not understand the problem well enough to get started or you did not show any work.

**❷**

**❸** You understood the problem well enough to make a plan and to work toward a solution.

**❹**

**❺** You made a plan, you used it to solve the problem, and you verified your solution.

### Mathematical Language

**❶** You did not use any mathematical vocabulary or symbols, or you did not use them correctly, or your use was not appropriate.

**❷**

**❸** You used appropriate mathematical language, but the way it was used was not always correct or other terms and symbols were needed.

**❹**

**❺** You used mathematical language that was correct and appropriate to make your meaning clear.

### Representations

**❶** You did not use any representations such as equations, tables, graphs, or diagrams to help solve the problem or explain your solution.

**❷**

**❸** You made appropriate representations to help solve the problem or help you explain your solution, but they were not always correct or other representations were needed.

**❹**

**❺** You used appropriate and correct representations to solve the problem or explain your solution.

### Connections

**❶** You attempted or solved the problem and then stopped.

**❷**

**❸** You found patterns and used them to extend the solution to other cases, or you recognized that this problem relates to other problems, mathematical ideas, or applications.

**❹**

**❺** You extended the ideas in the solution to the general case, or you showed how this problem relates to other problems, mathematical ideas, or applications.

### Presentation

**❶** The presentation of your solution and reasoning is unclear to others.

**❷**

**❸** The presentation of your solution and reasoning is clear in most places, but others may have trouble understanding parts of it.

**❹**

**❺** The presentation of your solution and reasoning is clear and can be understood by others.

Content Used: _____   **Computational Errors:** Yes ☐ No ☐

Notes on Errors: _____

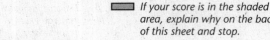 **STUDENT   SELF-ASSESSMENT SCALES**

*If your score is in the shaded area, explain why on the back of this sheet and stop.*

☆ *The star indicates that you excelled in some way.*

 ## Problem Solving

**❶**        **❷**        **❸**        **❹**        **❺**        ☆

**❶** I did not understand the problem well enough to get started or I did not show any work.

**❷** I understood the problem well enough to make a plan and to work toward a solution.

**❹** I made a plan, I used it to solve the problem, and I verified my solution.

 ## Mathematical Language

**❶**        **❷**        **❸**        **❹**        **❺**        ☆

**❶** I did not use any mathematical vocabulary or symbols, or I did not use them correctly, or my use was not appropriate.

**❸** I used appropriate mathematical language, but the way it was used was not always correct or other terms and symbols were needed.

**❺** I used mathematical language that was correct and appropriate to make my meaning clear.

 ## Representations

**❶**        **❷**        **❸**        **❹**        **❺**        ☆

**❶** I did not use any representations such as equations, tables, graphs, or diagrams to help solve the problem or explain my solution.

**❸** I made appropriate representations to help solve the problem or help me explain my solution, but they were not always correct or other representations were needed.

**❺** I used appropriate and correct representations to solve the problem or explain my solution.

 ## Connections

**❶**        **❷**        **❸**        **❹**        **❺**        ☆

**❶** I attempted or solved the problem and then stopped.

**❸** I found patterns and used them to extend the solution to other cases, or I recognized that this problem relates to other problems, mathematical ideas, or applications.

**❺** I extended the ideas in the solution to the general case, or I showed how this problem relates to other problems, mathematical ideas, or applications.

 ## Presentation

**❶**        **❷**        **❸**        **❹**        **❺**        ☆

**❶** The presentation of my solution and reasoning is unclear to others.

**❸** The presentation of my solution and reasoning is clear in most places, but others may have trouble understanding parts of it.

**❺** The presentation of my solution and reasoning is clear and can be understood by others.

## MODULE 5  SECTION 1  PRACTICE AND APPLICATIONS

### For use with Exploration 1

**Find the surface area of the cylinder with the given radius and height. Use π = 3.14.**

**1.** $r = 4$ cm, $h = 6$ cm

**2.** $r = 1$ m, $h = 1$ m

**3.** $r = 1$ ft, $h = 3$ ft

**4.** $r = 1.8$ m, $h = 9$ m

**5.** $r = 3.5$ cm, $h = 9.8$ cm

**6.** $r = 8$ ft, $h = 2$ ft

**7.** Containers that hold refined oil for use in cars are cylinders. Find the surface area of a cylinder that has a diameter of 30 feet and a height of 25 feet.

**Find the surface area of the following commonly used cylinders. Use π = 3.14.**

**8.**

1.5 in.

4.25 in.

15 oz can

**9.**

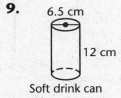

6.5 cm

12 cm

Soft drink can

**10.**

5 in.

$9\frac{3}{4}$ in.

42 oz oatmeal container

**11.**

1 in.

$3\frac{1}{4}$ in.

6 oz tomato paste

**12. Challenge** The surface area of a cylinder with circumference $24\pi$ cm is $300\pi$ cm$^2$. What is its height?

*(continued)*

**MODULE 5 SECTION 1**　　　　　　　　**PRACTICE AND APPLICATIONS**

## For use with Exploration 2

**Find the ratio of surface area to volume for each can.
Use π = 3.14.**

**13.**
1.5 in.
4 in.

**14.**
3 in.
12 in.

**15.**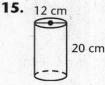
12 cm
20 cm

**16.** Use your answers for Exercises 13–15 to rank the cans shown above from the most efficient to the least efficient.

**Find the ratio of surface area to volume for each of the
following commonly used cylinders. Use π = 3.14.**

**17.**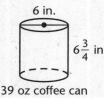
6 in.
$6\frac{3}{4}$ in
39 oz coffee can

**18.**
2 in.
$6\frac{7}{8}$ in.
46 fl oz juice can

**19.**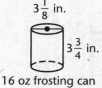
$3\frac{1}{8}$ in.
$3\frac{3}{4}$ in.
16 oz frosting can

**20. Challenge** A 10 ounce soup can has a diameter of $2\frac{1}{2}$ inches and a

height of $3\frac{7}{8}$ inches, while a 19 ounce soup can has a diameter of

3 inches and a height of $4\frac{7}{8}$ inches.

**a.** Which can is more efficient?

**b.** Find the ratio of the volumes of the soup cans.

**c.** How does the ratio of the volumes of the soup cans compare to
the ratio of the weights of the soup cans? Show the ratio of the
weights.

**d.** How does the ratio of the volumes of the soup cans compare to
the ratio of the diameters of the soup cans? Show the ratio of the
diameters.

**e. Writing** Use the answers to parts (a) – (d) to determine which
soup can you would manufacture if you had the opportunity.
Explain your choice.

**MODULE 5  SECTION 2**                    **PRACTICE AND APPLICATIONS**

## For use with Exploration 1

**Find the slope of each line.**

**1.**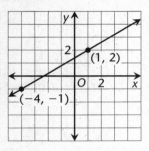

**2.**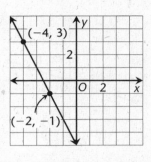

**3.**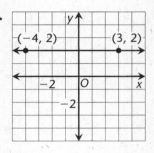

**Find the slope of the line through the given points. You may find it helpful to plot the points and draw a line through them first.**

**4.** (3, 5) and (5, −2)

**5.** (4, 6) and (8, 6)

**6.** (−2, −3) and (6, 0)

**7.** (−5, 7) and (−5, 9)

**8.** (2, −4) and (6, − 4)

**9.** (0, 2) and (0, −2)

**10.** Use the lines shown.

    **a.** Which line has a positive slope?

    **b.** Which line has a negative slope?

    **c.** Which line has a slope of zero?

    **d.** Which line has an undefined slope?

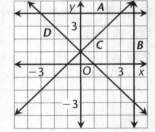

**The percentage of adult males who are overweight has increased dramatically from 1960 to 1994, as shown in the graph at the right.**

**11.** Estimate the rate of increase from 1980 to 1994.

**12.** Find the rate of increase in the percent of males who are overweight from 1976 to 1980.

**13.** Use slope to find the average rate of increase from 1960 to 1994.

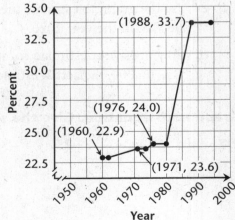

**Percentage of Males Who are Overweight**

*(continued)*

**MODULE 5  SECTION 2**                     **PRACTICE AND APPLICATIONS**

## For use with Exploration 2

**For each line, write an equation in slope-intercept form.**

**14.**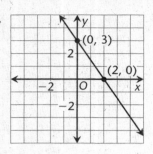

**15.**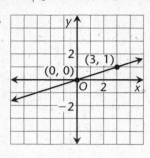

**16.**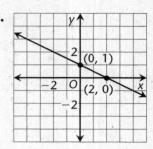

**Write an equation in slope-intercept form for the line through the given points. You may find it helpful to plot the points and draw a line through them first.**

**17.** $(0, 6)$ and $(1, 4)$

**18.** $(0, 3)$ and $(4, 9)$

**19.** $(-5, 5)$ and $(0, 5)$

**20.** $(1, 6)$ and $(3, 2)$

**21.** $(3, 7)$ and $(8, 9)$

**22.** $(-4, 0)$ and $(0, 5)$

**The graph shows a fitted line for the U.S. population for 1990 (year 0) and projections through the year 2040 (year 50).**

**23.** **a.** Find the line's slope and $y$-intercept. What information does the slope give you about the population of the U.S.? What information does the $y$-intercept give you about the population?

**b.** Write an equation for the line.

**c.** Use the graph to estimate the population of the U.S. in the year 2020.

**d.** How does your estimate compare with 322,700,000, the actual estimate?

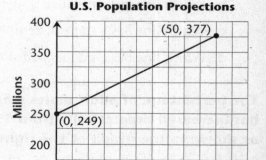

**Graph each equation. Give the slope of each line.**

**24.** $y = 4$

**25.** $y = -3$

**26.** $x = 2$

**27.** $x = -1$

## MODULE 5 SECTION 3                    PRACTICE AND APPLICATIONS

## For use with Exploration 1

**Write each product as a single power.**

**1.** $10^5 \cdot 10^3$      **2.** $10^2 \cdot 10^8$      **3.** $3^2 \cdot 3^5$      **4.** $5^4 \cdot 5^9$

**5.** $2^4 \cdot 2$      **6.** $6^3 \cdot 6^5 \cdot 6$      **7.** $x \cdot x^5$      **8.** $y^3 \cdot y^4$

**9.** $n^5 \cdot n^5$      **10.** $y^{12} \cdot y^{20}$      **11.** $w^{80} \cdot w^{12}$      **12.** $r^8 \cdot r \cdot r^5$

**13.** The "stopping" distance of a car is the distance it takes to stop after braking. The "stopping distance" is related to the speed of the car by the equation $d = k \cdot s^2$, where $d$ is the distance in feet, $s$ is the speed in miles per hour, and $k$ is a number that depends on the car and the road conditions.

    **a.** Since the exponent of the speed of the car is 2, the stopping distance depends on the square of the speed. Is this true?

    **b.** Suppose it is known that $k = 1.5$. What is the stopping distance of a car traveling at 30 mi/h? at 60 mi/h? How are these two answers related?

**Write each quotient as a single power.**

**14.** $\dfrac{10^8}{10^6}$      **15.** $\dfrac{10^{12}}{10^7}$      **16.** $\dfrac{5^5}{5}$      **17.** $\dfrac{8^7}{8^3}$

**18.** $\dfrac{6^{16}}{6^{12}}$      **19.** $\dfrac{4^5 \cdot 4^4}{4^2}$      **20.** $\dfrac{y^8}{y^5}$      **21.** $\dfrac{c^8}{c^7}$

**22.** $\dfrac{d^8}{d^4}$      **23.** $\dfrac{k^9}{k}$      **24.** $\dfrac{v^{99}}{v^{60}}$      **25.** $\dfrac{a^{42}}{a^{12} \cdot a^8}$

**26.** The annual number of cruise ship passengers $p$ (in millions) after $t$ years starting from 1960 can be modeled by the equation $p = 0.229(1.09)^t$.

    **a.** Find the ratio of the number of passengers in 1990 to the number of passengers in 1970. Hint: $t = 30$ for 1990, and $t = 10$ for 1970.

    **b.** The number of passengers in 1990 is how many times as much as the number of passengers in 1970?

    **c.** According to the equation, how many cruise ship passengers were there in 1970?

*(continued)*

**MODULE 5  SECTION 3**                                    **PRACTICE AND APPLICATIONS**

## For use with Exploration 2

**Write each power as a whole number or fraction without exponents.**

**27.** $10^0$          **28.** $4^{-2}$          **29.** $3^{-4}$          **30.** $2^{-1}$

**Write each expression without using zero or negative exponents.**

**31.** $r^0$          **32.** $g^{-4}$          **33.** $m^{-12}$          **34.** $3k^{-8}$

**35. Calculator** The monthly payment $P$ on a car loan of $10,000 at a rate of 4.8% over $t$ years is given by the equation $P = 10000(.004)/(1-(1.004)^{-12t})$.

   **a.** What is the monthly payment for a loan over 3 years? 4 years? 5 years?

   **b. Writing** Explain why paying the loan in the least number of years may be a better option if you are buying a car.

**Write each number in decimal notation.**

**36.** $6 \cdot 10^{-1}$          **37.** $5 \cdot 10^{-2}$          **38.** $3.2 \cdot 10^{-4}$

**39.** $5.1 \cdot 10^{-6}$          **40.** $1.47 \cdot 10^{-9}$          **41.** $6.023 \cdot 10^{-10}$

**42.** Cells are measured in units of 0.01 mm (one "micron"), as shown in the table.

   **a.** Rewrite each inequality in the table so that the numbers in the inequality are expressed in scientific notation.

   **b.** A cell measures $6 \cdot 10^{-2}$ mm. Tell what kind of cell it might be.

| Name | $s$ = size (mm) |
|---|---|
| lymphocyte | $0.05 < s < 0.08$ |
| bacteria | $0.005 < s < 0.015$ |
| virus | $0.0005 < s < 0.001$ |

**Write each number in scientific notation.**

**43.** 0.005          **44.** 0.0092          **45.** 0.00025

**46.** 0.000002234          **47.** 0.00000000007          **48.** 0.00000000415

| MODULE 5  SECTION 4 | PRACTICE AND APPLICATIONS |
|---|---|

## For use with Exploration 1

**Use mental math to find the complement of each angle.**

**1.** 44°     **2.** 15°     **3.** 72°     **4.** 89°

**5.** 10°     **6.** 30°     **7.** 56°     **8.** 28°

**Use the diagram.**

**9.** Name an angle that is the supplement of ∠AEB.
Find the measure of the angle.

**10.** Name an angle that is the complement of ∠AEB.
Find the measure of the angle.

**11. Writing** Suppose $m\angle ACD = 90°$. Find $m\angle ECD$.

**12.** Suppose $m\angle CEB = m\angle CDE$. Find $m\angle CDE$.

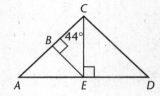

**Use mental math or a calculator to find the supplement of
each angle.**

**13.** 30°     **14.** 130°     **15.** 62°     **16.** 19°

**17.** 110°     **18.** 178°     **19.** 91°     **20.** 12°

**21.** $22\frac{1}{2}°$     **22.** 125.5°     **23.** 45°     **24.** $135\frac{2}{3}°$

**Algebra Connection For Exercises 25 and 26, write and solve an
equation to find the value of each variable.**

**25.** An angle equals four times its complement. Find the angle.

**26.** The supplement of an angle is twice the measure of the angle.
Find the angle.

(continued)

**MODULE 5  SECTION 4**                    **PRACTICE AND APPLICATIONS**

## For use with Exploration 2

**For Exercises 27–32, use the triangle to find the given tangent. Check each answer with a calculator. (Note: Side lengths are approximate.)**

**27.** tan 52°

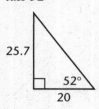

25.7

52°

20

**28.** tan 25°

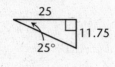

25

11.75

25°

**29.** tan 30°

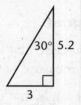

30° 5.2

3

**30.** tan 45°

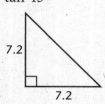

7.2

7.2

**31.** tan 49°

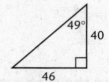

49°

40

46

**32.** tan 60°

8.1

60°

14

**33.** Namisha used an astrolabe to sight the top of the tallest residential tower in the world, Lake Point Tower in Chicago, Illinois.

   **a.** About how tall is Lake Point Tower?

   **b.** Suppose Namisha moves where she is standing so that the angle down from the top of the tower is 62°. About how far from the tower is she standing?

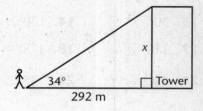

x

34°

292 m

Tower

**Find the value of each variable.**

**34.**

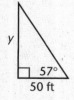

y

57°

50 ft

**35.**

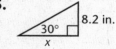

8.2 in.

30°

x

**36.**

m

18 cm

27°

Name _____ Date _____

**PRACTICE AND APPLICATIONS**

## For use with Exploration 1

1. Sundaes at a certain ice cream shop are available in 5 flavors: vanilla, strawberry, chocolate, raspberry, and butter pecan. There are also three toppings available: fudge, nuts, and fruit.

   **a.** Draw a tree diagram showing the different choices available for the ice cream and the toppings for a sundae.

   **b.** In how many ways can you choose one ice cream flavor and one topping for the sundae?

2. Maurice wants to buy a new stereo system and a new video game system. He limits his choices to 3 stereo systems and 4 video game systems. In how many ways can he choose a stereo system and a video game system?

3. Tanya rents all newly released movies. There are 10 movies on the "new release" list. In how many orders can she rent the movies if she chooses one at a time?

**Find the number of permutations of the letters of each word.**

4. GO          5. BUMPER          6. SEAT

7. TRUNK       8. CAR             9. GASOLINE

10. In professional football, there are 5 teams per division. In how many orders can the teams in a division finish at the end of the regular football season?

11. In basketball, 12 different teams participate in a holiday tournament. In how many orders can the teams finish the tournament?

12. A car repair person is supposed to do a "10-point inspection," or check 10 different items or settings in the engine or car. In how many different orders can the inspection be done?

13. Marjean made a list of 7 errands to do. In how many different orders can she do her errands?

14. Marty Jung rearranges the letters of his name to form a password for his computer. In how many different orders can he rearrange the letters of his name?

*(continued)*

Copyright © by McDougal Littell Inc. All rights reserved.          Math Thematics, Book 3 **177**

**MODULE 5 SECTION 5**             **PRACTICE AND APPLICATIONS**

## For use with Exploration 2

**15.** Mr. Junge grouped his class into 6 groups. Each day, two groups have to put homework problems on the board. How many combinations of two groups can be chosen?

**16.** Calin has strawberries, watermelon, grapes, pineapple, and peaches. How many combinations of fruits can she put in a salad if she uses:

    **a.** exactly 1 kind of fruit?            **b.** exactly 2 kinds of fruit?

    **c.** exactly 3 kinds of fruit?            **d.** exactly 4 kinds of fruit?

    **e.** exactly 5 kinds of fruit?            **f.** at least 3 kinds of fruit?

**17.** Students in Mrs. Jacobs' class have to answer 3 out of 5 essays on a test. How many combinations of 3 essays can be chosen?

**18.** There are 8 different toppings available at Papa Joe's pizza restaurant.

    **a.** How many different pizzas can be made with two toppings?

    **b.** How many different pizzas can be made with three toppings?

    **c.** A "supreme" pizza has six toppings. How many different pizzas can be made with six toppings?

**19.** A clothing inspector selects 2 pairs of socks at random from each box to check the production quality. How many different combinations of socks can be chosen from a box of 12 pairs?

**20.** **Challenge** Suppose Randy chooses 4 letters of his name to form a password for his computer.

    **a.** How many branches would a tree diagram have that shows the number of combinations of 4 letters?

    **b.** How many permutations of 3 letters can he make with the 4 letters he has chosen?

      

## MODULE 5  SECTION 6          PRACTICE AND APPLICATIONS

### For use with Exploration 1

**For Exercises 1–3, suppose two number cubes are rolled and the number of sixes are recorded.**

**1.** List all possible outcomes when two number cubes are rolled.

**2.** What is the probability of getting 0 sixes? 1 six? 2 sixes?

**3.** What is the probability of getting at least one six?

**4.** Your phone number is a 7-digit number (without the area code). The first three digits depend on your town, and the last 4 digits are chosen from the numbers 0–9.

    **a.** How many sequences are possible for the last four digits?

    **b.** What is the probability of getting a 1 or a 9 in the last digit?

    **c.** What is the probability of getting 2 zeros in the last two digits?

    **d.** What is the probability of getting 3 zeros in the last two digits?

    **e.** Suppose your entire phone number uses digits chosen from the numbers 0–9. How many sequences are possible for the seven digits?

**5.** Suppose two different color number cubes are rolled, one green and one red.

    **a.** How many outcomes are possible?

    **b.** How many outcomes have a sum of 9? 10?

    **c.** What is the probability that the sum of the numbers is 9 or 10?

**6. Open-ended** Suppose Randy chooses 3 letters of his name and other *characters* from the keyboard to complete his 4-character password for his computer (for example: "RNY." is a possibility).

    **a.** Draw a tree diagram to find the number of combinations of 3 letters and other characters from the keyboard.

    **b.** What is the probability that he chose "RNY." as his password?

**MODULE 5  SECTION 1**                    STUDY GUIDE

# Can Do!   Working with Cylinders

**GOAL**  **LEARN HOW TO:** • find the surface area of a cylinder
                  • find and interpret the ratio of a cylinder's surface area to
                    its volume

**As you:** • make a paper can
            • compare the efficiency of different cans

## Exploration 1: Surface Areas of Cylinders

### Finding Surface Area of a Cylinder

The **surface area** of a space figure is the combined area of the figure's
outer surfaces. The surface area, *S.A.*, of a cylinder with radius $r$ and
height $h$ is given by the formula $S.A. = 2\pi r^2 + 2\pi rh$.

---

**Example**

Find the surface area of the cylinder shown.

■ **Sample Response** ■

$S.A. = 2\pi r^2 + 2\pi rh$
$\quad = 2\pi(1.3)^2 + 2\pi(1.3)(5)$
$\quad \approx 10.6 + 40.8$
$\quad \approx 51.4$

The cylinder's surface area is about 51.4 in.$^2$.

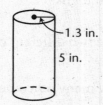

1.3 in.

5 in.

---

## Exploration 2: Surface Area and Volume

### Comparing Surface Area to Volume

For a container (such as a can) with surface area *S.A.* and volume *V*, the
ratio $\frac{S.A.}{V}$ is a measure of the object's **efficiency**. The smaller this ratio, the
more efficient the object.

Name _____  Date _____

### Example

Rank the cans shown from most efficient to least efficient.

**A.**  3 in.  16 in.

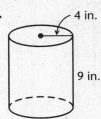
**B.**  4 in.  9 in.

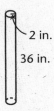
**C.**  2 in.  36 in.

### ■ Sample Response ■

**First** Find the ratio $\frac{S.A.}{V}$ for each can.

**A.** $\frac{S.A.}{V} \approx \frac{357.96}{452.16}$

$\approx 0.79$

**B.** $\frac{S.A.}{V} \approx \frac{326.56}{452.16}$

$\approx 0.72$

**C.** $\frac{S.A.}{V} \approx \frac{477.28}{452.16}$

$\approx 1.06$

**Then** Put the ratios in order from least to greatest.

$0.72 < 0.79 < 1.06$

Can B, Can A, Can C

## MODULE 5 SECTION 1    PRACTICE & APPLICATION EXERCISES

## Exploration 1

**Find the surface area of the cylinder with the given radius *r* and height *h*.**

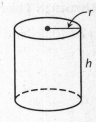

**1.** $r = 3$ ft, $h = 5$ ft

**2.** $r = 6$ mm, $h = 12$ mm

**3.** $r = 1.2$ cm, $h = 3.4$ cm

**4.** $r = 7.7$ yd, $h = 6.9$ yd

**5.** $r = 16$ m, $h = 10$ m

**6.** $r = 40$ ft, $h = 45$ ft

## MODULE 5 SECTION 1 | PRACTICE & APPLICATION EXERCISES | STUDY GUIDE

## Exploration 2

**Find the ratio of surface area to volume for each cylinder.**

**7.**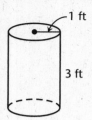
1 ft
3 ft

**8.**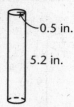
0.5 in.
5.2 in.

**9.**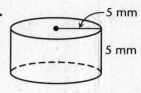
5 mm
5 mm

**10.**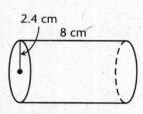
2.4 cm
8 cm

**11.**
12 in.
3 in.

**12.**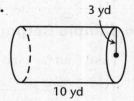
3 yd
10 yd

## Spiral Review

**13.** A dart is thrown randomly at the square target shown. Find the probability that the dart hits the shaded region. **(Module 4, p. 308)**

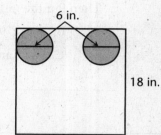
6 in.
18 in.

**Estimate each percent. (Module 2, p. 92)**

**14.** 12% of 500          **15.** 24% of 6000          **16.** 99% of 354

**Plot each pair of points on a coordinate plane and draw a line through them. Find the slope of the line. (Module 3, p. 195)**

**17.** (0, 2) and (3, 4)          **18.** (−1, −4) and (2, 5)          **19.** (4, 1) and (3, −2)

## MODULE 5 SECTION 2 | STUDY GUIDE

# Color My World   Slopes and Equations of Lines

**GOAL** **LEARN HOW TO:** • find and interpret positive and negative slopes
• identify slopes of horizontal and vertical lines
• identify the *y*-intercept of a line
• find an equation of a line in slope-intercept form

**As you:** • investigate TV sales
• model TV sales at an electronics store

## Exploration 1: Exploring Slope

### Finding and Comparing Slopes

The **slope** of a line is the ratio that measures the steepness of the line.

$$\text{slope} = \frac{\text{rise}}{\text{run}} = \frac{\text{vertical change}}{\text{horizontal change}}$$

The slope of a line can be *positive, negative, zero,* or *undefined.*

### Example

**Positive slope**

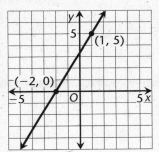

$$\frac{\text{vertical change}}{\text{horizontal change}} = \frac{5 - 0}{1 - (-2)} = \frac{5}{3}$$

**Negative slope**

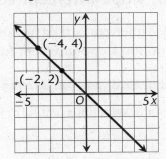

$$\frac{\text{vertical change}}{\text{horizontal change}} = \frac{4 - 2}{-4 - (-2)} = \frac{2}{-2} = -1$$

**Zero slope**

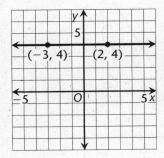

$$\frac{\text{vertical change}}{\text{horizontal change}} = \frac{4 - 4}{2 - (-3)} = \frac{0}{5} = 0$$

**Undefined slope**

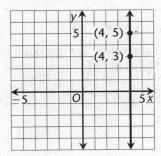

$$\frac{\text{vertical change}}{\text{horizontal change}} = \frac{5 - 3}{4 - 4} = \frac{2}{0} \leftarrow \text{undefined}$$

## MODULE 5  SECTION 2

## Exploration 2: Slope-Intercept Form

### Finding y-intercepts

The **y-intercept** of a line is the $y$-coordinate of the point where the line crosses the $y$-axis.

> **Example**
>
> Name the $y$-intercept of the line shown.
>
> The line crosses the $y$-axis at the point $(0, 5)$.
>
> The $y$-intercept is 5.

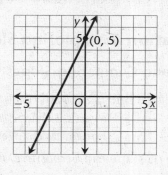

## Writing Equations in Slope-Intercept Form

If a line has slope $m$ and $y$-intercept $b$, then an equation of the line is $y = mx + b$. This equation is in **slope-intercept form**.

> **Example**
>
> Write an equation in slope-intercept form for the line shown.
>
> ■ **Sample Response** ■
>
> **First** Find the slope and the $y$-intercept.
>
> $$\text{slope} = \frac{5 - 0}{0 - (-3)} = \frac{5}{3}$$
>
> The $y$-intercept is 5.
>
> **Then** Substitute the values for the slope $m$ and the $y$-intercept $b$ into the equation $y = mx + b$.
>
> An equation is $y = \frac{5}{3}x + 5$.

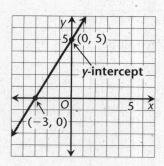

Name _____ Date _____

## MODULE 5  SECTION 2 | PRACTICE & APPLICATION EXERCISES | STUDY GUIDE

### Exploration 1

**Find the slope of the line through the given points. You may find it helpful to plot the points and draw a line through them first.**

**1.** (0, 3) and (2, 5)  **2.** (−2, 6) and (9, 5)  **3.** (−5, 7) and (−1, −2)

**4.** (−3, 5) and (5, 5)  **5.** (0, 6) and (9, 0)  **6.** (−2, 6) and (−2, 5)

**Use the lines shown for Exercises 7–9.**

**7.** Which line has a positive slope?

**8.** Which line has a negative slope?

**9.** Which line has an undefined slope?

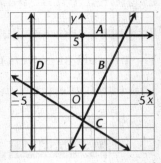

### Exploration 2

**For each line, write an equation in slope-intercept form.**

**10.**

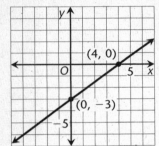

**11.**

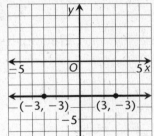

**12.**

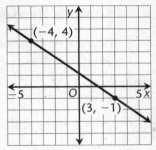

**Write an equation in slope-intercept form for the line through the given points. You may find it helpful to plot the points and draw a line through them first.**

**13.** (1, 4) and (4, 6)  **14.** (0, 3) and (3, 0)  **15.** (−1, −1) and (1, 1)

### Spiral Review

**16.** Find the surface area of a cylinder that has a radius of 8 in. and a height of 12 in. (Module 5, p. 324)

**Use an equation to find each percent or number.** (Module 2, p. 90)

**17.** 49 is what percent of 52?   **18.** What is 26% of 20?

**Write each number in scientific notation.** (Module 3, p. 218)

**19.** 800   **20.** 23,000,000   **21.** 3678

## MODULE 5 SECTION 3                                    STUDY GUIDE

# Big and Small    Working with Exponents

**GOAL**   **LEARN HOW TO:** • multiply and divide powers
• simplify powers with zero and negative exponents
• represent small numbers in scientific and decimal notation

**As you:** • work with astronomical distances
• investigate dimensions of real-world objects

## Exploration 1: Rules of Exponents

### Product of Powers Rule

The **product of powers** rule states:

To multiply powers with the same base, add the exponents.

$$b^m \cdot b^n = b^{m+n}$$

### Example

Find $4^5 \cdot 4^3$.

### ■ Sample Response ■

Because both factors have a base of 4, you can add the exponents.
$$4^5 \cdot 4^3 = 4^{5+3} = 4^8$$

### Quotient of Powers Rule

The **quotient of powers** rule states:

To divide powers with the same base, subtract the exponents.

$$\frac{b^m}{b^n} = b^{m-n}$$

### Example

Find $\dfrac{4^5}{4^3}$

### ■ Sample Response ■

Since both bases are 4, you can subtract the exponents.
$$\frac{4^5}{4^3} = 4^{5-3} = 4^2$$

Name _____                    Date _____

## Exploration 2: Zero and Negative Exponents

### Zero and Negative Exponents

Suppose $b$ is any positive number and $n$ is any positive integer.

Then $b^0 = 1$ and $b^{-n} = \dfrac{1}{b^n}$.

**Example**

**a.** Find $4^0$                                    **b.** Find $4^{-3}$.

**■ Sample Response ■**

**a.** Since 4 is a positive number, $4^0 = 1$.

**b.** Since 4 is a positive number and 3 is an integer, $4^{-3} = \dfrac{1}{4^3} = \dfrac{1}{64}$.

### Scientific Notation with Small Numbers

Given a small number in scientific notation, you can write the number in decimal notation. Given a small number in decimal notation, you can write the number in scientific notation.

**Example**

**a.** Write $2.5 \cdot 10^{-2}$ in decimal notation.      **b.** Write 0.00000045 in scientific notation.

**■ Sample Response ■**

**a.** $2.5 \cdot 10^{-2} = 2.5 \cdot \dfrac{1}{10^2}$

$\quad = \dfrac{2.5}{10^2}$

$\quad = 0.025 \longleftarrow$ 2 places

**b.** $0.00000045 = \dfrac{4.5}{10^7}$

$\quad = 4.5 \cdot \dfrac{1}{10^7}$

$\quad = 4.5 \cdot 10^{-7}$

7 places

**MODULE 5  SECTION 3** | PRACTICE & APPLICATION EXERCISES | **STUDY GUIDE**

## Exploration 1

**Write each product as a single power.**

**1.** $6^5 \cdot 6^7$      **2.** $9^2 \cdot 9^4$      **3.** $12^1 \cdot 12^5$      **4.** $7^5 \cdot 7^7 \cdot 7^7$

**5.** $y^8 \cdot y^2$      **6.** $g^5 \cdot g^3$      **7.** $h^{13} \cdot h^{24}$      **8.** $r^5 \cdot r^{75} \cdot r^{19}$

**Write each quotient as a single power.**

**9.** $\dfrac{5^4}{5^2}$      **10.** $\dfrac{8^{12}}{8^2}$      **11.** $\dfrac{3^4}{3}$      **12.** $\dfrac{7^{23}}{7^{20}}$

**13.** $\dfrac{b^8}{b^2}$      **14.** $\dfrac{x^{11}}{x^8}$      **15.** $\dfrac{m^{45}}{m^{28}}$      **16.** $\dfrac{k^{42}}{k^{12} \cdot k^3}$

## Exploration 2

**Write each power as a number without exponents.**

**17.** $35^0$      **18.** $4^{-2}$      **19.** $7^{-1}$      **20.** $3^{-3}$

**Write each expression without using zero or negative exponents.**

**21.** $g^{-5}$      **22.** $k^0$      **23.** $4t^{-2}$      **24.** $2r^{-45}$

**Write each number in decimal notation.**

**25.** $3 \cdot 10^{-3}$      **26.** $5.3 \cdot 10^{-5}$      **27.** $1.45 \cdot 10^{-6}$

**Write each number in scientific notation.**

**28.** 0.0009      **29.** 0.00123      **30.** 0.0000003      **31.** 0.0416

## Spiral Review

**32.** Give the slope and the $y$-intercept of the line with equation $y = -3x + 8$. **(Module 5, p. 338)**

**33.** Estimate $\sqrt{75}$ between two consecutive integers. **(Module 3, p. 170)**

**Solve each equation.** **(Module 1, p. 62)**

**34.** $\dfrac{x}{5} = 19$      **35.** $\dfrac{r}{20} + 3 = 8$      **36.** $9 = \dfrac{y}{24}$

## MODULE 5  SECTION 4                                    STUDY GUIDE

# Oh, What a Sight!   Complements, Supplements, and Tangents

**GOAL**  **LEARN HOW TO:** • identify special pairs of angles
                        • use the tangent ratio to find unknown side lengths in
                          right triangles

   **AS YOU:** • make and use an astrolabe
            • investigate heights of objects

## Exploration 1: Complementary and Supplementary Angles

### Identifying Complementary and Supplementary Angles

Two angles whose measures have a sum of 90° are **complementary angles**.
Each angle is called a **complement** of the other angle. Two angles whose
measures have a sum of 180° are **supplementary angles**. Each angle is
called a **supplement** of the other angle.

---

### ▪ Example

Find the complement and the supplement of ∠ABC.

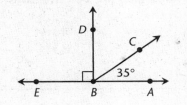

### ▪ Sample Response ▪

$m\angle ABC = 35°$

∠CBD is its complement.                    ∠CBE is its supplement.

$90 - 35 = 55$                             $180 - 35 = 145$

$m\angle CBD = 55°$                        $m\angle CBE = 145°$

---

## MODULE 5  SECTION 4

## Exploration 2: The Tangent Ratio

### Finding Unknown Side Lengths

In a right triangle, the **tangent** of an acute angle is the ratio of the length of the side opposite the angle to the length of the side adjacent to the angle. The tangent of an angle $A$ is written "tan $A$."

$$\tan A = \frac{\text{opposite}}{\text{adjacent}}$$

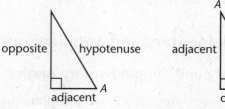

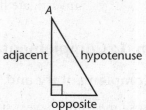

You can use the tangent ratio to find unknown side lengths in right triangles.

---

### Example

Find the value of $x$ in $\triangle ABC$.

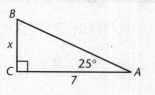

#### ■ Sample Response ■

$\tan 25° = \dfrac{\text{opposite}}{\text{adjacent}}$

$\tan 25° = \dfrac{x}{7}$  ← Use a calculator to find tan 25°.

$0.4663 \approx \dfrac{x}{7}$  ← Solve for $x$.

$3.3 \approx x$

---

## MODULE 5  SECTION 4 | PRACTICE & APPLICATION EXERCISES

## Exploration 1

### Find the complement of each angle.

**1.** 25°      **2.** 75°      **3.** 73°      **4.** 46°

**5.** 3°      **6.** 34°      **7.** 88°      **8.** 21°

| **MODULE 5  SECTION 4** | **PRACTICE & APPLICATION EXERCISES** | **STUDY GUIDE** |

**Find the supplement of each angle.**

**9.** 109°  **10.** 75°  **11.** 143°  **12.** 63°

**13.** 21°  **14.** 179°  **15.** 131°  **16.** 150°

## Exploration 2

**Use the triangles to find the given tangent. Check each answer with a calculator. (*Note:* Side lengths are approximate.)**

**17.** tan 39°  **18.** tan 45°  **19.** tan 27°

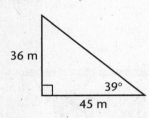

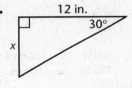

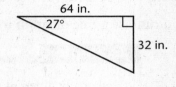

**Find the value of each variable.**

**20.**  **21.**  **22.**

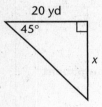

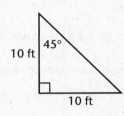

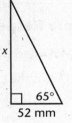

## Spiral Review

**23.** Write $4^6 \cdot 4^9$ and $\dfrac{x^{10}}{x^4}$ as single powers. **(Module 5, p. 350)**

**Write a rule for finding the next term of each sequence when you know the previous term. (Module 4, p. 247)**

**24.** 88, 77, 66, ...  **25.** $x + 1, 3x + 2, 5x + 3, ...$

**26.** Make a tree diagram to show the possible combinations you can make with 2 different pairs of jeans and 3 different T-shirts.

**(Module 2, p. 116)**

**MODULE 5 SECTION 5**                          STUDY GUIDE

# Reading is Believing   Counting Techniques

GOAL   **LEARN HOW TO:** • use the counting principle to count numbers of choices
                    • find the number of permutations of a group of objects
                    • find numbers of combinations

**As you:** • work with Braille symbols
          • investigate the first ten letters of the Braille alphabet

## Exploration 1: Counting and Permutations

### Using a Tree Diagram to Count Choices

You can use a tree diagram to count choices in a given situation.

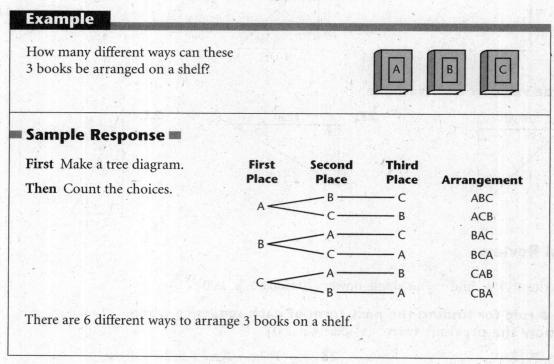

**Example**

How many different ways can these
3 books be arranged on a shelf?

**Sample Response**

**First**  Make a tree diagram.

**Then**  Count the choices.

| First Place | Second Place | Third Place | Arrangement |
|---|---|---|---|
| A | B | C | ABC |
|   | C | B | ACB |
| B | A | C | BAC |
|   | C | A | BCA |
| C | A | B | CAB |
|   | B | A | CBA |

There are 6 different ways to arrange 3 books on a shelf.

### Using the Counting Principle

The **counting principle** states that the total number of ways that a
sequence of decisions can be made is the product of the number of
choices for each decision.

**Example**

Use the counting principle to determine the number of ways the three books in the
above Example can be arranged.

## MODULE 5  SECTION 5                                STUDY GUIDE

### Sample Response

| Number of arrangements | = | Number of choices for 1st place 3 | × | Number of choices for 2nd place 2 | × | Number of choices for 3rd place 1 |
|---|---|---|---|---|---|---|

$$= 6$$

## Finding Permutations

A **permutation** of a group of items is an arrangement of the items in a definite order. You can find the number of permutations using the counting principle.

### Example

An arrangement of the books A, B, and C is an example of a permutation. The order in which the books are arranged is important.

## Exploration 2: Combinations

### Finding Combinations

A **combination** is a selection of items from a group where order is not important.

### Example

How many different ways could you choose 2 of the 3 books?

#### ■ Sample Response ■

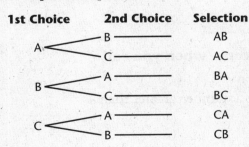

| 1st Choice | 2nd Choice | Selection |
|---|---|---|
| A | B | AB |
|   | C | AC |
| B | A | BA |
|   | C | BC |
| C | A | CA |
|   | B | CB |

The selections with the same letters are the same combination. BA is the same as AB, CA is the same as AC, and CB is the same as BC. There are 3 possible combinations.

## MODULE 5  SECTION 5 | PRACTICE & APPLICATION EXERCISES | STUDY GUIDE

### Exploration 1

1. Elizabeth has to choose 2 students, one for first place and one for second place, from the 5 who qualified to receive a scholarship. She wonders how many arrangements are possible. Use a tree diagram to determine how many.

2. Use the counting principle to answer Exercise 1.

3. Why is Exercise 1 an example of a permutation?

**How many ways can the letters of each word be arranged?**

4. BE                    5. TRY                    6. CAUGHT

### Exploration 2

7. How many ways can you choose 3 CDs from a group of 5?

8. How many different 2 card hands can be dealt from a stack of 6 cards?

9. A flower bouquet comes with any 3 of these flowers: rose, carnation, lily, iris. How many different bouquets are possible?

10. Why are Exercises 7–9 examples of combinations?

### Spiral Review

**Find the complement of each angle.** (Module 5, p. 363)

11. 26°                  12. 73°                  13. 68°

**Find the sum of the measures of the interior angles for each polygon.** (Module 4, p. 285)

14.                     15.

**Find the theoretical probability of each outcome when you roll a six-sided die.** (Module 2, p. 115)

16. rolling an odd number        17. rolling a number greater than 4

## MODULE 5  SECTION 6

# Lock It Up   Working with Probability

**GOAL**   **LEARN HOW TO:** • use the counting principle to determine the probability of an event

**AS YOU:** • solve the duplicate key problem

## Exploration 1: Probability and Counting

### Finding Probability

You can use the counting principle to find some probabilities.

---

**Example**

What is the probability that rolling four 6-sided dice will result in four different numbers?

---

■ **Sample Response** ■

$$\text{Probability} = \frac{\text{Ways to roll different numbers}}{\text{Total ways to roll dice}}$$

If different numbers are to be rolled, there are 6 numbers possible for the first die, 5 possible for the second die, 4 possible for the third die, and 3 possible for the fourth die.

$$\text{Probability} = \frac{6 \cdot 5 \cdot 4 \cdot 3}{6 \cdot 6 \cdot 6 \cdot 6}$$

Each die, when rolled has a total of 6 different outcomes.

$$= \frac{10}{36} \approx 0.28$$

The probability of rolling 4 dice and getting 4 different numbers is about 0.28.

---

## MODULE 5 SECTION 6 | PRACTICE & APPLICATION EXERCISES | STUDY GUIDE

## Exploration 1

**For Exercises 1–4, suppose two 6-sided dice are rolled and the outcomes are recorded.**

1. List all the possible outcomes when 2 dice are rolled.

2. Tell the probability of each outcome.

   **a.** two 1's            **b.** a 2 and a 3            **c.** doubles

3. What is the probability of getting at least one 6?

4. What is the probability that both dice will be even numbers?

**Suppose three spinners, with five equal-sized sectors labeled A, B, C, D, and E, are each spun once. Find the probability of each outcome.**

| | |
|---|---|
| 5. all A's | 6. all vowels |
| 7. all consonants | 8. no E's |
| 9. a number | 10. three letters |

## Spiral Review

11. Jackie needs to choose 3 of 5 types of flowers to make an arrangement. How many combinations of 3 types of flowers can Jackie choose? **(Module 5, p. 377)**

12. Some test scores for a history class are listed below. Display the scores either in a stem-and-leaf plot or a box-and-whisker plot. **(Module 1, p. 21 and Module 2, p. 152)**

    95, 93, 88, 78, 68, 97, 79, 55, 88, 89, 75, 93, 74

13. Find the surface area and the volume of a cube whose edges are 8 mm long. **(Toolbox, p. 605)**

Name _____     Date _____

## Isometric Dot Paper   (Use with Questions 6 and 10 on page 396, with Question 20 on page 399, with Exercises 2, 3, 5–7, and 12–14 on pages 400–402, and with Exercises 3–5, 8, and 9 on page 403.)

# MODULE 6

## Isometric Drawings   (Use with Question 7 on page 396.)

**Directions**   Copy each figure to the right of the given figure.

**a.**

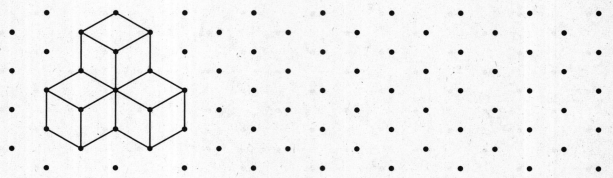

**b.**

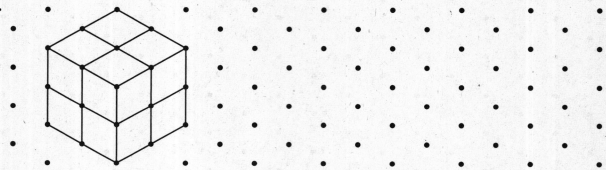

**c.**

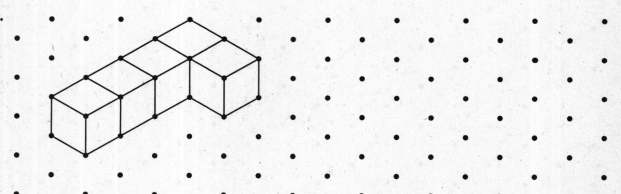

## Cube Figures (Use with Questions 8 and 9 on page 396.)

**Directions**  For each figure below, assume that there are no gaps on the bottom layer, and that there are no other hidden cubes.

- Remove the shaded cube in each figure and draw the new figure directly to its right.

- Count the number of cubes to find the volume (*V*) of each figure before and after removing the shaded cube. Record the results.

- Find the surface area (*S.A.*) of each figure before and after removing the shaded cube. Record the results. Remember to count all the faces on the outside of each figure, including those on the bottom.

**a.**

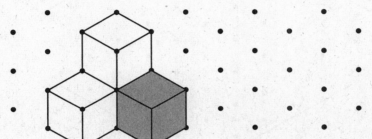

**Before**                                                    **After**

*V* = _____                                          *V* = _____

*S.A.* = _____                                      *S.A.* = _____

**b.**

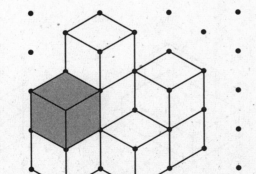

**Before**                                                    **After**

*V* = _____                                          *V* = _____

*S.A.* = _____                                      *S.A.* = _____

**MODULE 6**                                           **LABSHEET** **1D**

## Three Views of a Building  (Use with Question 14 on page 397.)

**Directions**  Look at the building in Question 14. Draw the
three-dimensional views of the building as specified below.

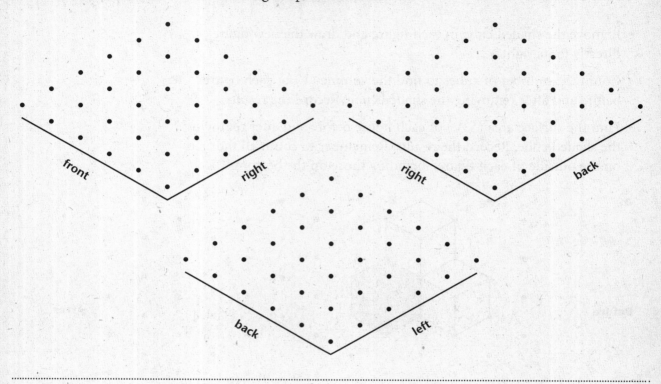

## Three Buildings  (Use with Exercise 15 on page 402.)

**Directions**  Follow the directions in your book to shade each building.

**a.** 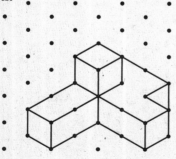       **b.** 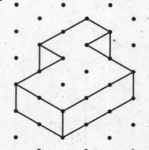       **c.**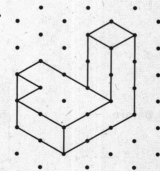

                          

**MODULE 6**

# Net for a House   (Use with Questions 8–10 on page 406.)

**Directions**   Cut out the net. Fold the net along the dashed lines and tape the edges together to form a model of a house with a modified mansard roof.

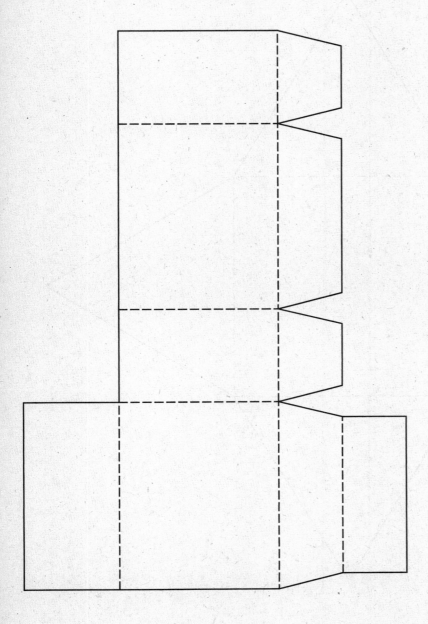

# MODULE 6                                              LABSHEET 3A

## Square Pyramid Net  (Use with Questions 6 and 7 on pages 420–421.)

**Directions**  Cut out the net and fold it to create a pyramid with
a square base.

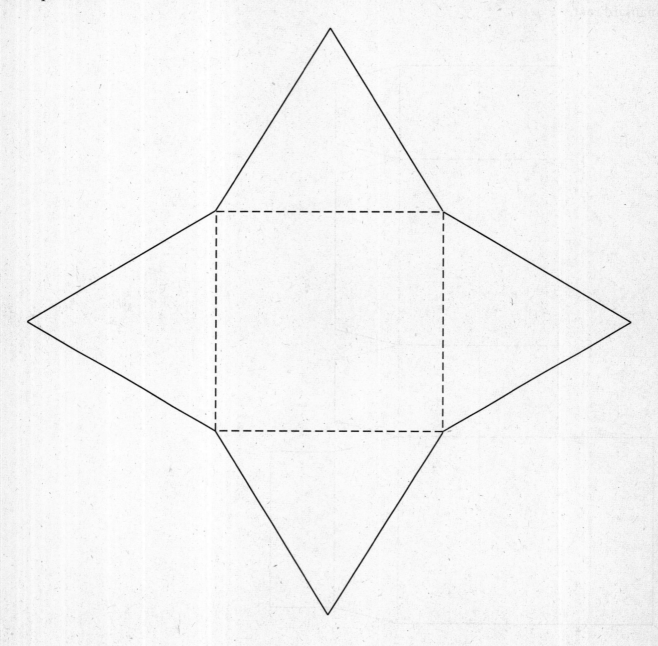

Name _____  Date _____

## Table of Volumes  (Use with Questions 12–14 on page 423.)

### Directions

• Find the height, the area of the base, and the volume of each block prism in the table.

• The block pyramids have the same heights and bases as the corresponding prisms. Complete the block pyramid portion of the table.

• For each row, find the ratio of the volume of the block pyramid to the volume of the prism. In the last column, write each answer in decimal form and round to the nearest thousandth.

| **Block Prisms** | | | | **Block Pyramids** | | | | **Volume Ratio** |
| --- | --- | --- | --- | --- | --- | --- | --- | --- |
| | Height $h$ | Area of base $B$ | Volume of prism $V = B \cdot h$ | | Height $h$ | Area of base $B$ | Volume of block pyramid | Volume of block pyramid ÷ Volume of prism |
| | 1 | 1 | 1 | | 1 | 1 | 1 | $1 \div 1 = 1.000$ |
| | 2 | 4 | 8 | | 2 | 4 | 5 | $5 \div 8 = 0.625$ |
| | | | | | | | | |
| | | | | | | | | |
| | | | | | | | | |
| | 6 | | | | | | | |
| | 7 | | | | | | | |
| | 8 | | | | | | | |
| | 9 | | | | | | | |
| | 10 | | | | | | | |

## MODULE 6    LABSHEET 3C

## Pattern for a Cone    (Use with Exercises 30 and 31 on page 430.)

**Directions**  Cut out the cone pattern. Then form a cone and secure it with a paper clip as shown.

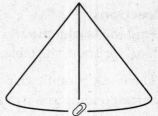

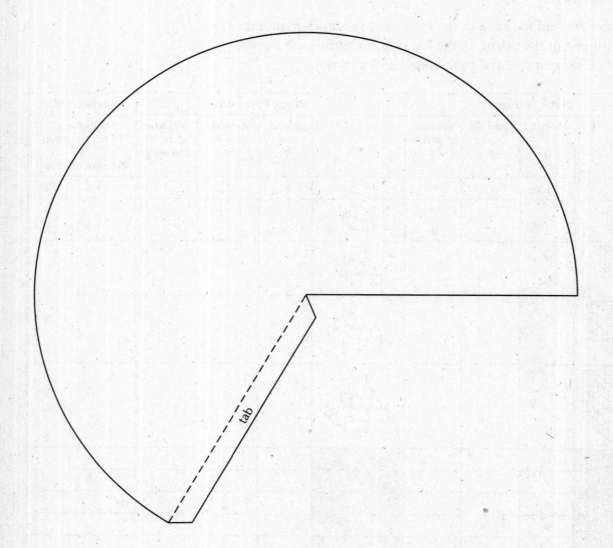

tab

## MODULE 6                                                      LABSHEET **3D**

## Dimensions of a Cone   (Use with Exercises 30 and 31 on page 430.)

**Directions**  Use the cone you formed with Labsheet 3C and the
diagram below to answer the following questions. The diagram
shows the cone with the slant height *s* and the radius *r* labeled.

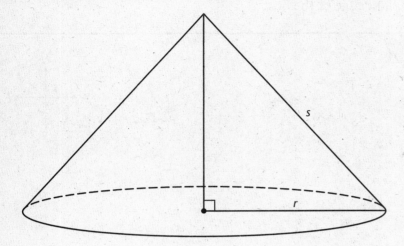

**a.** Write an expression for the circumference of the base of your cone
in terms of the radius *r* of the base.

**b.** Remove the paper clip from your cone and look at the partial circle.
Identify the part of the partial circle that became the circumference
of the base of the cone. Mark this part of the partial circle with the
expression from part (a).

**c.** Identify the part of the partial circle that corresponds to the slant height
of the cone. Label this part of the partial circle with the letter *s*.

Math Thematics, Book 3  **205**

## Chunnel Dig from England   (Use with Questions 1–2 on page 433.)

**Directions**   Starting at Folkestone Terminal in England, use your protractor to form a 72° angle with the vertical line. Use the Folkestone Terminal as the vertex of the angle. The ray you draw to form your angle should extend southeastward to the right edge of the box.

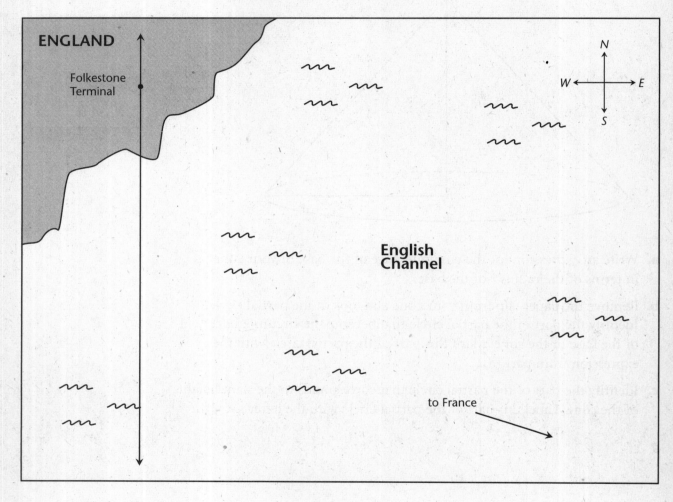

**MODULE 6**                                              LABSHEET **4B**

## Chunnel Dig from France  (Use with Questions 1–2 on page 433.)

**Directions**  Starting at Coquelles Terminal in France, use your
protractor to form a 72° angle with the vertical line. Use the Coquelles
Terminal as the vertex of the angle. The ray you draw to form your angle
should extend northwestward to the left edge of the box.

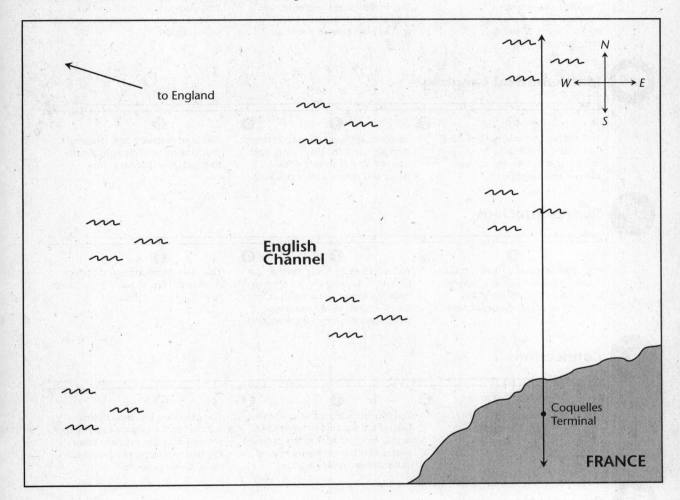

Name _____  Problem

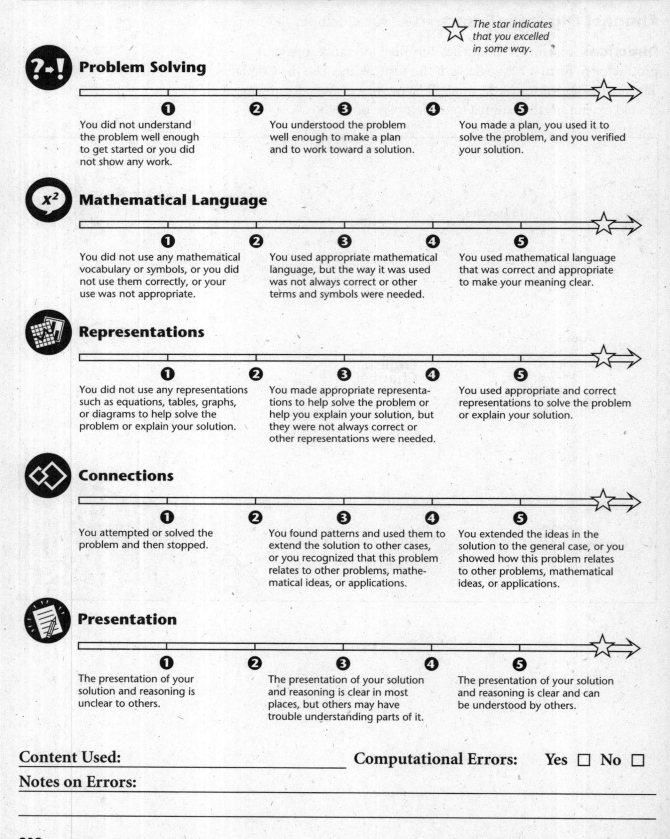

☆ *The star indicates that you excelled in some way.*

## ?→! Problem Solving

❶ You did not understand the problem well enough to get started or you did not show any work.

❷ ❸ You understood the problem well enough to make a plan and to work toward a solution.

❹ ❺ You made a plan, you used it to solve the problem, and you verified your solution.

## $x^2$ Mathematical Language

❶ You did not use any mathematical vocabulary or symbols, or you did not use them correctly, or your use was not appropriate.

❷ ❸ ❹ You used appropriate mathematical language, but the way it was used was not always correct or other terms and symbols were needed.

❺ You used mathematical language that was correct and appropriate to make your meaning clear.

## Representations

❶ You did not use any representations such as equations, tables, graphs, or diagrams to help solve the problem or explain your solution.

❷ ❸ ❹ You made appropriate representations to help solve the problem or help you explain your solution, but they were not always correct or other representations were needed.

❺ You used appropriate and correct representations to solve the problem or explain your solution.

## Connections

❶ You attempted or solved the problem and then stopped.

❷ ❸ ❹ You found patterns and used them to extend the solution to other cases, or you recognized that this problem relates to other problems, mathematical ideas, or applications.

❺ You extended the ideas in the solution to the general case, or you showed how this problem relates to other problems, mathematical ideas, or applications.

## Presentation

❶ The presentation of your solution and reasoning is unclear to others.

❷ ❸ ❹ The presentation of your solution and reasoning is clear in most places, but others may have trouble understanding parts of it.

❺ The presentation of your solution and reasoning is clear and can be understood by others.

Content Used: _____

Computational Errors:  Yes ☐  No ☐

Notes on Errors: _____

_____

## STUDENT   SELF-ASSESSMENT SCALES

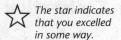 *If your score is in the shaded area, explain why on the back of this sheet and stop.*

*The star indicates that you excelled in some way.*

 ### Problem Solving

**❶** | **❷** | **❸** | **❹** | **❺** | ☆

**❶** I did not understand the problem well enough to get started or I did not show any work.

**❸** I understood the problem well enough to make a plan and to work toward a solution.

**❺** I made a plan, I used it to solve the problem, and I verified my solution.

 ### Mathematical Language

**❶** | **❷** | **❸** | **❹** | **❺** | ☆

**❶** I did not use any mathematical vocabulary or symbols, or I did not use them correctly, or my use was not appropriate.

**❸** I used appropriate mathematical language, but the way it was used was not always correct or other terms and symbols were needed.

**❺** I used mathematical language that was correct and appropriate to make my meaning clear.

 ### Representations

**❶** | **❷** | **❸** | **❹** | **❺** | ☆

**❶** I did not use any representations such as equations, tables, graphs, or diagrams to help solve the problem or explain my solution.

**❸** I made appropriate representations to help solve the problem or help me explain my solution, but they were not always correct or other representations were needed.

**❺** I used appropriate and correct representations to solve the problem or explain my solution.

 ### Connections

**❶** | **❷** | **❸** | **❹** | **❺** | ☆

**❶** I attempted or solved the problem and then stopped.

**❸** I found patterns and used them to extend the solution to other cases, or I recognized that this problem relates to other problems, mathematical ideas, or applications.

**❺** I extended the ideas in the solution to the general case, or I showed how this problem relates to other problems, mathematical ideas, or applications.

 ### Presentation

**❶** | **❷** | **❸** | **❹** | **❺** | ☆

**❶** The presentation of my solution and reasoning is unclear to others.

**❸** The presentation of my solution and reasoning is clear in most places, but others may have trouble understanding parts of it.

**❺** The presentation of my solution and reasoning is clear and can be understood by others.

## MODULE 6  SECTION 1                    PRACTICE AND APPLICATIONS

### For use with Exploration 1

1. Sketch a prism using the steps on page 395 of the textbook for drawing a rectangular prism.

2. Use isometric dot paper or other grid paper to draw the following.

   **a.** Draw a rectangular prism. Label the length and width.

   **b.** Draw a rectangular prism that is three times as wide as the one drawn in part (a).

   **c.** Draw a rectangular prism that is twice as tall as the one drawn in part (a).

   **d.** Find the number of cubes, the surface area, and the volume of each of the prisms you drew in parts (a) –(c). What relationships do you notice among these measurements?

3. How many different rectangular prisms can you draw that are made up of 16 cubes?

4. Use steps similar to the steps on page 395 of the textbook to draw the following.

   **a.** Sketch a parallelogram.

   **b.** Sketch a congruent parallelogram that is placed behind and to the right of the parallelogram in part (a).

   **c.** Connect corresponding vertices to form a prism.

   **d.** Sketch a prism as in parts (a)–(c) with a hexagon instead of a parallelogram.

**On isometric dot paper, draw the figure that results from removing the shaded cube(s). Then give the volume and the surface area before and after removing the cube(s). Assume there are no gaps on the bottom layer and that the only hidden cubes are directly beneath the cubes on the top layer.**

5.

6.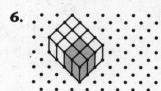

7. Using the figure from Exercise 6, redraw the figure with the shaded cubes moved to the right side of the bottom white cubes. This time, do not shade the cubes.

*(continued)*

Name _____ Date _____

## For use with Exploration 2

For Exercises 8–10, the top view of a building to the right is shown. Tell whether each view below is the left, right, front, or back view.

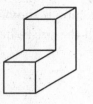

top view

**8.**

**9.**

**10.**

**11.** Assume the building at the right contains 12 cubes. Draw flat views of the building from each of the following viewpoints: front, back, left, right, and top.

**12.** Use isometric dot paper to draw and label front-left, right-back, and back-left views of the building in Exercise 11.

**13.** Suppose that the view shown in Exercise 11 is for a building containing 13 cubes. Think about where the hidden cube must be located if it shares a face with one other cube. Then carry out the steps in Exercises 11 and 12 for the 13-cube building.

**14.** Five flat views of a figure made with cubes are shown. On isometric dot paper, draw a view of the figure from the front-right corner.

front view     right-side     back     left-side     top

**MODULE 6 SECTION 2**                    **PRACTICE AND APPLICATIONS**

## For use with Exploration 1

1. A net for a cube is shown at the right. How many faces, edges, and vertices will the prism have?

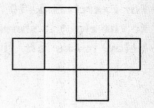

2. **Open-ended** Sketch a net for a triangular prism. How many faces, edges, and vertices will the prism have?

3. **Open-ended** Sketch a net for a square pyramid. How many faces, edges, and vertices will the pyramid have?

4. **Writing** Sketch a net for the cylinder at the right. How does it differ from a net for a prism?

5. The base of a barn or other large building used for storage can be an octagon or other polygon with a large number of sides. Follow the steps below to construct a regular octagon. Do not erase your compass marks.

  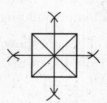 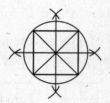 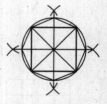

| **Step 1** | **Step 2** | **Step 3** | **Step 4** | **Step 5** |
|---|---|---|---|---|
| Start with a square. Draw the diagonals. | To construct the perpendicular bisector of two sides, draw arcs as shown by putting the compass at each vertex and using a radius greater than half the length of the sides. | Repeat Step (2) to construct the perpendicular bisector of the other two sides of the square. | Construct a circle whose radius is half the diagonal of the square and and whose center is the intersection of the diagonals. | Connect the 8 marked points of the circle to form a regular octagon. |

6. Draw a net for the sides of a barn using the octagon you constructed in Exercise 5.

*(continued)*

## MODULE 6 SECTION 2       PRACTICE AND APPLICATIONS

### For use with Exploration 2

**7.** Draw an angle larger than 90°. Use your compass and straightedge to bisect the angle. Do not erase your compass marks.

**8. Challenge** Describe how to repeat the construction of an octagon (see Exercise 5 of Exploration 1) using the angle bisector construction.

**For Exercises 9–11, choose the letter of the figure that matches each net.**

**A.** square pyramid      **B.** pentagonal pyramid      **C.** hexagonal pyramid

**9.**
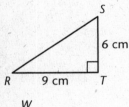

**10.**
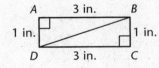

**11.**
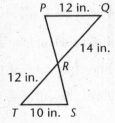

**Tell whether the triangles in each pair are congruent. Explain.**

**12.** △RST, △YWX      **13.** △ABD, △CDB      **14.** △RTS, △RQP

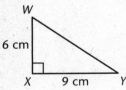

**MODULE 6  SECTION 3**                    **PRACTICE AND APPLICATIONS**

## For use with Exploration 1

**Find the surface area of each rectangular or triangular prism.**

**1.**
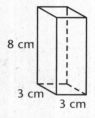
8 cm

3 cm
3 cm

**2.**
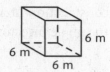
6 m
6 m
6 m

**3.**
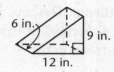
6 in.
9 in.
12 in.

**Find the surface area of each regular pyramid. Round each decimal answer to the nearest tenth. Use π = 3.14.**

**4.**
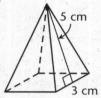
5 cm
3 cm

**5.**
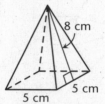
8 cm
5 cm
5 cm

**6.**
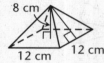
8 cm
12 cm   12 cm

**7. Home Involvement** Cereal is usually packaged in a box, a rectangular prism. Use a cereal box (or other box in your home) for each exercise below.

   **a.** Draw a net for the box.

   **b.** Find the surface area of the box.

   **c.** Sketch a view of the box that looks three-dimensional.

   **d.** Find the volume of the box.

**8.** Find products in your home that are packaged in containers that are prisms. Name each product, each container, and draw a sketch of the container. Find the volume and surface area of each container.

*(continued)*

**MODULE 6  SECTION 3**                    **PRACTICE AND APPLICATIONS**

## For use with Exploration 2

**Find the volume of each pyramid or cone with the given height and base. Round decimal answers to the nearest tenth. Use π = 3.14.**

**9.** height = 4 in.

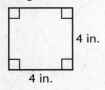
4 in.
4 in.

**10.** height = 6 cm

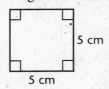
5 cm
5 cm

**11.** height = 3 m

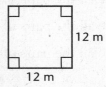
12 m
12 m

**12.** height = 12 mm

3 mm

**13.** height = 14.5 ft

30.4 ft

**14.** height = 12 yd

1.5 yd

**15. a.** A diagonal is drawn through the center of the hexagon. What two figures make up the hexagonal base of the prism?

**b.** If each side of the hexagon is 12 ft and the height of the prism is 24 ft, can the volume be found? Explain.

**c.** 20.8 ft is the approximate length of a shorter diagonal of the hexagon, and 24 ft is the length of the longer diagonal. Find the volume.

The diagram represents the base of a hexagonal prism.

**Find the surface area and volume of each composite figure.**

**16.**

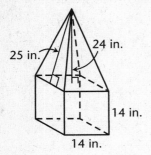
25 in.
24 in.
14 in.
14 in.

**17.**

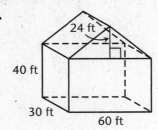
24 ft
40 ft
30 ft
60 ft

**MODULE 6 SECTION 4**          **PRACTICE AND APPLICATIONS**

## For use with Exploration 1

**The diagram at the right shows part of 3 roads in rural Illinois.**

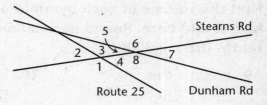

1. Name all the pairs of vertical angles.

2. Name all the pairs of corresponding angles.

3. Name all the pairs of alternate interior angles.

4. Name all the pairs of alternate exterior angles.

**In the diagram, line $p$ is parallel to line $q$ and line $r$ is parallel to line $s$. Find each angle measure.**

**5.** $m\angle 7$               **6.** $m\angle 4$

**7.** $m\angle 1$               **8.** $m\angle 5$

**9.** $m\angle 3$

**For Exercises 10 –12, use the diagram. Lines $m$ and $n$ are parallel.**

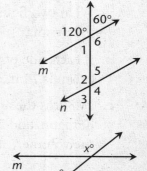

**10.** Find the measures of angles 1– 6.

**11.** What is the sum of the measures of angles 1 and 2?

**12.** What is the sum of the measures of angles 5 and 6?

**13. Algebra** Find the value of $x$ for parallel lines $m$ and $n$.

Name _____ Date _____

## For use with Exploration 1

**1.** Is 8 a solution of the inequality $-6 + y < 4$? Explain.

### Solve each inequality. Check and graph each solution.

**2.** $h + 8 < 19$       **3.** $6 + y \geq 2$       **4.** $-4 > d - 8$

**5.** $x - (-4) \geq 3$       **6.** $84 \leq 7n$       **7.** $-0.2a > -4.8$

**8.** $\dfrac{x}{4} > 3.2$       **9.** $-3 \geq \dfrac{r}{-4.5}$       **10.** $-\dfrac{3}{4}v < 8$

**11.** $\dfrac{y}{3} \geq 9.3$       **12.** $-9 < \dfrac{y}{3.5}$       **13.** $-8 \leq \dfrac{s}{4.8}$

### For Exercises 14–20, write and solve an inequality for each situation.

**14.** Eight more than a number is less than twelve.

**15.** Sixteen is less than or equal to the opposite of a number.

**16.** The minimum height of a cirrus cloud is 3000 m more than the highest cumulus cloud. The highest cumulus cloud is 2000 m. Find the minimum height of a cirrus cloud.

**17.** The cost of six cans of orange juice is greater than $2.30. Find the minimum cost of one can.

**18.** 86% of small companies in a town provide vacations as a benefit to their employees. If there are more than 50 small companies in a Midwestern town that provides vacations, find the least number of small companies in the town.

**19.** 130° F, the highest recorded temperature in the U.S. (at Greenland Ranch, CA), is more than 200° greater than the lowest recorded temperatures in the U.S. What is the range of the lowest recorded temperatures?

**20.** Sailfish, the fastest swimming fish, can travel more than 100 miles in 1 hour 30 minutes. What is an average fast speed for sailfish?

*(continued)*

**MODULE 6  SECTION 5**                          **PRACTICE AND APPLICATIONS**

## For use with Exploration 2

**For Exercises 21–24, write and solve an inequality for each situation.**

**21.** Three times a number minus 12 is less than 51.

**22.** Eighteen minus half of a number is greater than or equal to 112.

**23.** The sum of a 1.52 and 3 times a number is less than or equal to 13.52.

**24.** The difference when 8.2 is subtracted from twice a number is greater than or equal to 18.2.

**25.** You can rent a car for $24.95 a day plus $.10 per mile. For how many miles can you drive the rental car and still spend less than $40?

**Solve each inequality. Check and graph each solution.**

**26.** $-6x + 14 > 32$

**27.** $-6y + 16 \leq 22$

**28.** $-16 + (-12x) > 152$

**29.** $1.2h - 9.1 \geq 5.3$

**30.** $\frac{2}{3}m + \frac{5}{6} > \frac{11}{6}$

**31.** $6 - \frac{1}{4}c \leq \frac{5}{8}$

**32.** $6.42w - 55.23 < -3.87$

**33.** $52y + 420 \leq -932$

**34.** $-16x - 22 \leq -86$

**35.** $16d + 16 \leq 0$

| MODULE 6  SECTION 6 | PRACTICE AND APPLICATIONS |

## For use with Exploration 1

**In Exercises 1– 4, the dimensions of several objects are given. Make a scale drawing of the top view, the front view, and the right-side view of each object. Include the scale.**

1. A cereal box is $9\frac{3}{8}$ in. long, 3 in. wide, and $13\frac{1}{2}$ in. high.

2. A computer desk is 4 ft long, 2 ft wide, and 2.5 ft high.

3. The base of a triangular pyramid is a regular triangle with sides 90 mm. The height is 100 mm.

4. A textbook is 8 in. long, $1\frac{1}{2}$ in. wide, and $9\frac{1}{2}$ in. high.

5. Estimate and then find the dimensions of your classroom. Make a scale drawing of the floor plan and of one of the four walls. Include the scale(s).

6. **Open-ended** Choose an object that is more complex than a plain rectangular prism and make detailed scale drawings of the top view, the front view, and the right-side view.

7. Make a scale drawing of the floor plan of your ideal game room or athletic room. Include the doors, windows, closets, and furniture in your drawing, and identify the scale.

8. **Writing** Describe the process of choosing a scale to fit one of the scale drawings you did in Exercises 5 –7.

9. **Open-ended** Find a scale drawing in a newspaper or magazine. Cut it out and tape it to a piece of notebook paper. List the scale used and give the actual dimensions of each room that the drawing represents.

10. **Research** Find out how scale drawings are used to design hobby items like train sets, models, or doll houses. Give common scales used in hobbies.

*(continued)*

**MODULE 6  SECTION 6**                    **PRACTICE AND APPLICATIONS**

## For use with Exploration 2

**The perimeter of a room is 25 yd and the area of the room is 25 yd$^2$. What would be the perimeter and the area of the room in a scale drawing with each of the following scales?**

**11.** 5 cm to 1 yd          **12.** 1 ft to 5 yd          **13.** 3 in. to 5 yd

**14. Writing** Describe the process you went through to answer Exercise 12.

**The two figures in each diagram are similar. Use the given information to replace each ___?___ with the correct measurement.**

**15.** Area of $\triangle ABC = 8.5$ cm$^2$
Area of $\triangle XYZ = $ ___?___

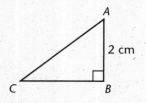

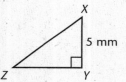

**16.** Perimeter of $RSTU = 90$ ft
Perimeter of $ABCD = $ ___?___

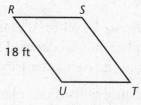

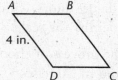

**17.** Area of $PENTA = 3124$ ft$^2$
Area of $HOUSE = $ ___?___

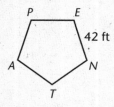

**18.** Perimeter of $RSTU = 18$ yd
Perimeter of $NOPQ = $ ___?___

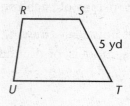

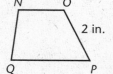

**MODULE 6  SECTION 1**                                        **STUDY GUIDE**

# Where Do You Stand?   Geometry and Perspective

**GOAL**   **LEARN HOW TO:** • draw rectangular prisms and figures made with cubes
                              • find volumes and surface areas of figures made with cubes
                              • draw three-dimensional figures and flat views

   **AS YOU:** • use isometric dot paper
                 • model simple buildings with cubes

## Exploration 1: Cubes and Prisms

**Isometric Drawings**

**Isometric dot paper** is paper with dots spaced at an equal distance
from each other. Isometric dot paper can be helpful in drawing
space figures.

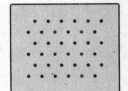

**Example**

Four different views of a space figure whose volume is 5 cubic units are shown.

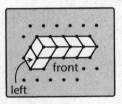

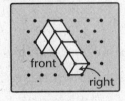

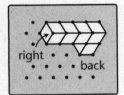

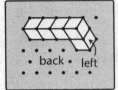

The surface area of the figure is 22 square units.

## Exploration 2: Points of View

**Flat Views**

Flat views of a space figure can be used to show what the space figure will
look like when viewed from the front, back, left, or right sides, or from the
top (directly above).

## MODULE 6  SECTION 1                                    STUDY GUIDE

### Example

These are the flat views of the space figure modeled in the first Example.

front view

back view

left-side view

right-side view

front

left

back

left [ ][ ][ ][ ] right

front

top view

## MODULE 6  SECTION 1 | PRACTICE & APPLICATION EXERCISES

### Exploration 1

**1.** Sketch a rectangular prism whose length is three times its height.

**2.** Sketch a rectangular prism whose height is one half its length.

### Exploration 2

**For Exercises 3 and 4, draw three different models of a building containing 6 cubes.**

**3.** Record the number of cubes, the surface area, and the volume of each building you drew. What relationships do you notice among the measurements?

**4.** Draw flat views of each building from each of the following viewpoints: front, back, left, right, and top.

**5.** Draw the figure that results from removing the shaded cube. Then give the volume and the surface area of the figure before and after removing the cube. Assume there are no gaps on the bottom layer. Also assume that the only hidden cubes are directly beneath the cubes on the top layer.

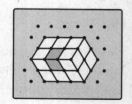

## MODULE 6  SECTION 1 | PRACTICE & APPLICATION EXERCISES | STUDY GUIDE

### Spiral Review

6. Linda, Samuel, and Julio have been chosen as winners of a bike, CD player, and $100 savings bond. The winner of each prize will be determined by a random drawing. What is the probability that Linda will receive the bike? that Samuel will not receive the CD player?
   (Module 5, pp. 376–377)

### Write each product or quotient as a single power.
(Module 5, p. 350)

7. $(t^8)(t^7)$         8. $(5g^2)(g^{-1})$         9. $(3x^8)(6x^5)$

10. $\dfrac{b^8}{b^7}$         11. $(20t^{25})(t^{-3})$         12. $\dfrac{5y^9}{15y^7}$

### Construct a triangle with the given side lengths.
(Module 4, p. 242)

13. 4 in., 3 in., 5 in.         14. 8 cm, 3 cm, 6 cm

**MODULE 6  SECTION 2**                                    **STUDY GUIDE**

# Building Blocks    Geometry and Constructions

**GOAL**    **LEARN HOW TO:** • identify and count parts of space figures
             • create nets for pyramids and prisms
             • bisect an angle using a compass
             • compare triangles using two sides and the included angle

**AS YOU:** • build a house with a mansard roof
            • construct a net for a pyramid

## Exploration 1: Constructing Nets

### Nets for Pyramids and Prisms

A two-dimensional pattern that can be folded into a space figure is a **net**.
A **pyramid** is a space figure with a polygon-shaped base. The other faces are
triangles that meet at a common vertex. Pyramids can be built from nets.

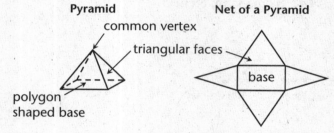

A pyramid with four triangular faces, including the base, is a **tetrahedron**.
A tetrahedron has 4 faces, 6 edges, and 4 vertices.

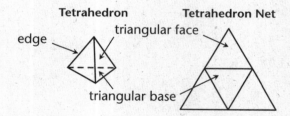

A **prism** is a space figure that has two parallel and congruent bases in the
shape of polygons. A rectangular prism has 6 faces, 12 edges, and 8 vertices.

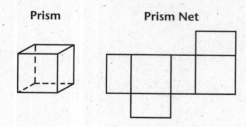

## MODULE 6  SECTION 2 STUDY GUIDE

## Exploration 2: Angles and Triangles

### Bisecting Angles

You can use a compass and a straightedge to bisect an angle. A ray that divides an angle into two equal angles is called an **angle bisector**.

**First**

**Next**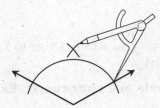

**Then**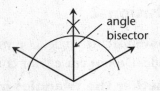

| Place the compass point on the vertex on the angle. Draw an arc that intersects both sides of the angle. | Place the compass point at one of the points where the original arc intersects the sides of the angle. Draw an arc inside the angle. Use the same compass setting to draw an arc from the other intersection point as shown. | Use a straightedge to draw a ray from the vertex of the angle through the point where the two arcs intersect. |

### Congruent Triangles

The angle formed by two sides of a figure is called an **included angle**. If two sides and the included angle of one triangle are congruent to two sides and the included angle of another triangle, then the triangles are congruent. This is known as the side-angle-side rule (SAS).

**Example**

△ABC ≅ △RST by the SAS rule.

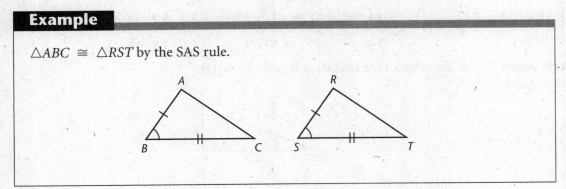

## MODULE 6 SECTION 2 | PRACTICE & APPLICATION EXERCISES | STUDY GUIDE

## Exploration 1

1. Sketch a net for a pentagonal prism. How many faces, edges, and vertices does the prism have?

2. Sketch a net for an octagonal pyramid. How many faces, edges, and vertices does the pyramid have?

## Exploration 2

3. Draw an acute angle. Use your compass and straightedge to bisect the angle. Do not erase your compass marks.

**Tell whether the triangles in each pair are congruent. Explain.**

4. △STU, △SVU

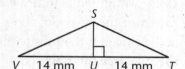

5. △PQR, △LMN

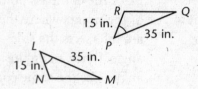

## Spiral Review

6. Draw a model of a building made from 5 cubes. Draw it so that at least one cube is hidden. Then draw flat views of the building from each of the following viewpoints: front, back, left, right, and top. (Module 6, p. 399)

**Solve each equation.** (Module 3, p. 218; Module 4, p. 274)

7. $5y - \dfrac{2}{3} = \dfrac{5}{9}$

8. $\dfrac{1}{2}t + 10 = 45$

9. $-9x = 45$

10. $-0.8y + 2.3 = 7.42$

11. $48 = -1.9f - (-48.95)$

12. $77 = 11x$

13. $\dfrac{2}{3}r - 9 = 3$

14. $3.7x + 17 = 30.69$

15. $16 - 9x = 17$

**For each right triangle, find the unknown side length.**
(Module 4, p. 297)

16.

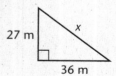

17.

26 ft

24 ft

$x$

**MODULE 6  SECTION 3**                                          **STUDY GUIDE**

# Where You Live   Surface Area and Volume

**GOAL**  **LEARN HOW TO:** • find surface areas of prisms and pyramids
                          • find volumes of prisms, pyramids, and cones

  **As you:** • explore the shape of an adobe house
              • look at models of block pyramids and prisms

## Exploration 1: Surface Areas of Prisms and Pyramids

### Finding Surface Areas

The surface area of a prism or a pyramid is the sum of the areas of the
faces of the figure, including the base or bases. You can use a net to help
you find the surface area.

**Example**

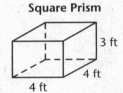

**Square Prism**

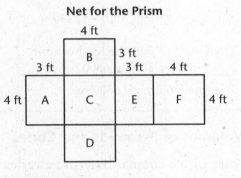

**Net for the Prism**

$S.A.$ = area A + area B + area C + area D + area E + area F
  = $(3 \cdot 4) + (4 \cdot 3) + (4 \cdot 4) + (4 \cdot 3) + (3 \cdot 4) + (4 \cdot 4)$
  = $12 + 12 + 16 + 12 + 12 + 16$
  = $80$

The surface area of the prism is 80 ft$^2$.

The base of a **regular pyramid** is a regular polygon, and its other faces
are congruent isosceles triangles. The height of a triangular face is the
**slant height** of the pyramid. You use the slant height of a pyramid to
find its surface area.

$S.A.$ = **(area of base)** + $4 \times$ **(area of one triangular face)**

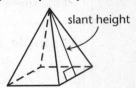

**Regular Square Pyramid**
slant height

Math Thematics, Book 3  **227**

## MODULE 6 SECTION 3 — STUDY GUIDE

## Exploration 2: Volumes of Prisms, Pyramids, and Cones

### Finding Volumes of Prisms

You can use the formula **Volume = area of base × height**, or $V = Bh$, to find the volume of any prism. Many buildings consist of two or more space figures. To find the volume, you add the volumes of the parts.

**Example**

Find the volume of the building shown below.

**■ Sample Response ■**

**First** Find the volume of the rectangular prism.

$V = Bh = (10 \cdot 30)15 = 4500$

**Next** Find the volume of the triangular prism.

$V = Bh = \left(\frac{1}{2} \cdot 10 \cdot 12\right)30 = 1800$

**Then** Add to find the total volume.
    $4500 + 1800 = 6300$

The total volume is 6300 m$^3$.

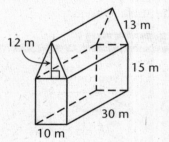

### Finding Volumes of Pyramids and Cones

A space figure with a circular base and a vertex is a circular **cone**. The volume of a cone is one third the volume of a cylinder with the same base and height. The volume of a pyramid is one third the volume of a prism with the same base and height.

The formula **Volume = $\frac{1}{3}$ × area of base × height**, or $V = \frac{1}{3}Bh$, can be used to find the volume of a pyramid or a cone.

**Example**

Find the volume of the cone shown below.

**■ Sample Response ■**

$V = \frac{1}{3} Bh$

$= \frac{1}{3} \cdot \pi r^2 \cdot h \approx \frac{1}{3} \cdot (3.14) \cdot 4^2 \cdot 6 \approx 100.5$

The volume of the cone is about 100.5 yd$^3$.

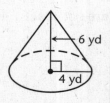

| MODULE 6  SECTION 3 | PRACTICE & APPLICATION EXERCISES | STUDY GUIDE |

## Exploration 1

**Find the surface area of each right prism or regular pyramid.**

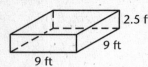

**1.** 2.5 ft, 9 ft, 9 ft

**2.** 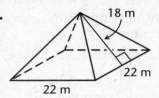 18 m, 22 m, 22 m

**3.** 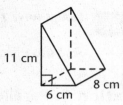 11 cm, 6 cm, 8 cm

## Exploration 2

**For Exercises 4 and 5, round decimal answers to the nearest tenth.**

**4.** The height of a cone is 4 m and the radius of the base is 8 m. Find the volume.

**5.** The height of a square pyramid is 10 cm and the length of each side of the base is 0.9 cm. Find the volume.

**Find the surface area and the volume of each composite figure. Round decimal answers to the nearest tenth.**

**6.** 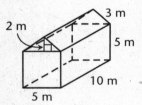 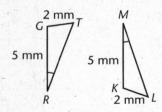 2 m, 3 m, 5 m, 10 m, 5 m

**7.** 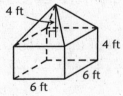 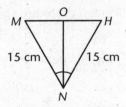 4 ft, 4 ft, 6 ft, 6 ft, 6 ft

## Spiral Review

**Tell whether the triangles in each pair are congruent. Explain.** (Module 6, p. 411)

**8.** △GTR, △KLM

2 mm, G, T, M, 5 mm, 5 mm, R, K, 2 mm, L

**9.** △MNO, △HNO

M, O, H, 15 cm, 15 cm, N

**Write an equation in slope-intercept form of a line that has the given slope and y-intercept.** (Module 5, p. 338)

**10.** slope = 5, y-intercept = 4

**11.** slope = −3, y-intercept = −2

**Find the supplement of each angle measure.** (Module 5, p. 363)

**12.** 29°

**13.** 111°

**14.** 164°

**15.** 8°

# Meet Me in the Middle   Angles Formed by Intersecting Lines

**GOAL**   **LEARN HOW TO:** • identify and find the measures of pairs of angles formed by intersecting lines

**AS YOU:** • learn about the construction of the Chunnel

## Exploration 1: Parallel Lines and Transversals

### Angles Formed by Intersecting Lines and Transversals

When two lines intersect they form four angles. Angles that have the same vertex and whose sides are opposite rays are called **vertical angles**, and they are always congruent.

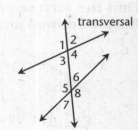

$m\angle 1 = m\angle 2 \quad m\angle 3 = m\angle 4$

A **transversal** is a line that intersects two or more lines in a plane at separate points. When two lines are cut by a transversal, various angles are formed.

• **Alternate interior angles** are between the two lines and are on opposite sides of the transversal. $\angle 3$, $\angle 6$ and $\angle 4$, $\angle 5$ are pairs of alternate interior angles.

• **Alternate exterior angles** are outside of the two lines and are on opposite sides of the transversal. $\angle 1$, $\angle 8$ and $\angle 2$, $\angle 7$ are pairs of alternate exterior angles.

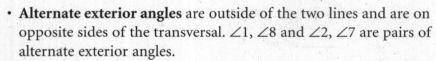

• **Corresponding angles** are in the same position with respect to two lines and a transversal. $\angle 1, \angle 5$; $\angle 2$, $\angle 6$; $\angle 3$, $\angle 7$; and $\angle 4$, $\angle 8$ are pairs of corresponding angles.

### Angles Formed by Parallel Lines and Transversals

When parallel lines are cut by a transversal, there are special relationships formed among the angles.

• Alternate interior angles are congruent.
  $m\angle 3 = m\angle 6 \qquad m\angle 4 = m\angle 5$

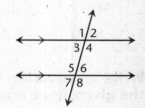

• Alternate exterior angles are congruent.
  $m\angle 1 = m\angle 8 \qquad m\angle 2 = m\angle 7$

• Corresponding angles are congruent.
  $m\angle 1 = m\angle 5 \qquad m\angle 2 = m\angle 6$
  $m\angle 3 = m\angle 7 \qquad m\angle 4 = m\angle 8$

## MODULE 6  SECTION 4 | PRACTICE & APPLICATION EXERCISES | STUDY GUIDE

### Exploration 1

**For Exercises 1–5, use the diagram.**

1. Which line is the transversal?

2. Identify each pair of vertical angles.

3. Identify each pair of corresponding angles.

4. Identify each pair of alternate exterior angles.

5. Identify each pair of alternate interior angles.

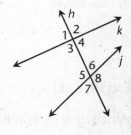

**In the diagram, line *t* is parallel to line *s*. Find each measure.**

6. $m\angle 3$

7. $m\angle 1$

8. $m\angle 7$

9. $m\angle 2$

10. $m\angle 5 + m\angle 3$

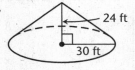

### Spiral Review

**Find the volume of each cone or regular pyramid. Round decimal answers to the nearest tenth.** (Module 6, p. 426)

11.
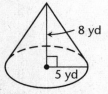
8 yd
5 yd

12.
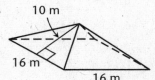
10 m
16 m
16 m

13.
24 ft
30 ft

**Graph each inequality on a number line.** (Module 2, p. 152)

14. $x \geq 3$

15. $b < 6$

16. $j \leq -2$

17. $t > 0$

**MODULE 6  SECTION 5**                                    **STUDY GUIDE**

# The Human Factor    Solving Inequalities

**GOAL**  **LEARN HOW TO:** • write and solve inequalities that involve one operation
                            • solve inequalities that have more than one operation

**As you:** • study the seat heights of chairs
            • plan the arrangement of seats in a theater

## Exploration 1: Solving Simple inequalities

### Writing and Solving Inequalities

All the values of a variable that make an inequality true are the **solutions
of the inequality**. When you find them you are **solving the inequality**.

You can use inverse operations to solve inequalities. However, you must be
sure to reverse the inequality symbol whenever you multiply or divide
both sides by a negative number.

---

**Example**

Solve each inequality. Check and graph each solution.

**a.** $x - 8 \leq -1$                     **b.** $-3y > 6$

---

**Sample Response**

**a.**          $x - 8 \leq -1$
        $x - 8 + 8 \leq -1 + 8$
              $x \leq 7$

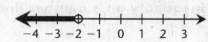

Adding or subtracting the same
number from both sides of the
inequality *does not affect the
inequality*.

**b.**          $-3y > 6$

              $\dfrac{-3y}{-3} < \dfrac{6}{-3}$
                $y < -2$

Dividing or multiplying by a
negative number *reverses the
inequality*.

---

## MODULE 6  SECTION 5 STUDY GUIDE

## Exploration 2: Multi-Step Inequalities

### Solving Inequalities with More than One Operation

You can solve multi-step inequalities the same way you solve multi-step equations. However, you must be sure to reverse the inequality sign whenever you multiply or divide both sides by a negative number.

---

**Example**

Solve the inequality. Graph the solution.

$-5x + 7 < -3$

---

**■ Sample Response ■**

$-5x + 7 \leq -3$

$-5x + 7 - 7 \leq -3 - 7$  ← Subtracting the same number does not affect the inequality.

$\phantom{-5x + 7 - 7} -5x \leq -10$

$\dfrac{-5x}{-5} \geq \dfrac{-10}{-5}$  ← Dividing by a negative number reverses the inequality.

$\phantom{----} x \geq 2$

```
<———+———+———+———●———+———+———+———>
   -1   0   1   2   3   4   5   6
```

---

## MODULE 6  SECTION 5 | PRACTICE & APPLICATION EXERCISES

### Exploration 1

**Solve each inequality. Check and graph each solution.**

**1.** $y + 5 \leq 3$

**2.** $-4t > -8$

**3.** $22b \geq 12$

**4.** $\frac{2}{3}b \leq 5$

**5.** $33 \geq 6k$

**6.** $y + 4 \leq 7$

**7.** $y + 20 \leq 23$

**8.** $\frac{-4}{5}x > -12$

**9.** $4m > -24$

**10.** $y - 7 \leq 4$

**11.** $\frac{f}{2} < 29$

**12.** $\frac{y}{-3} \geq 4$

Name                                                    Date

**Write and solve an inequality for each situation.**

**13.** Six more than a number is less than eight.

**14.** Five minus a number is greater than or equal to four.

**15.** Twice a number added to 18 is less than 20.

## Exploration 2

**Solve each inequality.**

**16.** $3y + 5 \leq 3$

**17.** $-2t + 4 > -10$

**18.** $2.2m - 1 \leq 1.2$

**19.** $-3x + 1 \geq 4$

**20.** $\dfrac{-4}{7t} - 5 < -1$

**21.** $7y + 6 \geq -13$

**22.** $6y + 3 \leq -9$

**23.** $\dfrac{r}{2} + 6 > -18$

**24.** $-t + (-13) \leq 45$

**25.** $\dfrac{x}{-2} + 4 \leq -7$

**26.** $-2.9h - (-2.7) < -8.5$

**27.** $\dfrac{2}{3}k + \dfrac{1}{2} \geq \dfrac{1}{6}$

## Spiral Review

**Use the diagram to find each angle measure.** (Module 6, p. 436)

**28.** $m\angle 2$

**29.** $m\angle 5$

**30.** $m\angle 8$

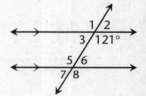

**Solve each proportion.** (Module 2, p. 90)

**31.** $\dfrac{x}{100} = \dfrac{5}{20}$

**32.** $\dfrac{8}{y} = \dfrac{7}{8}$

**33.** $\dfrac{1}{2} = \dfrac{5.8}{t}$

**MODULE 6  SECTION 6**                                              **STUDY GUIDE**

# Building Models   Scale Drawings and Similar Figures

**GOAL**  **LEARN HOW TO:** • make a scale drawing
                       • find relationships between perimeters and areas of two
                         similar figures

           **AS YOU:** • measure and draw your classroom
                       • find the perimeter and area of your classroom floor

## Exploration 1: Scale Drawings

### Making Scale Drawings

A scale drawing shows the parts of whatever it represents in proportion to
one another. The ratio of each pair of corresponding lengths is the **scale**.
To find out how long to make a segment in a scale drawing, you can use
a proportion.

---

**Example**

The dimensions of a bedroom are 12 ft by 9.2 ft. The scale in a scale drawing will be
0.75 in. to 1 ft. What will be the dimensions of the bedroom in the scale drawing?

**Sample Response**

$x$ = length on scale drawing (inches)        $y$ = width on scale drawing (inches)

inches → $\dfrac{x}{12} = \dfrac{0.75}{1}$              inches → $\dfrac{y}{9.2} = \dfrac{0.75}{1}$
feet  →                                   feet  →
$\qquad x = (0.75)(12)$                         $\qquad y = (0.75)(9.2)$
$\qquad x = 9$                                  $\qquad y = 6.9$

In the scale drawing, the dimensions of the bedroom will be 9 in. by 6.9 in.

---

## Exploration 2: Perimeters and Area of Similar Figures

### Comparing Perimeters and Areas of Similar Figures

If the ratio between corresponding sides of similar figures is $\dfrac{a}{b}$, then the

ratio of their perimeters is $\dfrac{a}{b}$ and the ratio of their areas is $\dfrac{a^2}{b^2}$.

Math Thematics, Book 3  **235**

**MODULE 6  SECTION 6**                                    STUDY GUIDE

### Example

Rectangle $ABCD$ is similar to rectangle $QRST$.
Use ratios to find the perimeter and area of
rectangle $QRST$.

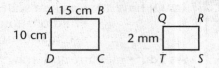

### ■ Sample Response ■

**First** Find the scale. It is the ratio of $QT$ to $AD$.

$$\frac{QT}{AD} = \frac{2}{10} = \frac{1}{5}$$

The scale is $\frac{1 \text{ mm}}{5 \text{ cm}}$.

**Next** Use the fact that the ratio of the perimeters is the same as the scale to write
a proportion.

$$\frac{\text{perimeter of rectangle } QRST}{\text{perimeter of rectangle } ABCD} = \frac{1 \text{ mm}}{5 \text{ cm}}$$

**Then** Find the perimeter of rectangle $ABCD$ and let $p$ = the perimeter of
rectangle $QRST$. Solve the proportion.

$$\frac{p}{15 \text{ cm} + 10 \text{ cm} + 15 \text{ cm} + 10 \text{ cm}} = \frac{1 \text{ mm}}{5 \text{ cm}}$$

$$\frac{p}{50 \text{ cm}} = \frac{1 \text{ mm}}{5 \text{ cm}}$$

$$50 \text{ cm} \cdot \frac{p}{50 \text{ cm}} = 50 \text{ cm} \cdot \frac{1 \text{ mm}}{5 \text{ cm}}$$

$$p = 10 \text{ mm}$$

The perimeter of rectangle $QRST$ is 10 mm.

**Now** Use the fact that the ratio of the areas is the square of the scale to find the area
of rectangle $QRST$. Find the area of rectangle $ABCD$ and let $x$ = area of rectangle
$QRST$.

$$\frac{\text{area of rectangle } QRST}{\text{area of rectangle } ABCD} = \frac{1^2 \text{ mm}^2}{5^2 \text{ cm}^2}$$

$$\frac{x}{15 \text{ cm} \cdot 10 \text{ cm}} = \frac{1 \text{ mm}^2}{25 \text{ cm}^2}$$

$$150 \text{ cm}^2 \cdot \frac{x}{150 \text{ cm}^2} = 150 \text{ cm}^2 \cdot \frac{1 \text{ mm}^2}{25 \text{ cm}^2}$$

$$x = 6 \text{ mm}^2$$

The area of rectangle $QRST$ is 6 mm$^2$.

## MODULE 6  SECTION 6 | PRACTICE & APPLICATION EXERCISES | STUDY GUIDE

## Exploration 1

**1.** A 12 ft statue is drawn 10 in. tall in a scale drawing. What is the scale?

**2.** The dimensions of a room in a scale drawing are 45 mm × 36 mm. The scale is 9 mm to 4 m. Find the dimensions of the actual room.

**3.** Make a scale drawing of the top view, the front view, and the right-side view of a rectangular prism that is 12 ft long, 8 ft wide, and 50 ft high.

## Exploration 2

**The two polygons in each diagram are similar. Find the unknown perimeter or area.**

**4.** Perimeter of larger triangle = 60 cm

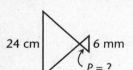

24 cm   6 mm   $P = ?$

**5.** Area of larger rectangle = 36 ft$^2$

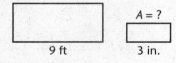

9 ft   $A = ?$   3 in.

## Spiral Review

**Solve each inequality. Graph the solution.** (Module 6, p. 447)

**6.** $3 + x \leq 4$

**7.** $y - 5 > 7$

**8.** $-1.5b < 20$

**9.** $18 - 5m > -7$

**10.** $2.5t + 3.1 \geq 5.6$

**11.** $-9r + \frac{1}{2} > 5$

**The spinner is equally divided into 5 sections. Use it to find the probability of each event.** (Module 4, p. 308)

**12.** The pointer lands in a section labeled A on the first spin and a section labeled B on the next.

**13.** The pointer lands in a section labeled C on the first spin and a section labeled A on the second spin.

**Graph each equation.** (Module 3, p. 183)

**14.** $y = x + 7$

**15.** $y = -1$

**16.** $y = 8 - 4x$

**MODULE 7**

## Graphs without Labels   (Use with Exercise 5 on page 477.)

**Directions**   Each of the graphs models one of the verbal descriptions or data tables below. Decide which graph goes with which description or table. Choose an appropriate title for the graph. Label the axes to show which quantities are being compared.

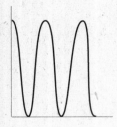    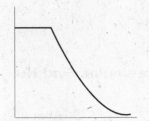    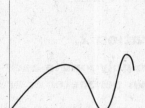

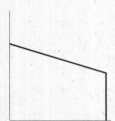    

- The length of a firecracker (including the fuse) after the fuse is lit

- The depth of water in a child's swimming pool that suddenly gets a hole in the bottom

- The height of a sandcastle you build at the beach

| • Time (h) | 0 | 1 | 2 | 3 | 4 | 5 | 6 | 7 | 8 | 9 | 10 |
|---|---|---|---|---|---|---|---|---|---|---|---|
| Speed (mi/h) | 0 | 1 | 2 | 2.5 | 2.3 | 1 | 0.5 | 0 | 4 | 5 | 3 |

| • Time (seconds) | 0 | 1 | 2 | 3 | 4 | 5 | 6 | 7 | 8 | 9 | 10 |
|---|---|---|---|---|---|---|---|---|---|---|---|
| Distance of yo-yo from ground (ft) | 4 | 2 | 0 | 2 | 4 | 2 | 0 | 2 | 4 | 2 | 0 |

**MODULE 7**                                                    LABSHEET  **4A**

## Sequence of Transformations  (Use with Question 9 on page 513.)

### Sequence I

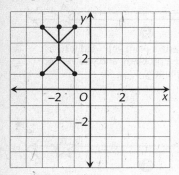

$(x, y)$

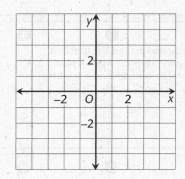

$(x', y') = ( \quad , \quad )$

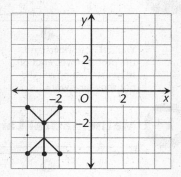

$(x'', y'') = ( \quad , \quad )$

### Sequence II

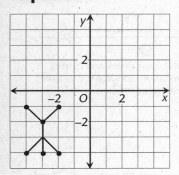

$(x, y)$

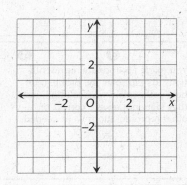

$(x', y') = ( \quad , \quad )$

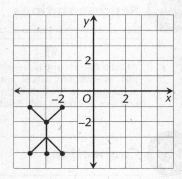

$(x'', y'') = ( \quad , \quad )$

### Sequence III

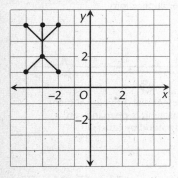

$(x, y)$

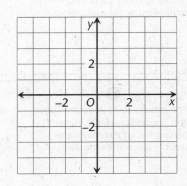

$(x', y') = ( \quad , \quad )$

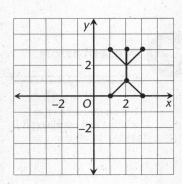

$(x'', y'') = ( \quad , \quad )$

Name _____                                    Problem _____

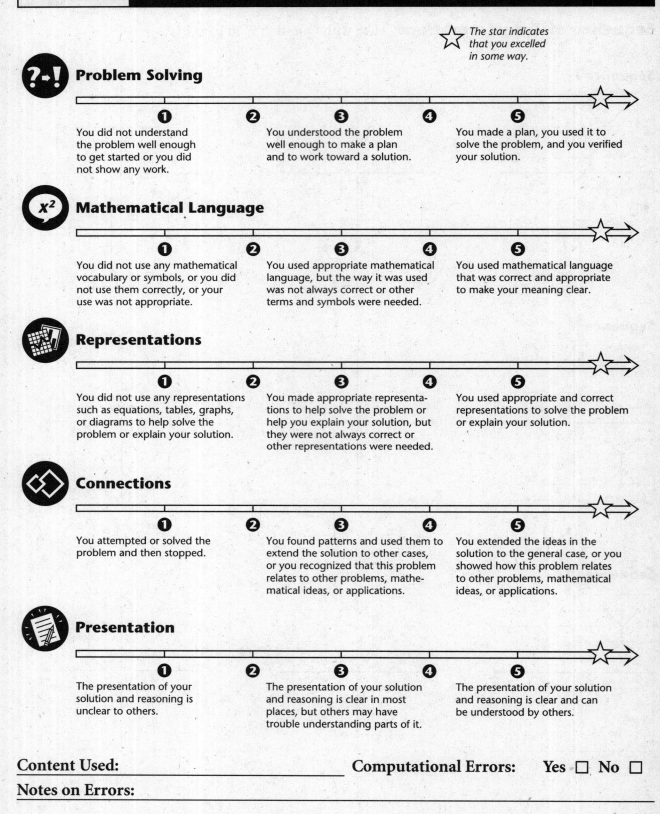

☆ The star indicates that you excelled in some way.

### ?→! Problem Solving

**❶** You did not understand the problem well enough to get started or you did not show any work.

**❷**

**❸** You understood the problem well enough to make a plan and to work toward a solution.

**❹**

**❺** You made a plan, you used it to solve the problem, and you verified your solution.

### $x^2$ Mathematical Language

**❶** You did not use any mathematical vocabulary or symbols, or you did not use them correctly, or your use was not appropriate.

**❷**

**❸** You used appropriate mathematical language, but the way it was used was not always correct or other terms and symbols were needed.

**❹**

**❺** You used mathematical language that was correct and appropriate to make your meaning clear.

### Representations

**❶** You did not use any representations such as equations, tables, graphs, or diagrams to help solve the problem or explain your solution.

**❷**

**❸** You made appropriate representations to help solve the problem or help you explain your solution, but they were not always correct or other representations were needed.

**❹**

**❺** You used appropriate and correct representations to solve the problem or explain your solution.

### Connections

**❶** You attempted or solved the problem and then stopped.

**❷**

**❸** You found patterns and used them to extend the solution to other cases, or you recognized that this problem relates to other problems, mathematical ideas, or applications.

**❹**

**❺** You extended the ideas in the solution to the general case, or you showed how this problem relates to other problems, mathematical ideas, or applications.

### Presentation

**❶** The presentation of your solution and reasoning is unclear to others.

**❷**

**❸** The presentation of your solution and reasoning is clear in most places, but others may have trouble understanding parts of it.

**❹**

**❺** The presentation of your solution and reasoning is clear and can be understood by others.

**Content Used:** _____

**Notes on Errors:** _____

**Computational Errors:**  Yes ☐  No ☐

Name _____ Problem _____

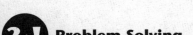 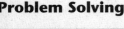 SELF-ASSESSMENT SCALES

⬛ *If your score is in the shaded area, explain why on the back of this sheet and stop.*

☆ *The star indicates that you excelled in some way.*

 ## Problem Solving

**①**     **②**     **③**     **④**     **⑤**     ☆→

**①** I did not understand the problem well enough to get started or I did not show any work.

**③** I understood the problem well enough to make a plan and to work toward a solution.

**⑤** I made a plan, I used it to solve the problem, and I verified my solution.

 ## Mathematical Language

**①**     **②**     **③**     **④**     **⑤**     ☆→

**①** I did not use any mathematical vocabulary or symbols, or I did not use them correctly, or my use was not appropriate.

**③** I used appropriate mathematical language, but the way it was used was not always correct or other terms and symbols were needed.

**⑤** I used mathematical language that was correct and appropriate to make my meaning clear.

 ## Representations

**①**     **②**     **③**     **④**     **⑤**     ☆→

**①** I did not use any representations such as equations, tables, graphs, or diagrams to help solve the problem or explain my solution.

**③** I made appropriate representations to help solve the problem or help me explain my solution, but they were not always correct or other representations were needed.

**⑤** I used appropriate and correct representations to solve the problem or explain my solution.

## Connections

**①**     **②**     **③**     **④**     **⑤**     ☆→

**①** I attempted or solved the problem and then stopped.

**③** I found patterns and used them to extend the solution to other cases, or I recognized that this problem relates to other problems, mathematical ideas, or applications.

**⑤** I extended the ideas in the solution to the general case, or I showed how this problem relates to other problems, mathematical ideas, or applications.

 ## Presentation

**①**     **②**     **③**     **④**     **⑤**     ☆→

**①** The presentation of my solution and reasoning is unclear to others.

**③** The presentation of my solution and reasoning is clear in most places, but others may have trouble understanding parts of it.

**⑤** The presentation of my solution and reasoning is clear and can be understood by others.

**MODULE 7  SECTION 1**                    **PRACTICE AND APPLICATIONS**

## For use with Exploration 1

**Suppose water is poured into each of the containers below.
Which graph models the water level in each container
over time?**

1.    2.    3.    4.

A.    B.    C.    D.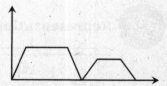

5. **Open-ended** Suppose the graph at the right represents a car trip
   to the grocery store. The horizontal axis is time in minutes
   and the vertical axis is the speed of the car. Write a story to
   match the graph.

6. Which graph would you expect to model the change in the height of
   sand as it is being poured into a container like in Exercise 2 above?

   A.           B.           C.

7. **Create Your Own** Write a story or a poem that describes how the
   level of sand changes as it fills an hour glass.

## For use with Exploration 2

8. Suppose you have $420 saved before you start spending
   $15 per week.

   **a.** Describe a function based on this situation. Identify the
   input and the output.

   **b.** Write an equation to model the function.

*(continued)*

**MODULE 7  SECTION 1**                    **PRACTICE AND APPLICATIONS**

**For each pair of variables, tell whether $y$ is a function of $x$. Explain your thinking.**

**9.** $x$ = the number of tickets sold to the school play
    $y$ = the amount of money made by selling the tickets

**10.** $x$ = the number of miles driven on a rental car
    $y$ = the cost of renting a rental car

**11.** $x$ = the average speed of a car
    $y$ = the distance traveled in one hour

**12.** $x$ = the height of a student in your class
    $y$ = the weight of a student in your class

**For each equation or graph, tell whether $y$ is a function of $x$.**

**13.** $6x^2 = y$         **14.** $2x = y$         **15.** $3x = y^2$         **16.** $-4x + 1 = y$

**17.** 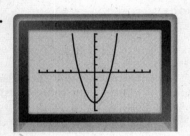         **18.** 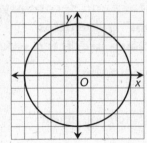         **19.**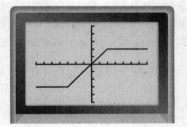

**For Exercises 20–22, a rule for a function is given. Write an equation to model the function.**

**20.** Multiply a number by 4.                    **21.** Divide a number by –6.

**22.** Find the square root of a number, then add 2 to the result.

**23.** A leak in a 50 gallon container causes it to drain steadily at the rate of one gallon per hour.

  **a.** Let $y$ = the amount of water that is left in the container.
      Let $x$ = the number of hours the container has been draining.
      Explain why the value of $y$ is a function of $x$.

  **b.** Write an equation that models this function.

  **c.** Graph your equation.

Name _____     Date _____

## MODULE 7 SECTION 2 — PRACTICE AND APPLICATIONS

### For use with Exploration 1

**1.** The equation $y = 140 + 5x$ models Toni's savings after $x$ weeks. Describe her savings plan in words.

**Graphing Calculator** **Graph each pair of equations on the same pair of axes. Show the point where the graphs intersect and label its coordinates.**

**2.** $y = 8x$ and $y = 7x + 3$

**3.** $y = 8 - 3x$ and $y = x + 16$

**4.** $y = 10x - 25$ and $y = 40 - 3x$

**5.** $y = 12 - 4x$ and $y = -6x + 4$

**6.** $y = 20x - 30$ and $y = 50 - 20x$

**7.** $y = 12 - 2x$ and $y = -4x + 14$

**Education** **Economists use graphs to help them explain trends in population. For example, the graph below can be used to predict the resurgence in elementary and secondary school enrollment due to the "baby boom" generation having children. Totals after 1995 are predicted values.**

**8.** Explain how to use the graph to predict the enrollment in the year 2000.

**9.** Explain what the points $A$, $B$, and $C$ tell you about the enrollment.

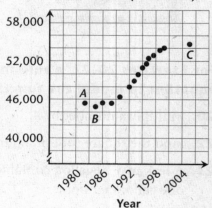

Elementary and Secondary Enrollment (thousands)

**10.** Suppose you have $10,000 in savings for college. You start spending your savings at a rate of $250 per month. Your brother is working and starts saving for college at the same time with $500 already in savings. He saves $350 per month. Use a table or graph to answer the questions below.

  **a.** When do you run out of money? How much has your brother saved by that time?

  **b.** When will you and your brother have the same amount in savings?

*(continued)*

| MODULE 7  SECTION 2 | PRACTICE AND APPLICATIONS |

## For use with Exploration 2

**Use the distributive property to rewrite each expression.**

**11.** $-4(x + 15)$  **12.** $8 + 16w$  **13.** $6(-2 - 3s)$

**14.** $50(0.1 - 0.5g)$  **15.** $12f + 24$  **16.** $8 - 32k$

**17.** It only costs $1 to swim at the community pool if you buy a summer pass. A summer pass costs $40 and can be used all summer. It costs $3 to swim without a summer pass.

   **a.** Write two equations that model the cost of swimming at the community pool $n$ times, one if you have a pass, and one if you do not have a pass.

   **b. Writing** Under what circumstances would you want to swim without buying a summer pass? Explain your thinking.

   **c.** How many times would you have to use your summer pass in order to "break even" and start saving money?

**18. a.** Use an equation to find a common solution of $y = 2x$ and $y = 3x - 4$. Are there other common solutions? How do you know?

   **b.** Graph the equations from part (a) on the same pair of axes. How can you use a graph to find a common solution of the two equations?

**Solve each equation.**

**19.** $15x + 25 = 18x - 10$  **20.** $6c = -8c - 14$

**21.** $36 = 3(v - 8)$  **22.** $-14 - 8d = 2(6d + 4)$

**23.** $10g + 12 - 2g = 6g$  **24.** $6(3k - 2) = -8(k + 4)$

**25.** $3(2 - x) = -x - 10$  **26.** $10 - 2(6 - w) = 3(w - 1)$

**27. Graphing Calculator** You can use graphs to solve equations like $2x + 16 = 3(x - 4)$.

   **a.** Graph $y = 2x + 16$ and $y = 3(x - 4)$ on the same pair of axes. Find the $x$-coordinate of the point where the graphs intersect.

   **b.** Check to see that the $x$-coordinate you found in part (a) is the solution of $2x + 16 = 3(x - 4)$.

   **c.** Use graphs to solve $-8 = -2(-3 - x) + 4$.

**MODULE 7  SECTION 3**                    **PRACTICE AND APPLICATIONS**

## For use with Exploration 1

**For Exercises 1–3, use the graphs below.**

A. 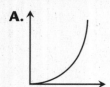   B. 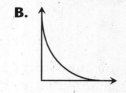   C. 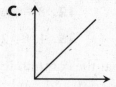   D.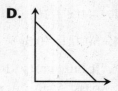

1. In an experiment, bacteria that double their numbers every hour are allowed to grow and be studied. Which graph could represent their growth? Explain your choice.

2. The population of a certain town is decreasing at a rate of 1.8% each year. Which graph could represent the population decrease? Explain your choice.

3. Ten new students sign up for intramural sports every month. Which graph could represent the number of new students in intramural sports? Explain your choice.

4. **a.** Refer to Exercise 1. If there are 100 bacteria at the start of the experiment, how many bacteria are there in one hour? two hours?

   **b.** Make a table for the first ten hours of their growth.

   **c.** Use the table to help you write an equation to find the number of bacteria after 24 hours of growth.

   **d.** **Challenge** Use the information in parts (a) – (c) above to write an equation that models the total number of bacteria after $x$ hours.

   **e.** **Writing** Explain how the equation can be used to find the number of bacteria after 48 hours.

5. **a.** **Graphing Calculator** Graph the equation you found in Exercise 4, part (d). Verify that your answer to Exercise 1 is correct.

   **b.** **Writing** Explain how the graph can be used to find how long it takes for the number of bacteria to reach 10,000.

   **c.** Verify your answer to part (b) in the equation you found in Exercise 4, part (d).

6. **Open-ended** Write about a growth experiment or growth situation you are familiar with. Explain how it can be modeled by the growth formulas given in this lesson.

*(continued)*

## MODULE 7  SECTION 3                    PRACTICE AND APPLICATIONS

### For use with Exploration 2

**7. a.** Suppose you deposit $250 into an account that earns 5% annual interest. Write an equation that shows the amount of money $y$ in the account after $x$ years.

**b.** How much money will be in the account after 10 years?

**c.** About how many years will it take for the amount of money in the account to reach $1000?

**d. Graphing Calculator** Graph the equation you found in part (a). Explain how to use it to verify the answer in part (d).

**8.** Write an equation in the form $y = a \cdot b^x$ to model each situation. Tell what the variables $x$ and $y$ represent.

**a.** A town with 55,000 people is predicted to grow at a rate of 1.7% each year over a period of $x$ years.

**b.** A ball dropped from 9 ft bounces to 80% of its previous height. In $x$ bounces, its height will be $y$ ft.

**c.** Describe a situation like the ones in parts (a) and (b). Write a word problem about the situation that you could use an exponential equation to solve. Give the solution to your problem.

### Evaluate each expression for the given value of the variable.

**9.** $2 \cdot 4^x$, $x = 3$

**10.** $2 \cdot \left(\dfrac{1}{3}\right)^x$, $x = 3$

**11.** $100(0.2)^x$, $x = 4$

**12.** $\dfrac{1}{3} \cdot 3^x$, $x = 4$

**13.** $6 \cdot \left(\dfrac{1}{2}\right)^x$, $x = 6$

**14.** $\dfrac{1}{3}(5)^x$, $x = 4$

**15.** Refer to your answer to Exercise 8, part (a).

**a. Graphing Calculator** Graph your equation. Your graph should show the town's population for the next 25 years.

**b.** Explain how to use the graph to help you find how many years it will take for the population of the town to double.

**c. Challenge** Suppose the growth rate of the town is 3.4%. Predict how many years it will take for the population to double. Check your prediction by writing an equation, graphing it, and using the graph.

**MODULE 7  SECTION 4**                    **PRACTICE AND APPLICATIONS**

## For use with Exploration 1

**Reflect each figure across the given axis or axes. Draw the original figure and the reflection(s) in the same coordinate plane.**

**1.** the *y*-axis

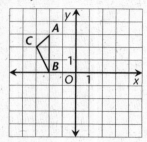

**2.** the *x*-axis

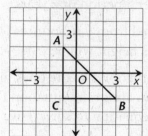

**3.** the *x*-axis, then the *y*-axis

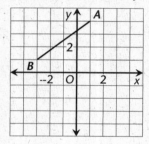

**4.** the *y*-axis, then the *x*-axis

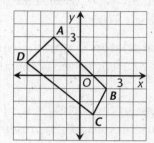

**Write an algorithm that can be used to create each transformation.**

**5.**

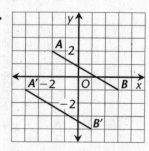

**6.**

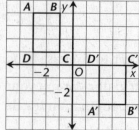

**7.** In the diagram at the right, △*A′B′C′* was created by rotating △*ABC* 90° about the origin. Describe how to transform △*ABC* to △*A′B′C′* using reflections.

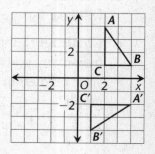

**MODULE 7  SECTION 5**                          **PRACTICE AND APPLICATIONS**

## For use with Exploration 1

**Match each equation with one of the parabolas.**

**1.** $y = x^2$

**2.** $y = -x^2$

**3.** $y = -0.05x^2$

**4.** $y = 0.3x^2$

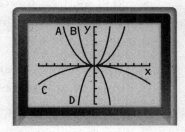

**5. a. Graphing Calculator** Graph the three equations below on the same pair of axes.

$y = -x^2 + 1$ $\qquad\qquad$ $y = -x^2 + 2$ $\qquad\qquad$ $y = -x^2 + 3$

**b.** Predict how the graph of $y = -x^2 + 4$ will compare with the graphs from part (a).

**c.** Predict how the graphs of $y = -0.1x^2 - 1$, $y = -0.1x^2 - 2$ and $y = -0.1x^2 - 3$ will compare with the graph of $y = -0.1x^2$. Then check your predictions.

**6. Physics** The Ritz Tower in New York is one of the tallest residential towers in the world at 540 ft. You can use the formula $h = 540 - 16t^2$ to find the height $h$ (in feet) of an object $t$ seconds after it is dropped from the top of the tower.

**a.** Find the values of $h$ for $t = 0, 1, 2, 3, 4, 5$.

**b.** Use your answer to part (a) to plot 6 ordered pairs $(t, h)$ on the same pair of axes. Connect the points with a smooth curve.

**c.** About how long does it take an object dropped from the top of the tower to hit the ground? Explain how you know.

**d.** Reflect the curve you drew in part (a) across the $y$-axis. Does this part make sense in this real-life situation?

**e.** Give the coordinates of the vertex of the parabola you drew in parts (b) and (d).

**f. Challenge** Reflect the curve you drew in part (b) across the $x$-axis. Predict an equation for this curve. Check your prediction with a graphing calculator.

*(continued)*

## MODULE 7  SECTION 5                         PRACTICE AND APPLICATIONS

### For use with Exploration 2

7. **Graphing Calculator**  A ball is thrown upward with an initial
   speed of 40 ft/s. The equation $h = -16t^2 + 40t + 6$ gives the
   height $h$ (in feet) of the ball $t$ seconds after it is thrown from an
   initial height of 6 feet.

   **a.** Explain why this equation is a quadratic function. Identify the
   values of $a$, $b$, and $c$ in the equation.

   **b.** Graph the equation. Show where the equation crosses each axis.
   Sketch the line of symmetry.

   **c.** About how high does the ball go? After about how many seconds
   does it begin to fall? About how long does it stay in the air?

**Identify the values of $a$, $b$, and $c$ in the equation of the form
$y = ax^2 + bx + c$ below.**

8. $y = 6x^2 - 4x + 3$                    9. $y = 0.01x^2 - 0.5x + 1.8$

10. $y = -12x^2 - 8x - 6$                 11. $y = -x^2 - 5x$

**Rewrite each equation in the form $y = ax^2 + bx + c$. Tell
whether the equation models a quadratic function.**

12. $y = 2x(x - 2)$                       13. $y = 3x(x - 2) - 2x^2$

14. $y = 4x + x - 12$                     15. $y = 6x^2 - 5x^2 + 3$

16. $y = 6x^2 + x - 6x^2$                 17. $3x^2 + 5(x - 1) - 2x^2 = y$

18. $9x^2 - 8x^2 = y - 4$                 19. $2x^2 + 6(x + 2) - 2x^2 = y + x^2$

20. **a.** **Graphing Calculator**  Graph the quadratic function
    $y = 4(x - 1)^2 + 3$.

    **b.** Sketch the axis of symmetry.

    **c.** Find the vertex.

    **d.** Predict the vertex for the quadratic function $y = 2(x - 4)^2 - 5$.
    Check your predictions with a graphing calculator.

| **MODULE 7  SECTION 1** | **STUDY GUIDE** |

# Time for a Change   Graphs and Functions

**GOAL**  **LEARN HOW TO:** • use tables and graphs to model changes in data
• use equations, tables, and graphs to represent functions

**AS YOU:** • explore how the shape of a container affects changes in water level
• compare different rainfall data

## Exploration 1: Modeling Change

### Modeling Changes in Data

You can use tables and graphs to model and analyze changes in data.

---

### Example

Suppose you were to pour water in equal amounts into containers A and B. How can you use a graph to show the change in water level inside each container?

---

### ▰ Sample Response ▰

**First** Make a table of values.

**A.**

| Water poured in | Level in container |
|---|---|
| 1 c | 1 in. |
| 2 c | 2 in. |
| 3 c | 3 in. |
| 4 c | 4 in. |
| 5 c | 5 in. |

**B.**

| Water poured in | Level in container |
|---|---|
| 1 c | $\frac{1}{2}$ in. |
| 2 c | $\frac{3}{4}$ in. |
| 3 c | $1\frac{1}{4}$ in. |
| 4 c | $2\frac{1}{4}$ in. |
| 5 c | $3\frac{1}{4}$ in. |

**Then** Plot the ordered pairs and connect the points.

The data for container A lie in a straight line because the water level increases at a constant rate.

The data for container B do not lie in a straight line until 3 cups of water have been added. The water level increases at different rates.

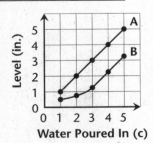

---

## MODULE 7 SECTION 1

### Exploration 2: Functions

**Representing Functions**

A **function** is a relationship between input and output. It is a rule that
pairs each input value with *exactly one* output value. Given an equation,
you can tell whether $y$ is a function of $x$ by analyzing input and output
values in a table or a graph.

---

**Example**

Write and graph an equation for the following statement. Tell whether $y$ is a
function of $x$.

A number $y$ is 1 less than 2 times a number $x$.

---

**Sample Response**

Equation: $y = 2x - 1$

Table:

| x | y |
|----|----|
| −2 | −5 |
| −1 | −3 |
| 0 | −1 |
| 1 | 1 |

Graph:

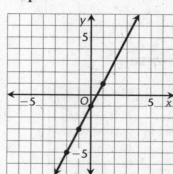

$y$ is a function of $x$ because there is exactly one $y$-value for each $x$-value.

---

Name _____     Date _____

## Exploration 1

**Match each container with a graph that shows the water level as a function of the amount of water in the container.**

**1.** 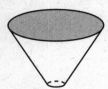     **2.** 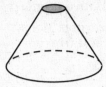     **3.**

**A.**      **B.** 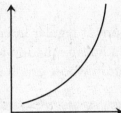     **C.**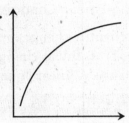

## Exploration 2

**For each pair of variables, tell whether $y$ is a function of $x$. Explain your thinking.**

**4.** $x$ = the height of a person
$y$ = the age of a person

**5.** $x$ = number of movies seen
$y$ = amount spent

**For each equation or graph, tell whether $y$ is a function of $x$.**

**6.** $3x = 5y$     **7.** $3y = x^3$     **8.** $y^2 = x$

**9.** 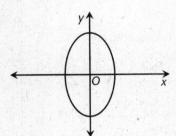     **10.**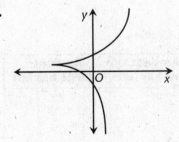

## Spiral Review

**11.** The actual perimeter of a rectangular garden is 44 ft. Its actual area is 120 ft$^2$. Find the perimeter and area of a scale drawing of the garden with a scale of 2 in. to 3 ft. **(Modules 6, p. 457)**

**12.** Find the value of $x$ in the diagram. **(Module 5, p. 363)**

**Graph each equation. Give the slope of each line.**
**(Module 5, pp. 337–338)**

**13.** $y = -3x + 3$     **14.** $y = 3x - 2$     **15.** $y = \frac{1}{2}x + 1$

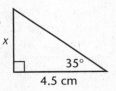

**MODULE 7  SECTION 2**                                 **STUDY GUIDE**

# A Penny Saved   Linear Equations and Problem Solving

**GOAL**  **LEARN HOW TO:** • use tables, graphs, and equations to solve problems
• solve equations that involve simplifying
• use the distributive property

**AS YOU:** • investigate different savings plans
• model savings plans and trips

## Exploration 1: Linear Change

### Modeling Linear Change

When a quantity changes by the same amount at regular intervals, the quantity shows **linear change**. You can use a linear equation to represent linear change. A **linear equation** is an equation whose graph is a line.

### Example

Kara has 8 oz of medicine. She has been instructed to take 1 oz per day until it is gone. George has 22 oz of medicine. He has been instructed to take 3 oz per day until it is gone. When will they have the same amount of medicine left and who will finish their medicine first?

### ■ Sample Response ■

**First** Write an equation for each person. Let $y$ = the amount each has left after $x$ days.

Kara:
$y = 8 - 1x$

George:
$y = 22 - 3x$

**Next** Make a table of values.

**Then** Make a graph.

| Number of days taken | Amount Kara has left | Amount George has left |
|:---:|:---:|:---:|
| 0 | 8 | 22 |
| 1 | 7 | 19 |
| 2 | 6 | 16 |
| ... | ... | ... |
| 6 | 2 | 4 |
| 7 | 1 | 1 |

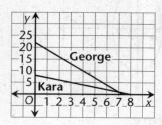

After 7 days, they each have 1 oz left. They both can take medicine on the 8th day; however, George will have only $\frac{1}{3}$ of his dosage to take.

**MODULE 7  SECTION 2**                    **STUDY GUIDE**

## Exploration 2: Multi-Step Equations

### Solving Equations

The **distributive property** states that for all numbers $a$, $b$, and $c$:

$a(b + c) = ab + ac$ and $ab + ac = a(b + c)$
$3(4 + 5) = 3(4) + 3(5)$ and $12 + 15 = 3(4 + 5)$
$2(x + 5) = 2x + 2(5)$ and $2x + 10 = 2(x + 5)$

To solve some multi-step equations, you may need to use the distributive property and combine like terms.

---

**Example**

Solve $4(x - 3) = x + 5$.

**Sample Response**

$$4(x - 3) = x + 5$$
$$4(x + (-3)) = x + 5 \qquad \text{Rewrite } (x - 3) \text{ as } (x + (-3)).$$
$$4x + 4(-3) = x + 5 \qquad \text{Use the distributive property.}$$
$$4x - 12 = x + 5$$
$$4x + 12 - 12 = x + 12 + 5 \qquad \textbf{Add 12} \text{ to both sides.}$$
$$4x = x + 17 \qquad \text{Combine like terms.}$$
$$4x - x = x - x + 17 \qquad \textbf{Subtract } x \text{ from both sides.}$$
$$3x = 17 \qquad \text{Combine like terms.}$$
$$\frac{3x}{3} = \frac{17}{3} \qquad \textbf{Divide} \text{ both sides } \textbf{by 3}.$$
$$x = \frac{17}{3} \text{ or } 5\frac{2}{3}$$

---

**MODULE 7  SECTION 2** | **PRACTICE & APPLICATION EXERCISES**

## Exploration 1

**Graph each pair of equations on the same pair of axes. Show the point where the graphs intersect and label its coordinates.**

**1.** $y = 3x$ and $y = x + 2$

**2.** $y = 2x - 3$ and $y = 3x - 5$

**3.** $y = -3x + 1$ and $y = x + 4$

**4.** $y = x - 2$ and $y = 2x$

## MODULE 7  SECTION 2 | PRACTICE & APPLICATION EXERCISES | STUDY GUIDE

### Exploration 2

**Solve each equation.**

**5.** $5x + 1 = x + 3$      **6.** $-2 + 2x = 6x + 2$      **7.** $15 + x = -6 + 8x$

**8.** $11x + 7 = 6x + 18$      **9.** $-7x - 6 = 13x + 4$      **10.** $-9x + 2 = -3x - 10$

**Use the distributive property to rewrite each expression.**

**11.** $7(x + 2)$      **12.** $-5(-3 + 4x)$      **13.** $5x + 15$

**Solve each equation.**

**14.** $3(x + 2) = 4x + 1$      **15.** $8y + 1 + 2y = 2(y - 3)$

**16.** $3 + 7(m + 2) = -9$      **17.** $x(3 - x) = x(5 - x)$

**18.** $-y(9 + 7y) = 7(-2 - y^2) + 5$      **19.** $2 + 3t = 5(3t + 7)$

### Spiral Review

**Write a rule for finding a term of each sequence when you know the previous term.** (Module 4, p. 246)

**20.** $6, 12, 18, 24, \ldots$      **21.** $5, 4\frac{3}{4}, 4\frac{1}{2}, 4\frac{1}{4}, 4, \ldots$

**22.** $100, 20, 4, \frac{4}{5}, \ldots$      **23.** $1, 9, 17, 25, 33, \ldots$

**Rewrite each product as a power.** (Toolbox, p. 600)

**24.** $3.4 \cdot 3.4 \cdot 3.4$      **25.** $5 \cdot 5 \cdot 5 \cdot 5 \cdot 5 \cdot 5$

**26.** $45 \cdot 45 \cdot 45 \cdot 45 \cdot 45$      **27.** $\frac{5}{6} \cdot \frac{5}{6} \cdot \frac{5}{6} \cdot \frac{5}{6} \cdot \frac{5}{6} \cdot \frac{5}{6}$

## MODULE 7 SECTION 3                                        STUDY GUIDE

# How Sweet It Is    Modeling Exponential Change

**GOAL**   **LEARN HOW TO:** • describe exponential change
• write an equation to model compound interest
• use equations and tables to solve problems

**AS YOU:** • use paper folding to model eating a chocolate bar
• model price changes and the growth of a savings account

## Exploration 1: Exponential Change

### Using an Equation for Exponential Change

Some **exponential equations** have the form $y = b^x$, where $b > 0$ and $x \geq 0$.
You can use an equation in this form to model some types of
exponential change.

### Example

How many regions will there be in a 1 square unit piece of paper that is repeatedly
folded in half after 5 folds? Find the area of one of those regions.

### ■ Sample Response ■

| **Steps** | **Results** |
|---|---|
| **1.** Fold a piece of paper in half. | 2 regions |
| **2.** Fold it in half again. | 4 regions |
| **3.** Fold it in half again. | 8 regions |

Let $x$ be the number of steps, $y$ be the regions in the result, and $z$ be the area of
one region.

Use $y = b^x$ to write a formula.

Number of regions after $x$ steps $= 2^x$. So, $y = 2^5$ or 32.

Area of each region after $x$ steps $= \left(\frac{1}{2}\right)^x$. So, $z = \left(\frac{1}{2}\right)^5$ or $\frac{1}{32}$.

After 5 folds of the piece of paper into halves, there would be 32 regions, each having
an area of $\frac{1}{32}$ square unit.

**MODULE 7  SECTION 3**

## Exploration 2: Exponential Models

### Exponential Models for Growth of Money

You can also model certain kinds of exponential change with an
exponential equation that has the form:

$$\overset{\displaystyle \text{starting amount}}{\underset{\displaystyle \underset{\text{rate of change}}{\uparrow}}{\text{amount after } x \text{ years} \rightarrow \ y = a \cdot b^{\,x}}}$$

An equation of this type models the growth of money in an account if the
interest earned is left in the account.

---

**Example**

Suppose you deposit $600 into an account that earns 8% annual interest. Find how
much money you will have after 3 years if you do not make any withdrawals from
the account.

---

**Sample Response**

Use the formula $y = a \cdot b^{\,x}$.

Let $a = \$600$
  $b = 1 + 0.08 = 1.08$
  $x = 3$

  $y = 600 \cdot (1.08)^3$
    $\approx 600 \cdot 1.26$
    $\approx 756$

You will have about $756 after 3 years.

---

## MODULE 7  SECTION 3 | PRACTICE & APPLICATION EXERCISES | STUDY GUIDE

## Exploration 1

**Match each equation with one of the graphs below.**

**1.** $y = 3^x$

**2.** $y = \left(\dfrac{1}{4}\right)^x$

**A.**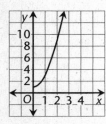

**B.**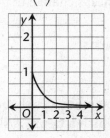

## Exploration 2

**Write an equation in the form $y = a \cdot b^x$ to model each situation. Tell what the variables $x$ and $y$ represent.**

**3.** A school has 522 students. The superintendent predicts the number will increase by 3% a year over the next $x$ years.

**4.** A bakery produces 500 cookies an hour. The owner wants to increase production by 20% an hour over the next $x$ hours.

**5.** A painting worth $50 is projected to increase in value by 25% a year over the next $x$ years.

**Evaluate each expression for the given value of the variable.**

**6.** $22 \cdot 3^x$; $x = 2$

**7.** $\dfrac{2}{5} \cdot 5^x$; $x = 4$

**8.** $0.02 \cdot \left(\dfrac{1}{2}\right)^x$; $x = 3$

**Write and solve an equation to find out how much money you will have in each situation.**

**9.** You deposit $400 into an account for 2 years at 6% interest.

**10.** You deposit $1200 into an account for 5 years at 7% interest.

## Spiral Review

**Solve each equation.** (Module 7, p. 491)

**11.** $14x + 12 = 250 - 7x$

**12.** $-7 - 9x = 11x - 6(1 + x)$

**13.** After the translation $(x - 3, y + 4)$, the image of a point is $(5, 11)$. What are the coordinates of the original point? (Module 2, p. 130)

## MODULE 7 SECTION 4                                                    STUDY GUIDE

# Moving Around    Algorithms and Transformations

**GOAL**   **LEARN HOW TO:** • use algorithms to transform geometric shapes
                          • reflect geometric shapes

**As you:** • model a gymnast's change in positions

## Exploration 1: Using Algorithms

### Geometric Transformations

A **transformation** is a change made to an object's shape or position.
A **translation** is a transformation in which a figure is slid horizontally,
vertically, or both.

---

### Example

Translate $A(3, 2)$ 2 units to the right and 1 unit down.

---

#### ■ Sample Response ■

The coordinates of $A'$ are
$(x + 2, y - 1)$, or $(3 + 2, 2 - 1)$.

So, the coordinates of $A'$ are $(5, 1)$.

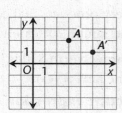

---

A **reflection** is a transformation in which a figure is flipped across a line
such as the $x$- or $y$-axis.

---

### Example

Reflect $A(3, 2)$ across the $y$-axis.

---

#### ■ Sample Response ■

Multiply the $x$-coordinate by $-1$, or find the opposite
of the $x$-coordinate.
$A'(-1x, y)$

The coordinates of $A'$ are $(-3, 2)$.

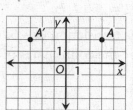

---

## MODULE 7  SECTION 4                                    STUDY GUIDE

### Writing Algorithms

An **algorithm** is a set of steps that you can follow to accomplish a goal.
You can use an algorithm to describe a transformation that involves
several steps.

---

**Example**

Write an algorithm to describe the transformation
shown.

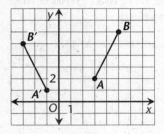

---

**■ Sample Response ■**

**Step 1**  Reflect each point across the $y$-axis. $(x', y') = (-x, y)$

**Step 2**  Translate each point down 1 unit. $(x'', y'') = (x', y - 1)$

**Step 3**  Translate each point right 2 units. $(x''', y''') = (x'' + 2, y'')$

Use $A(3, 2)$ and $B(5, 6)$ to check the algorithm.

**Step 1**  $(-3, 2); (-5, 6)$

**Step 2**  $(-3, 2 - 1); (-5, 6 - 1)$ or $(-3, 1); (-5, 5)$

**Step 3**  $(-3 + 2, 1); (-5 + 2, 5)$ or $(-1, 1); (-3, 5)$

The coordinates of $A'$ and $B'$ are $(-1, 1)$ and $(-3, 5)$.

---

## MODULE 7  SECTION 4 | PRACTICE & APPLICATION EXERCISES

### Exploration 1

**Write an algorithm for moving the point as specified.**

**1.** from $(1, 2)$ to $(4, 5)$        **2.** from $(-2, 7)$ to $(8, 4)$

**3.** from $(3, -6)$ to $(0, 0)$ and then to $(1, 2)$

Name _____  Date _____

## MODULE 7 SECTION 4 | PRACTICE & APPLICATION EXERCISES | STUDY GUIDE

**Explain how to perform the following transformations.**

**4.** Reflect the point $(-2, 5)$ across the $x$-axis.

**5.** Reflect the point $(3, 0)$ across the $y$-axis.

**6.** Describe two different ways to transform point $A(1, 3)$ to point $A'(1, -3)$.

**Sketch the original figure and the final image of the transformation.**

**7.** reflect across the $x$-axis

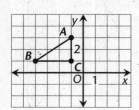

**8.** reflect across the $y$-axis

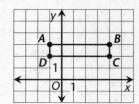

## Spiral Review

**Evaluate each of the following equations for $x = 4$.**
(Module 7, p. 504)

**9.** $y = 5^x$

**10.** $y = 8 \cdot \left(\dfrac{1}{2}\right)^x$

**11.** $y = 1^x$

**12.** In the diagram, line $s$ is parallel to line $t$. Find each angle measure. (Module 6, p. 436)

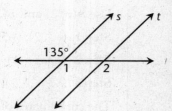

**Use mental math to find each value.** (Module 3, p. 170)

**13.** $-\sqrt{121}$

**14.** $\sqrt{0.0009}$

**15.** $\sqrt{\dfrac{1}{49}}$

**16.** $-\sqrt{\dfrac{25}{400}}$

**MODULE 7  SECTION 5**                                                    **STUDY GUIDE**

# It's All in the Curve   Exploring Quadratic Functions

**GOAL**   **LEARN HOW TO:** • predict the shape of a parabola
• simplify expressions in order to recognize quadratic equations

**AS YOU:** • use equations to model events and objects
• explore the physics of sports

## Exploration 1: Parabolas

### Analyzing Parabolas

A **parabola** is a type of curve. The parabola's **line of symmetry** is a line that divides the curve into two parts that are reflections of one another. The **vertex** of a parabola is the point at which the line of symmetry intersects the curve. Many parabolas can be modeled by equations in the form $y = ax^2$, where $a \neq 0$. The value of $a$ determines the shape of the parabola.

---

**Example**

Graph the following equations. The vertex of each parabola is $(0, 0)$. The line of symmetry for each parabola is the $y$-axis.

**a.** $y = 2x^2$      **b.** $y = -2x^2$      **c.** $y = \frac{1}{2}x^2$

**Sample Response**

**First** Make a table of values.

**a.**

| x | y |
|----|----|
| –2 | 8 |
| –1 | 2 |
| 0 | 0 |
| 1 | 2 |
| 2 | 8 |

**b.**

| x | y |
|----|----|
| –2 | –8 |
| –1 | –2 |
| 0 | 0 |
| 1 | –2 |
| 2 | –8 |

**c.**

| x | y |
|----|----|
| –2 | 2 |
| –1 | $\frac{1}{2}$ |
| 0 | 0 |
| 1 | $\frac{1}{2}$ |
| 2 | 2 |

**Then** Graph the points and connect them with a smooth curve.

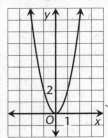

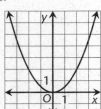

---

Math Thematics, Book 3 **263**

**MODULE 7  SECTION 5**

## Exploration 2: Quadratic Equations

### Quadratic Equations for Quadratic Functions

A **quadratic function** can be modeled by an equation in the form $y = ax^2 + bx + c$, where $a \neq 0$. The graph of a quadratic function is a parabola.

---

**Example**

Determine if $y = 3x^2 + 2x(-2x + 7)$ is a quadratic function.

**■ Sample Response ■**

If possible, rewrite the equation in the form $y = ax^2 + bx + c$.

$y = 3x^2 + 2x(-2x + 7)$
$y = 3x^2 + (-4)x^2 + 14x$
$y = (-1)x^2 + 14x$

The equation is a quadratic function because it has an $x^2$ term.

---

**Example**

Determine if $y + 2x^2 = 5 - 3x + 2x^2$ is a quadratic function.

**■ Sample Response ■**

If possible, rewrite the equation in the form $y = ax^2 + bx + c$.

$y + 2x^2 = 5 - 3x + 2x^2$
$y + 2x^2 - 2x^2 = 5 - 3x + 2x^2 - 2x^2$
$y = 5 - 3x$

The equation is not a quadratic function because it does not have an $x^2$ term.

---

| MODULE 7  SECTION 5 | PRACTICE & APPLICATION EXERCISES | STUDY GUIDE |

## Exploration 1

**Match each equation with one of the parabolas.**

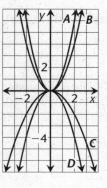

**1.** $y = x^2$

**2.** $y = -x^2$

**3.** $y = 1.5x^2$

**4.** $y = -\frac{4}{9}x^2$

**For each parabola give the coordinates of the vertex and describe the line of symmetry.**

**5.**

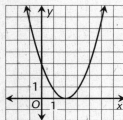

**6.**

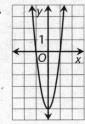

## Exploration 2

**Rewrite each equation in the form $y = ax^2 + bx + c$. Tell whether the equation models a quadratic function.**

**7.** $y = 3x^2 + 7x + 4x^2$

**8.** $y = 3(x^2 - 2) + 4x + (-3)x^2$

**9.** $y + 6x^2 = 3x^3 + 2x - 3$

**10.** $y + 5x^2 = 4x^2 - 8 - 2x + 7x$

## Spiral Review

**11.** The points $A$ (3, 4), $B$ (3, 2), and $C$ (0, 5) are vertices of a triangle. Plot $\triangle ABC$ and reflect it over the $x$-axis. **(Module 7, p. 514)**

**Find the complement of each angle. (Module 5, p. 363)**

**12.** 23°          **13.** 11°          **14.** 45°          **15.** 89°

**A survey is given to find out how the summer programs sponsored by the Youth Group are rated. The survey is given to parents of the children who attended last year. (Module 2, p. 92)**

**16.** What is the population? What is the sample?

**17.** Is this a representative sample? Why or why not?

**MODULE 8**                                                    LABSHEET **1A**

## Table and Scatter Plot   (Use with Question 11 on page 539.)

**Directions** Make a scatter plot of the data pairs in the last two columns of the table.

| Year | Registered boats (in ten thousands) | Manatees killed |
|------|-------------------------------------|-----------------|
| 1975 | 44 | 6 |
| 1976 | 45 | 10 |
| 1977 | 46 | 13 |
| 1978 | 48 | 21 |
| 1979 | 50 | 24 |
| 1980 | 51 | 16 |
| 1981 | 51 | 24 |
| 1982 | 53 | 20 |
| 1983 | 56 | 15 |
| 1984 | 59 | 34 |
| 1985 | 61 | 33 |
| 1986 | 64 | 33 |
| 1987 | 68 | 39 |
| 1988 | 71 | 43 |
| 1989 | 72 | 50 |
| 1990 | 72 | 47 |

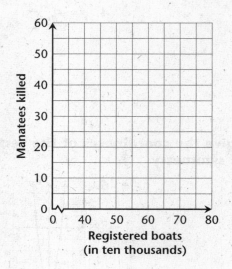

**MODULE 8**                                                    **LABSHEET** 2A

## Circle Graph  (Use with Question 3 on page 552.)

**Directions**  Follow the directions in your book to complete the table.

| Feature | Number of students | Percent of all students | Angle measure of sector | Percent of total measure (360°) |
|---------|--------------------|-----------------------|------------------------|-------------------------------|
| A | 8 | | | |
| B | 4 | | | |
| C | 5 | | | |
| D | 3 | | | |

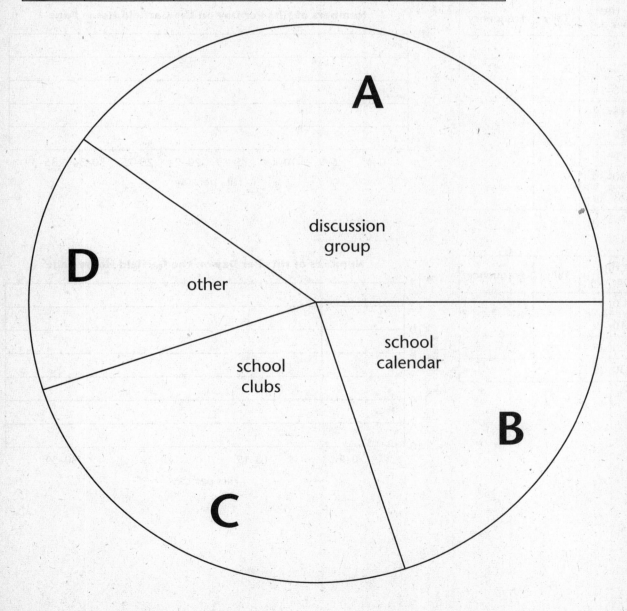

**MODULE 8**                                                        **LABSHEET** **2B**

## Histograms  (Use with Questions 10–15 on page 555.)

**Directions** Follow the directions in your book to complete the frequency tables and draw the histograms.

### Numbers of Hits Per Day on the Garfield Home Page

16, 27, 26, 5, 11, 33, 23, 17, 15, 20, 3, 14, 29, 21, 23,
31, 16, 8, 14, 28, 19, 20, 24, 35, 7, 12, 22, 27, 18, 20

| Hits per day | Tally | Frequency |
|---|---|---|
| 0–4 | I | 1 |
| 5–9 | III | 3 |
| 10–14 | | |
| 15–19 | | |
| 20–24 | | |
| 25–29 | | |
| 30–34 | | |
| 35–39 | | |

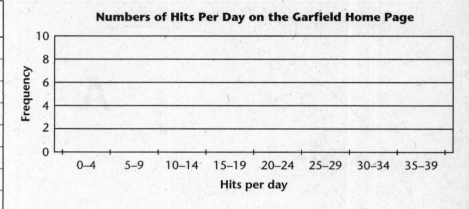

Numbers of Hits Per Day on the Garfield Home Page

| Hits per day | Tally | Frequency |
|---|---|---|
| 0–9 | | |
| 10–19 | | |
| 20–29 | | |
| 30–39 | | |

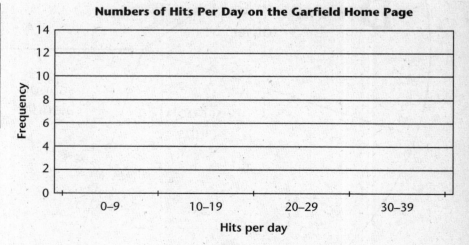

Numbers of Hits Per Day on the Garfield Home Page

**MODULE 8**                                                        LABSHEET **3A**

# Longevity of United States Presidents

(Use with Questions 15 and 16 on page 565.)

| Ages at Death of United States Presidents | | | | | | | | |
|---|---|---|---|---|---|---|---|---|
| President | Year of birth | Age at death | President | Year of birth | Age at death | President | Year of birth | Age at death |
| Washington | 1732 | 67 | Fillmore | 1800 | 74 | T. Roosevelt | 1858 | 60 |
| J. Adams | 1735 | 90 | Pierce | 1804 | 64 | Taft | 1857 | 72 |
| Jefferson | 1743 | 83 | Buchanan | 1791 | 77 | Wilson | 1856 | 67 |
| Madison | 1751 | 85 | Lincoln | 1809 | 56 | Harding | 1865 | 57 |
| Monroe | 1758 | 73 | A. Johnson | 1808 | 66 | Coolidge | 1872 | 60 |
| J. Q. Adams | 1767 | 80 | Grant | 1822 | 63 | Hoover | 1874 | 90 |
| Jackson | 1767 | 78 | Hayes | 1822 | 70 | F. Roosevelt | 1882 | 63 |
| Van Buren | 1782 | 79 | Garfield | 1831 | 49 | Truman | 1884 | 88 |
| W. Harrison | 1773 | 68 | Arthur | 1829 | 57 | Eisenhower | 1890 | 78 |
| Tyler | 1790 | 71 | Cleveland | 1837 | 71 | Kennedy | 1917 | 46 |
| Polk | 1795 | 53 | B. Harrison | 1833 | 67 | L. Johnson | 1908 | 64 |
| Taylor | 1784 | 65 | McKinley | 1843 | 58 | Nixon | 1913 | 81 |

**Game Cards 1 and 2** (Use with Question 2 on page 579.)

Fact: A cheetah can run at a maximum speed of about 70 mi/h.

The maximum speed of a cheetah is about 146 ft/s. — Deven

The maximum speed of a cheetah is about 2053 yd/min. — Jean

In 12 s, a cheetah running at maximum speed covers about 0.68 mi. — Elisa

To cover 500 ft, a cheetah running at maximum speed needs about 4.9 s. — Brian

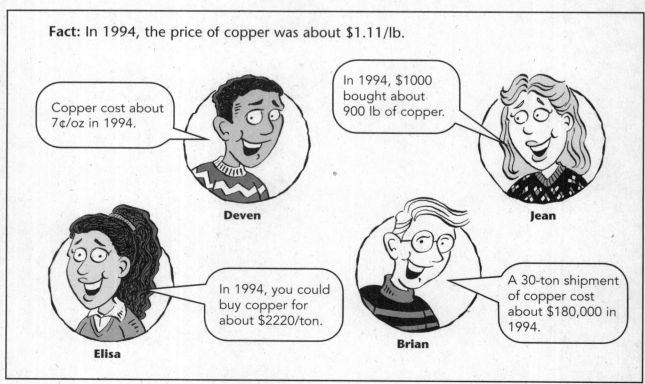

Fact: In 1994, the price of copper was about $1.11/lb.

Copper cost about 7¢/oz in 1994. — Deven

In 1994, $1000 bought about 900 lb of copper. — Jean

In 1994, you could buy copper for about $2220/ton. — Elisa

A 30-ton shipment of copper cost about $180,000 in 1994. — Brian

**MODULE 8**                                              LABSHEET **4B**

## Game Cards 3 and 4   (Use with Question 2 on page 579.)

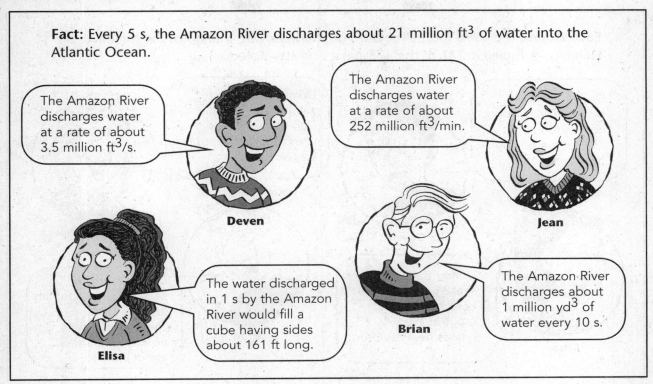

**Fact:** Every 5 s, the Amazon River discharges about 21 million ft³ of water into the Atlantic Ocean.

The Amazon River discharges water at a rate of about 3.5 million ft³/s.

**Deven**

The Amazon River discharges water at a rate of about 252 million ft³/min.

**Jean**

The water discharged in 1 s by the Amazon River would fill a cube having sides about 161 ft long.

**Elisa**

The Amazon River discharges about 1 million yd³ of water every 10 s.

**Brian**

**Fact:** In 1995, about 5400 of the 13,800 junior high schools in the United States had computers with modems.

In 1995, the probability that a junior high school had computers with modems was about 0.39.

**Deven**

In a random sample of 350 junior high schools taken in 1995, you would expect about 137 to have computers with modems.

**Jean**

About 47% of junior high schools had computers with modems in 1995.

**Elisa**

About 1 out of every 5 junior high schools had computers with modems in 1995.

**Brian**

**MODULE 8**                                                    **LABSHEET 4C**

## Game Cards 5 and 6  (Use with Question 2 on page 579.)

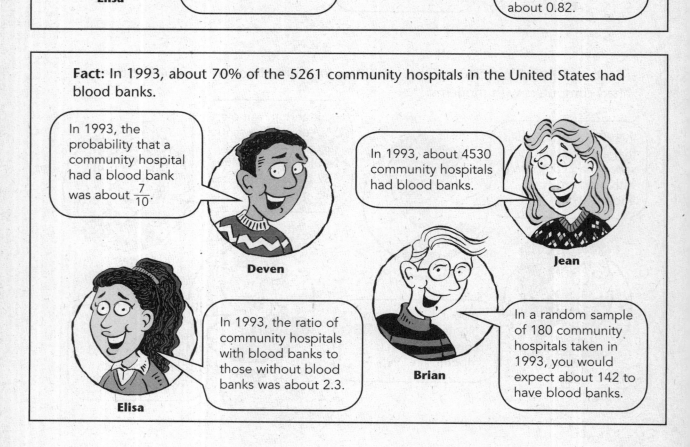

**Fact:** During the 1996 football season, quarterback Dan Marino of the Miami Dolphins completed 221 of the 373 passes he attempted.

During the 1996 season, Dan Marino completed about 75% of the passes he attempted.

**Deven**

During the 1996 season, the ratio of Dan Marino's pass completions to attempts was about 0.51.

**Jean**

During the 1996 season, Dan Marino completed about 6 out of every 10 passes he attempted.

**Elisa**

During the 1996 season, the probability that Dan Marino completed a pass he attempted was about 0.82.

**Brian**

**Fact:** In 1993, about 70% of the 5261 community hospitals in the United States had blood banks.

In 1993, the probability that a community hospital had a blood bank was about $\frac{7}{10}$.

**Deven**

In 1993, about 4530 community hospitals had blood banks.

**Jean**

In 1993, the ratio of community hospitals with blood banks to those without blood banks was about 2.3.

**Elisa**

In a random sample of 180 community hospitals taken in 1993, you would expect about 142 to have blood banks.

**Brian**

Name _____    Problem _____

☆ *The star indicates that you excelled in some way.*

### Problem Solving

① ② ③ ④ ⑤ ☆

**①** You did not understand the problem well enough to get started or you did not show any work.

**③** You understood the problem well enough to make a plan and to work toward a solution.

**⑤** You made a plan, you used it to solve the problem, and you verified your solution.

### Mathematical Language

① ② ③ ④ ⑤ ☆

**①** You did not use any mathematical vocabulary or symbols, or you did not use them correctly, or your use was not appropriate.

**③** You used appropriate mathematical language, but the way it was used was not always correct or other terms and symbols were needed.

**⑤** You used mathematical language that was correct and appropriate to make your meaning clear.

### Representations

① ② ③ ④ ⑤ ☆

**①** You did not use any representations such as equations, tables, graphs, or diagrams to help solve the problem or explain your solution.

**③** You made appropriate representations to help solve the problem or help you explain your solution, but they were not always correct or other representations were needed.

**⑤** You used appropriate and correct representations to solve the problem or explain your solution.

### Connections

① ② ③ ④ ⑤ ☆

**①** You attempted or solved the problem and then stopped.

**③** You found patterns and used them to extend the solution to other cases, or you recognized that this problem relates to other problems, mathematical ideas, or applications.

**⑤** You extended the ideas in the solution to the general case, or you showed how this problem relates to other problems, mathematical ideas, or applications.

### Presentation

① ② ③ ④ ⑤ ☆

**①** The presentation of your solution and reasoning is unclear to others.

**③** The presentation of your solution and reasoning is clear in most places, but others may have trouble understanding parts of it.

**⑤** The presentation of your solution and reasoning is clear and can be understood by others.

Content Used: _____    Computational Errors:   Yes ☐  No ☐

Notes on Errors: _____

Name _____  Problem _____

▭ *If your score is in the shaded area, explain why on the back of this sheet and stop.*

☆ *The star indicates that you excelled in some way.*

## Problem Solving

**❶** I did not understand the problem well enough to get started or I did not show any work.

**❷** I understood the problem well enough to make a plan and to work toward a solution.

**❸** I made a plan, I used it to solve the problem, and I verified my solution.

## Mathematical Language

**❶** I did not use any mathematical vocabulary or symbols, or I did not use them correctly, or my use was not appropriate.

**❷** I used appropriate mathematical language, but the way it was used was not always correct or other terms and symbols were needed.

**❸** I used mathematical language that was correct and appropriate to make my meaning clear.

## Representations

**❶** I did not use any representations such as equations, tables, graphs, or diagrams to help solve the problem or explain my solution.

**❷** I made appropriate representations to help solve the problem or help me explain my solution, but they were not always correct or other representations were needed.

**❸** I used appropriate and correct representations to solve the problem or explain my solution.

## Connections

**❶** I attempted or solved the problem and then stopped.

**❸** I found patterns and used them to extend the solution to other cases, or I recognized that this problem relates to other problems, mathematical ideas, or applications.

**❺** I extended the ideas in the solution to the general case, or I showed how this problem relates to other problems, mathematical ideas, or applications.

## Presentation

**❶** The presentation of my solution and reasoning is unclear to others.

**❸** The presentation of my solution and reasoning is clear in most places, but others may have trouble understanding parts of it.

**❺** The presentation of my solution and reasoning is clear and can be understood by others.

# MODULE 8  SECTION 1                    PRACTICE AND APPLICATIONS

## For use with Exploration 1

**Tell whether each graph shows a positive correlation, a negative correlation, or no correlation between the two variables.**

**1.**

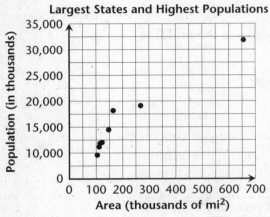

Largest States and Highest Populations

**2.**

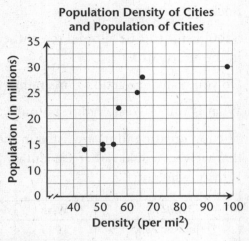

Population Density of Cities and Population of Cities

**Use each table below to tell whether there is a positive correlation, a negative correlation, or no correlation between length and body weight.**

**3.**

| Animal | Length (m) | Body weight (kg) |
|---|---|---|
| Elephant | 7.3 | 7000 |
| Rhinoceros | 4.2 | 3600 |
| Elephant seal | 5.8 | 3364 |
| Giraffe | 5.8 | 16 |

**4.**

| Whale | Length (ft) | Body weight (tons) |
|---|---|---|
| Blue | 110 | 143 |
| Fin | 82 | 50 |
| Right | 58 | 44 |
| Sperm | 59 | 40 |
| Gray | 46 | 36 |

**5.** Tell whether there is a positive correlation, a negative correlation, or no correlation between the percentage of total area and the number of thousands of square kilometers of water area in a country.

| Percentage of Water Area | | |
|---|---|---|
| Country | Total area | 1000 km² |
| Canada | 7.6 | 755 |
| India | 9.6 | 314 |
| China | 2.8 | 271 |
| U.S. | 2.2 | 106 |
| Ethiopia | 9.9 | 121 |

*(continued)*

## MODULE 8  SECTION 1                          PRACTICE AND APPLICATIONS

### For use with Exploration 2

**Tell whether each question is biased. Rewrite each biased question so that it is no longer biased.**

6. Would not football be a better sport for you to play than field hockey?

7. Should students be allowed to eat their lunches outside the building in the courtyard?

8. Do you really like action films rather than dramas?

9. What is your favorite radio station?

10. The top grossing films are listed in the table below. Can you conclude that viewers would rather see fantasy films than other types of films? Why or why not?

| Movie | Year | World gross receipts |
|---|---|---|
| Jurassic Park | 1993 | $913,000,000 |
| Independence Day | 1996 | $798,000,000 |
| The Lion King | 1994 | $772,000,000 |
| Star Wars | 1977–1997 | $740,000,000 |
| E.T.: The Extra Terrestrial | 1982 | $701,000,000 |

11. Suppose you did a survey of 34 car owners and asked them to list their preference of color for a car. The results are shown in the table at the right. Can you conclude that most people prefer dark green cars? Explain your answer.

| Color | Number | Percent |
|---|---|---|
| Dark green | 10 | 29.4 |
| White | 8 | 23.5 |
| Light brown | 6 | 17.6 |
| Medium red | 5 | 14.7 |
| Black | 5 | 14.7 |

### For use with Exploration 3

**For Exercises 12–15, tell what observations you could make to answer each question.**

12. On what day of the week are students absent the most?

13. What is the most popular radio station?

14. Which football team scored the most points in a single season?

15. What food do students like best for lunch?

## MODULE 8 SECTION 2                    PRACTICE AND APPLICATIONS

### For use with Exploration 1

**Technology Use the circle graph shown for Exercises 1–3.**

**1.** What percentage of European households are on-line?

**2.** Give the angle measure that corresponds to each section of the circle graph.

**3.** If there were 100,000,000 households in the U.S. in 1996, how many of them would you expect to be on-line?

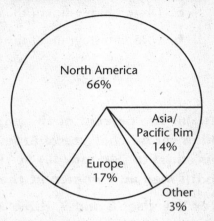

**World On-line Households, 1996**

**4.** The chart at the right shows how the population of the world was distributed in 1996. Draw a circle graph of the data.

| Country | Percent |
|---------|---------|
| China | 21.3 |
| India | 16.5 |
| U.S. | 4.6 |
| Indonesia | 3.6 |
| Other | 54.0 |

**5.** **Social Studies** The age structure of a country is used as an indicator of the health of the population of the country. The age structure of selected countries is shown in the table below. For each country in the table, draw a circle graph that shows the age structure of the country.

| Country | 0–14 years | 15–64 years | 65 years & older |
|---------|-----------|-------------|------------------|
| Afghanistan | 43% | 54% | 3% |
| Denmark | 17% | 67% | 16% |
| U.S. | 22% | 65% | 13% |
| Russia | 21% | 67% | 12% |

**6.** **Writing** Charlene said that the data she collected would not make a good circle graph. Her data were the birth year and height of students in her class. Was she right? How do you know? How could she restructure the data so that a circle graph would be appropriate?

*(continued)*

## MODULE 8 SECTION 2        PRACTICE AND APPLICATIONS

### For use with Exploration 2

**7.** The data table at the right represents the test grades for an eighth grade class.

   **a.** Draw a histogram of the data set using categories of 10 points.

   **b.** Draw a histogram of the data set using categories of 25 points.

| | | | |
|---|---|---|---|
| 48 | 52 | 55 | 56 |
| 57 | 58 | 59 | 60 |
| 62 | 65 | 68 | 69 |
| 70 | 71 | 71 | 78 |
| 80 | 85 | 87 | 89 |
| 91 | 91 | 92 | 95 |
| 98 | 98 | 99 | 99 |

**Health** **The percent of the population with high serum cholesterol (a level greater than or equal to 240 mg/dL) in 1994 is shown for both men and women at the right.**

**For Exercises 8 and 9, draw a histogram of the given data set. Use the same intervals for both histograms. Note: the over 75 years category is omitted.**

| | Men | Women |
|---|---|---|
| 25–34 years | 8.2 | 7.3 |
| 35–44 years | 19.4 | 12.3 |
| 45–54 years | 26.6 | 26.7 |
| 55–64 years | 28 | 40.9 |
| 65–74 years | 21.9 | 41.3 |

**8.** percent of men with high cholesterol      **9.** percent of women with high cholesterol

**10. Interpreting Data** Use the histograms from Exercises 8 and 9 to draw a conclusion about how the percent of men with high cholesterol compares with the percent of women with high cholesterol.

**11.** The age category "75 and older" was omitted from the table. Explain why you cannot use this interval to make a histogram.

**12.** For Exercises 8 and 9, the mean serum cholesterol in mg/dL could have been given instead of the percent. For example, in the 35–44 age category for men, the mean serum cholesterol is 206 mg/dL, while the female mean serum cholesterol is 195 mg/dL. Would these have been better statistics to convey information about high cholesterol levels? Why or why not?

## MODULE 8 SECTION 3          PRACTICE AND APPLICATIONS

## For use with Exploration 1

**Science** **The tables below give the weight and length of the nine smallest bats in the world.**

| Weight (g) | Length (cm) |
|:---:|:---:|
| 2.0 | 2.9 |
| 2.5 | 3.8 |
| 3.0 | 3.8 |
| 3.0 | 3.8 |
| 3.5 | 4.0 |

| Weight (g) | Length (cm) |
|:---:|:---:|
| 3.5 | 4.0 |
| 4.0 | 3.6 |
| 5.0 | 3.7 |
| 5.0 | 4.3 |

**For Exercises 1–4, make a data display that shows the information specified. Tell why you chose that type of display.**

1. the number of bats that weigh between 2.0 and 2.9 grams

2. the number of bats listed that have a length of 3.8 cm

3. the relationship between the weight and length of the bats

4. the median length of the bats listed

5. **Open-ended** Describe a data set that can be shown using the given type of display.

    **a.** a line graph                        **b.** a stem-and-leaf plot

    **c.** a circle graph                     **d.** a scatter plot

6. **Open-ended** Suppose you conduct a survey asking the participants their age and the type of music they like most. Also note if the participant is male or female.

    **a.** Suppose you want to display the survey results in a histogram. What are four age categories you could use?

    **b.** Suppose you want to display the survey results in a circle graph. What are some categories you could use?

    **c.** Suppose you want to display the survey results in a bar graph. What are sample responses you could use as categories?

*(continued)*

| MODULE 8  SECTION 3 | PRACTICE AND APPLICATIONS |

## For use with Exploration 2

The graphs below show the mean SAT college entrance test scores for 1985–1997. Use these graphs for Exercises 7–9.

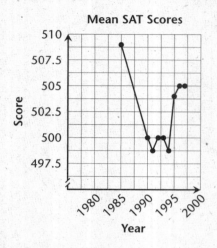

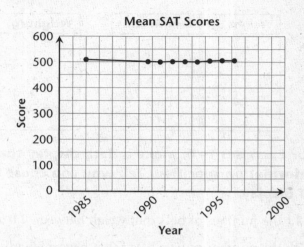

7. Describe how the two graphs give different impressions.

8. Which graph would you use to persuade people that the mean score on the SAT test changes little over time.

9. Explain how a bar graph of the data could also be misleading.

## For use with Exploration 3

10. The "scanning tunneling microscope" (STM), invented in 1981, has the capability of magnifying an object 100 million times. It can also resolve down to one-hundredth the diameter of an atom ($3 \times 10^{-10}$ m).

   a. Draw a picture showing the relative sizes of objects using powers of ten. For example, a pen may be 10 times the length of a fingernail. Put as many objects into the picture as possible.

   b. Sometimes a common object is put into the foreground of a picture. Why do you think this is done?

**The table at the right shows the number of turkeys and the number of people in the United States and France in 1996.**

11. How would you draw a pictorial model that compares the number of turkeys? the population?

| Country | Number of turkeys | Number of people |
|---|---|---|
| United States | 88,000,000 | 265,300,000 |
| France | 36,000,000 | 58,300,000 |

## MODULE 8  SECTION 4                    PRACTICE AND APPLICATIONS

### For use with Exploration 1

**For Exercises 1– 4, use the Table of Measures on page 607 of the textbook. Tell whether the given rates are *equivalent* or *not equivalent*.**

**1.** 60 mi/h; 1 mi/min

**2.** 3 oz/h;  72 oz/day

**3.** 4.4 gal/week; 2 qt/day

**4.** 2000 cars/day; 80 cars/h

**5.** Use an equivalent rate to rewrite this statement so that it has a more powerful impact: "The fastest bird in the world can fly at 171 km/h."

**6.** Use an equivalent rate to rewrite this statement so that it has a more powerful impact: "The ratio of sheep to people in the Falkland Islands is 710,000 to 2121."

**Education** **The table below shows the total fall enrollment in higher education for the years 1980 and 1995. Use the table for Exercises 7–10.**

| Classification | 1980 | 1995 |
|---|---|---|
| Total (in thousands) | 12,086 | 14,262 |
| White, non-Hispanic | 9,833 | 10,311 |
| Total minority | 1,949 | 3,496 |
| Black, non-Hispanic | 1,107 | 1,474 |
| Hispanic | 472 | 1,094 |
| Asian or Pacific Islander | 287 | 797 |
| American Indian/Alaskan native | 84 | 131 |
| Nonresident alien | 305 | 454 |

**7.** In 1980, what was the relative frequency of students enrolled in institutions of higher education that were

  **a.** white, non-Hispanic?

  **b.** minorities?

  **c.** Asian or Pacific Islander?

  **d.** Hispanic?

**8.** Repeat Exercise 7 for the year 1995.

**9.** For which category in the table did the number of people increase but the relative frequency decrease from 1980 to 1995?

**10.** What is the probability that a college student chosen at random

  **a.** was black, non-Hispanic in 1980?

  **b.** was a nonresident alien in 1995?

**MODULE 8  SECTION 1**                                    **STUDY GUIDE**

# Getting the Facts    Collecting Data

**GOAL** | **LEARN HOW TO:** • find and interpret information given in data sources
• determine if there is a correlation between two variables
• identify and correct biased survey questions
• identify representative and biased samples
• collect data by making observations and performing experiments

**AS YOU:** • read about the Florida manatee
• read about conducting a survey to choose a fundraising activity
• learn how the sizes of animal populations are estimated

## Exploration 1: Using Data Sources

### Using Graphs and Other Data Sources

You can gather data from magazines and newspapers as well as from
encyclopedias, almanacs, and other books. Data can be presented in text,
in tables, and in graphs.

### Correlation

Two variables that are related in some way are said to be correlated. There
is a **positive correlation** if one variable tends to increase as the other
increases. There is a **negative correlation** if one variable tends to decrease
as the other increases.

Positive correlation        Negative correlation        No correlation

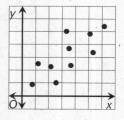  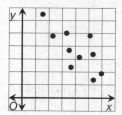  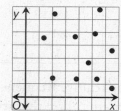

## Exploration 2: Surveys and Sampling

### Conducting Surveys

You can conduct a survey to get information about a population. When a
question produces responses that do not accurately reflect the opinions of
the people surveyed, it is a **biased question**. A survey should contain no
biased questions. You should also avoid using a biased sample for a survey.
A **biased sample** is a sample that is not representative of the population.

## MODULE 8  SECTION 1                          STUDY GUIDE

### Exploration 3: Observations and Experiments

**Using Observations and Experiments**

Sometimes you can collect data by recording observations of events, objects, or people. You can also perform an experiment to generate data.

## MODULE 8  SECTION 1 | PRACTICE & APPLICATION EXERCISES

### Exploration 1

**For Exercises 1 and 2, tell whether there is a _positive correlation_, a _negative correlation_, or _no correlation_ between x and y.**

**1.**

**2.**

| x | 3 | 5 | 7 | 9 |
|---|---|---|---|---|
| y | −1 | −2 | −3 | −4 |

### Exploration 2

**Tell whether each question is biased. Rewrite each biased question so that it is no longer biased.**

**3.** Wouldn't Kelly make a better class president than Rachel?

**4.** Should students use pen, which is hard to erase, or pencil to do math?

**5.** Which type of book do you like better, fiction or nonfiction?

### Exploration 3

**Tell what observations you could make to answer each question. List any factors that may affect your observations and conclusions.**

**6.** How many people like airplane food?

**7.** How is a child's growth affected by not drinking milk?

### Spiral Review

**Rewrite each equation in the form $y = ax^2 + bx + c$.
Tell whether each equation is quadratic.** (Module 7, p. 526)

**8.** $y = 5x(x + 7) + 1$

**9.** $y - 9x = 11x^2 + 6x(1 + x)$

**10.** Find the surface area of a cylinder whose radius is 2 in. and whose height is 10 in. **(Module 5, p. 324)**

**11.** Find 40% of 840. **(Module 2, p. 90)**

**MODULE 8  SECTION 2**                                                  **STUDY GUIDE**

# On the Web   Making Data Displays

**GOAL**   **LEARN HOW TO:** • draw and interpret circle graphs
                            • draw and interpret histograms

   **AS YOU:** • read about home pages and computer software
             • read about a school's home page on the World Wide Web

## Exploration 1: Circle Graphs

### Making Circle Graphs

A **circle graph** shows the division of a whole into parts, each represented
by a slice of the whole circle, called a **sector**.

> ### Example
>
> A rug company asked 40 customers in which room the carpet is cleaned most often.
> Of these, 20 said the family room, 10 said the dining room, 6 said the kitchen, and
> 4 said their child's bedroom. Use a circle graph to display these results.

**■ Sample Response ■**

**Step 1:** Organize the data in a table.

| Response | Number | Percent | Angle measure |
|---|---|---|---|
| family room | 20 | $\frac{20}{40}$ = 50% | $0.5 \times 360° = 180°$ |
| dining room | 10 | $\frac{10}{40}$ = 25% | $0.25 \times 360° = 90°$ |
| kitchen | 6 | $\frac{6}{40}$ = 15% | $0.15 \times 360° = 54°$ |
| child's bedroom | 4 | $\frac{4}{40}$ = 10% | $0.10 \times 360° = 36°$ |

To find each angle measure, multiply the percent expressed as a decimal by 360°.

**Step 2:** Use a compass to draw a circle. Use a protractor to draw sectors having the angle measures found in the table.

Give the graph a title.

Label each sector with the corresponding response and percent.

**Carpet Cleaned Most Often**

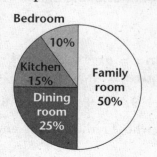

The sum of the percents in a circle graph must be 100%.

The sum of the angle measures in a circle must be 360°.

**MODULE 8  SECTION 2**

## Exploration 2: Histograms

### Histograms

A **frequency table** shows the **frequency,** or number, of items in each category or numerical interval. A **histogram** shows the frequencies of values that fall within intervals of equal width.

**Example**

The histogram below displays the temperature data given in the frequency table.

The height of each bar is the frequency of temperatures in the corresponding interval.

The intervals in the graph are the same as the intervals in the table.

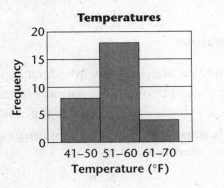

| Temp. (°F) | Frequency |
|------------|-----------|
| 41–50      | 8         |
| 51–60      | 18        |
| 61–70      | 4         |

**MODULE 8  SECTION 2** | **PRACTICE & APPLICATION EXERCISES**

## Exploration 1

### Use the circle graph at the right.

1. What percent of families surveyed own 3 or more TVs?

2. Without measuring, give the angle measure of the sector for families owning 2 TVs.

3. Draw a circle graph that shows the percent of truck sales at Auto World for the years listed in the table. Round each percent to the nearest whole percent.

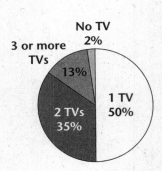

| 1993 | 1994 | 1995 | 1996 | 1997 |
|------|------|------|------|------|
| 34   | 27   | 27   | 36   | 46   |

| MODULE 8   SECTION 2 | PRACTICE & APPLICATION EXERCISES | STUDY GUIDE |

## Exploration 2

**The cost of groceries for the Morales family for each month of 1997 are given below.**

$420  $509  $225  $235  $350  $400  $450  $250  $315  $480  $505  $335

**4.** Draw a histogram of the data using intervals of $100.

**5.** Draw a histogram of the data using intervals of $50.

**6.** Can you make a histogram of the cost of groceries for each week?
Explain.

## Spiral Review

**7.** Do you think there is a positive correlation, a negative correlation, or
no correlation between the amount of snowfall and the amount of
gas used to heat homes? **(Module 8, p. 544)**

**Write each expression without using zero or negative
exponents.** **(Module 5, p. 350)**

**8.** $x^{-3}$        **9.** $m^{-4}$        **10.** $5t^{-7}$        **11.** $8r^{0}$

**12.** Make a box-and-whisker plot of these data values:
8, 8, 9, 9, 10, 10, 3, 4, 5, 3, 4, 7, 8, 12 **(Module 2, p. 152)**

## MODULE 8  SECTION 3                                    STUDY GUIDE

# Displaying the News     Representing Data

**GOAL**   **LEARN HOW TO:** • choose the best data display for a given situation
• recognize a misleading graph
• interpret graphs with different vertical scales
• illustrate a fact with a pictorial model
• understand data by taking part in a demonstration

**As you:** • look at math scores of students from different countries
• look at the amount of waste generated in the United States
• look at water resources and world population

## Exploration 1: Choosing a Data Display

### Choosing an Appropriate Data Display

You can use bar graphs, histograms, box-and-whisker plots, stem-and-leaf
plots, scatter plots, line graphs, and circle graphs to display data. When
deciding what type of display to use, consider the type and number of
data sets you have, as well as the aspect of the data you want to emphasize.

## Exploration 2: Misleading Graphs

### Analyzing Misleading Graphs

Sometimes graphs can give misleading impressions. For example, a bar
graph or histogram can be misleading if the heights of the bars are not
proportional to the values they represent. The vertical scale of a line graph
can be altered to make changes in data seem small or large.

### Example

These two graphs are displays of the same data. Only the vertical scales are different. The
graph on the left makes the changes in data seem greater than the graph on the right.

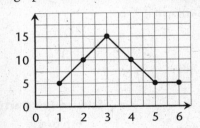   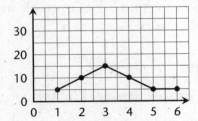

## Exploration 3: Pictorial Models and Demonstrations

### Using Pictorial Models and Demonstrations

Pictorial models and demonstrations can be used to present information
in very visual and dramatic ways.

| MODULE 8  SECTION 3 | PRACTICE & APPLICATION EXERCISES | STUDY GUIDE |

## Exploration 1

**Tell which type of data display would be best in each of the following situations. Explain your thinking.**

1. shows the relationship between the number of patents applied for and the number obtained in the past four years

2. compares the acreage of park systems in Texas, Florida, Washington, and California

3. shows that a company's sales have decreased each month since June

## Exploration 2

4. Use the data from this graph to draw a graph that shows that the price of gasoline has not changed very much since 1973.

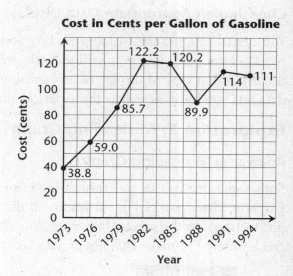

**Cost in Cents per Gallon of Gasoline**

## Exploration 3

5. The number of operable U.S. nuclear power plants in 1976 was 61. The number in 1996 was 110. Sketch or describe a pictorial model that compares the number of operable nuclear power plants in 1976 to the number in 1996.

## Spiral Review

**Use the circle graph.** (Module 8, p. 557)

6. What percent of the students entering the science fair were sixth graders?

7. Without measuring, give the angle measure of the sector that represents students in the eighth grade entering the science fair.

**Copy and complete each equation.** (Module 1, p. 9)

8. $32 \text{ mi/h} = \underline{\quad?\quad} \text{ mi/min}$

9. $\$.13/\text{in.} = \$\underline{\quad?\quad}/\text{ft}$

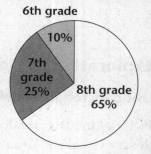

**Science Fair Participants**

6th grade 10%
7th grade 25%
8th grade 65%

## MODULE 8  SECTION 4                                    STUDY GUIDE

# State Your Case   Equivalent Rates and Relative Frequency

**GOAL**   **LEARN HOW TO:** • use equivalent rates to make an impact
                    • find relative frequencies
       **AS YOU:** • analyze data about donating blood

## Exploration 1: Rates and Frequency

### Equivalent Rates

**Equivalent rates** are equal ratios of two quantities. The units for the rates
may be different. You can use equivalent rates to express data in more
powerful or more understandable ways.

### Example

Mr. Gregory's doctor has put him on a 14,000 Cal per week diet. How might you state
this in a way that might be more useful?

$$14{,}000 \text{ Cal/wk} = \frac{14{,}000 \text{ Cal}}{\text{wk}} \cdot \frac{1 \text{ wk}}{7 \text{ days}} = \frac{14{,}000 \text{ Cal}}{7 \text{ days}} = 2000 \text{ Cal/day}$$

### Finding Relative Frequency

The **relative frequency** of an item is defined as:

$$\text{Relative frequency} = \frac{\text{Number of occurrences of item}}{\text{Total number of occurrences}}.$$

### Example

Use the table of results of a phone survey of 500 people. Find the relative frequency of
those surveyed who voted *Yes* to making Groundhog Day a national holiday.

| Choice | Votes |
|--------|-------|
| No | 455 |
| Yes | 41 |
| Undecided | 4 |

$$\text{Relative frequency} = \frac{\text{Yes votes}}{\text{Total votes}}$$

$$= \frac{41}{500}$$

$$= 0.082, \text{ or } 8.2\%$$

## MODULE 8  SECTION 4 | PRACTICE & APPLICATION EXERCISES | STUDY GUIDE

## Exploration 1

**Tell whether the given rates are *equivalent* or *not equivalent*.**

**1.** 300 mi/h;  50 mi/min

**2.** $9/h;  $.15/min

**3.** 20 gal/km;  0.02 gal/m

**4.** 3 g/day;  0.021 kg/week

**5.** Use an equivalent rate to rewrite this statement so that it makes a more powerful impact: "A cricket chirps 10 times every 15 seconds when the temperature is 50°F."

**The table shows the number of students enrolled in each of the world language classes at a certain high school.**

| Type of language | Spanish | Italian | French | Latin | Japanese |
|---|---|---|---|---|---|
| Number of students | 245 | 121 | 350 | 47 | 56 |

**For Exercises 6 –9, find the relative frequency of students enrolled in the given program(s). Write each answer as a decimal or as a percent.**

**6.** Spanish

**7.** Italian

**8.** Latin or Japanese

**9.** French

## Spiral Review

**Choose a type of data display that you could use for each data set. Explain each choice of display.** (Module 8, p. 571)

**10.** the amounts of snowfall during the days of a certain month

**11.** the percentages of people who shopped at The Corner Market, You Bag It, and The Food Place

**Find the complement and the supplement of each angle.**
(Module 5, p. 363)

**12.** 23°                **13.** 90°                **14.** 1°                **15.** 50°